Prentice-Hall International, Inc., *London*
Prentice-Hall of Australia Pty. Limited, *Sydney*
Prentice-Hall Canada Inc., *Toronto*
Prentice-Hall of India Private Limited, *New Delhi*
Prentice-Hall of Japan, Inc., *Tokyo*
Prentice-Hall of Southeast Asia Pte. Ltd., *Singapore*
Whitehall Books Limited, *Wellington, New Zealand*
Editora Prentice-Hall do Brasil Ltda., *Rio de Janeiro*

GAVIN KENNEDY

EVERYTHING
IS
NEGOTIABLE

How to Get
a Better Deal

A SPECTRUM BOOK

Prentice-Hall, Inc., Englewood Cliffs, New Jersey 07632

Library of Congress Cataloging in Publication Data

Kennedy, Gavin.
    Everything is negotiable.

    "A Spectrum Book."
    Includes index.
    1. Negotiation in business.   I. Title.
HD58.6.K46 1983   658.4   83-3187
ISBN 0-13-293597-X
ISBN 0-13-293571-6 (pbk.)

For Patricia

First published in 1982 by Business Books: an imprint
of the Hutchinson Publishing Group. Revised American
edition © Gavin Kennedy 1983.

10 9 8 7 6 5 4 3 2 1

ISBN 0-13-293597-X

ISBN 0-13-293571-6 (PBK.)

Editorial/production supervision by Chris McMorrow
Cover design © 1983 by Jeannette Jacobs
Manufacturing buyers: Christine Johnston and Doreen Cavallo

This book is available at a special discount when ordered in
bulk quantities. Contact Prentice-Hall, Inc., General
Publishing Division, Special Sales, Englewood Cliffs, N.J. 07632.

CONTENTS

PREFACE

The topics and issues discussed in this book feature in my international negotiating seminar: *Everything Is Negotiable!*

I have been running this seminar (and its workshop version) since 1980, and it has been attended by managers in and from Scandinavia, Britain, continental Europe, North America, the Middle and Far East, and Australia.

Many managers who attend the seminars—particularly the Negotiators' "Confessional" and "Clinics"—revise their negotiating approach afterward. But not all need to do so: Others return to their work more than refreshed, having had their individual approaches endorsed.

Almost universally, there has been an emphatic demand for written materials on the topics of the seminars. These have been provided (for a negotiated fee!) on a small scale.

This book can be thought of as a collection of some of the seminar materials. It is aimed at a wider readership than I can possibly reach through the seminars, frequent as they may be.

By reading this book you will be able to improve your negotiating performance by appreciating your own individual strengths as a negotiator (through the Self-Assessment Tests) and seeing how typical negotiating situations are tackled by professionals.

Like the seminars, my intention is to make the difficult task of learning as enjoyable as possible; hence, there is a certain streak of lightness running through the text. I hope that you do not think me flippant about a serious subject—I know how deadly earnest a negotiation can get and I chose this approach only because I am convinced it is more effective than the alternatives.

John Benson has influenced much of my thinking on negotiating over the years and it is appropriate that I acknowledge his contribution here.

I also acknowledge the support of Professor Keith Lumsden of the Esme Fairbairn Research Centre at Heriot–Watt University in Edinburgh for the negotiating seminar.

In this context I should also mention Lars Johannesen and Kris Helgersen of the Norwegian Ship Research Institute, Oslo, and Colin Bass and Kate Brown of Colin Bass Human Resources, Sydney.

Others have made their contributions at the seminars. They include the hundreds of managers who have attended and made them lively and productive activities.

Professor Anthony Clunies-Ross at the University of Strathclyde, Glasgow, kindly allowed me time to work on the book at a critical moment in its gestation.

My family, as ever, has indulged my wandering attentions while the book was written and has gone to extraordinary lengths to support the project. Florence, Beatrice, and Gavin have been their normal admirable selves, and my appreciation of Patricia is evidenced in the dedication.

Finally, a plea to the reader. As an author I am always delighted to hear what you think of my work, both critically and otherwise. If you have any suggestions on how the book can be improved or any comments at all on negotiating, why not drop me a line?

Strathclyde Business School
130 Rottenrow
Glasgow, Scotland

"How much do I want, sir?"

"Yes. Give it a name. We won't haggle."

He pursed his lips. "I'm afraid," he said, having unpursed them, "I couldn't do it as cheap as I'd like, sir . . . I'd have to make it twenty pounds."

I was relieved. I had been expecting something higher. He, too, seemed to feel he had erred on the side of moderation, for he immediately added:

"Or rather thirty."

"Thirty?"

"Thirty, sir."

"Let's haggle," I said.

But when I suggested twenty-five, a nicer looking sort of number than thirty, he shook his grey head regretfully, so we went on haggling, and he haggled better than me, so that eventually we settled on thirty-five.

It wasn't one of my best haggling days.

Aunts Aren't Gentlemen, by P. G. Wodehouse

INTRODUCTION

Surviving in these tough recessionary times is one good reason for reading this book, and there is no surer way to survive than to improve your negotiating performance.

This book shows you how. Its message is clear and unambiguous:

Everything is negotiable

Assume this until circumstances prove otherwise, and you will get better deals time and time again. That is the central message of this book.

If you go about your daily business assuming that nothing is negotiable unless the other party indicates otherwise, you are missing opportunities galore to get better deals both for yourself *and* for the people you deal with.

Ironic, isn't it? Not only are *you* poorer as a result of not trying to negotiate, but so are those you deal with. Why? Because in many cases there is a better deal than the one on offer that is waiting to be discovered. A deal that is better for *you* can also be better for *them*. So, if working for your own interests strikes you as being selfish (perish the thought!), then consider it a favor to them.

However, you don't have to be a dedicated altruist to be a negotiator. Far from it. It is my belief that persons who strive to look after

1

their own interests are more likely to contribute to the common good than those who assume the world owes them a living. By striving to negotiate a better deal than the one that is on offer, you can make our world a more pleasant place to be in. Everything is negotiable—but only if *you* make it so. On some issues you may choose not to negotiate. That is your right, and it is perfectly sensible, too, if you haven't the time to look for a different deal or if the outcome isn't worth the effort on some occasions. But if you do decide to negotiate and you want to do the best you can, you should know that your negotiating behavior can make or blow the deal.

This book shows you how to avoid basic negotiating errors that are committed everywhere and every day by someone or other (and even the world's best negotiators screw up a deal occasionally).

In business, you can be intimidated into believing that certain things are not negotiable, and if you give in without a struggle, you will pay whatever they demand or do without whatever they have to offer.

As a result, you can get only what they want you to have in the form they decide is good for you and for a price that they decide will make them—not you—better off.

This book will show you how to recognize intimidation and how to overcome it. You are challenged in this book to consider testing the prices you come across, no matter how prestigious the vendor, no matter what the "normal rules" of business. Indeed, the more prestigious (read: intimidating) the vendor's reputation, the more vulnerable they are to the methods outlined in this book.

And what is true of the big guys is also true of all the smaller guys who also want to secure your business.

Hence the challenge: *Do not be intimidated by fixed prices.* Never mind what the price tag says or what the vendor tells you—just keep haggling. Somewhere, sooner or later, a better deal will emerge, and that's got to be good for you (and for them).

This book is about finding those better deals, about getting them irrespective of the obstacles put in your way by whoever is trying (or expecting) to intimidate you. You will be shown how to find those better deals and how to make a negotiator happy by haggling.

This is a practical book, packed with advice on how to handle negotiations. It is not a theoretical treatise.

The methods outlined in the text are the methods tried and tested where it matters—in face-to-face negotiations in the real world of international business.

Negotiating as a technique can be applied no matter what the issues or their gravity, no matter who the parties are, or their cultures, or the amounts at stake. But the particular principles applicable to each

2

negotiation can differ for each culture, depending on local business and social norms.

In scores of examples throughout the text you will see different ways to play the same shots, depending on the circumstances. When you change the issues, parties, cultures, or amounts, only the *way* you play the shots needs to be different.

The book discusses negotiations for *big* stakes (ships, real estate, long-term contracts, rent reviews, mainframe computers, companies, high-volume outputs, airlines, territory, hostages, your life, etc.) and *smaller* stakes (accommodation, travel, food and drink, low volumes, small offices, and such like).

Sometimes I demonstrate the appropriate moves to get results by illustrations from everyday domestic negotiations, many of which are essential to domestic happiness and security. And yet hardly any attention is given to domestic negotiations, even by those experienced in handling big deals for their companies.

Top company negotiators, handling accounts in the $10 million plus range, often confess at the Negotiators' Clinics that they are hopeless when it comes to negotiating for a set of tires, or a discount off a case of wine, or Christmas without mother-in-law. Somehow the skills they use professionally are forgotten when it is their own personal interests at stake and not their company's.

For these people, this book has an important message: What works when buying tankers or selling refineries works when getting your car fixed, the roof repaired, and the garden tilled.

Why?

Because Everything Is Negotiable!

And for those more familiar with the smaller deals, remember that the moves that work for those tires also work for the buying of tankers, options on land, or a million gross of widgets.

Hence, we look at how to get better deals when buying or selling a new or used car, or getting it fixed at the garage; buying or selling your house; getting plumbers, plasterers, electricians, and painters to improve it, plus getting them to do what they promised to do for the money.

You will also read how to negotiate with such people to get them to do even more for the same money.

NEGOTIATING IS A BIG ACTIVITY

Over 40,000 international agreements have been negotiated in the twentieth century so far, and they are increasing at the rate of over 1100 a year (up from 550 a year in the late 1940s).

At present about 15,000 agreements between governments are still in force; the United States is party to about 7000 of them.

But nobody knows exactly how many international agreements there are, and even the United Nations has great difficulty keeping track of them all.

The League of Nations published 205 volumes of Treaties before its demise, and the United Nations series was running at 862 volumes in 1979.

With 250 international organizations operating around the world, we can expect the number of negotiated agreements to keep rising throughout the rest of this century—and the next!

[Details from R. D. Bilder, *Managing the Risks of International Agreement*, The University of Wisconsin Press, Wisconsin, 1981]

We also look at negotiations to buy refrigerators, TVs, video recorders, furniture, washing machines, cookers, and so on.

En passant, I show you how to negotiate a night out without provoking a divorce; how to get discounts for poor service in hotels and restaurants; how to negotiate disputes with spouses, lovers, in-laws, friends, neighbors, strangers, work forces, bosses, and bureaucrats.

There is even some advice on negotiating with kidnappers, hijackers, burglars, and pests!

In life everybody negotiates about almost everything.

We don't always realize we are negotiating—that is one reason why we get worse deals than we need to, and why sometimes we don't realize we are being screwed into the bargain, too!

In business we negotiate with customers and suppliers. We also negotiate within our organizations with colleagues *and* rivals. Behind our every move as a business negotiator there is a whole hierarchy of interested parties watching, not all of them benevolently inclined to enhance our own interests, or even grateful for our efforts.

Because negotiating is such a common activity you probably hardly think about it. You may think that you only negotiate on big deals. But if you look more closely at the hundreds of little deals you make every year—with your boss, your customers, your suppliers, your spouse, your children, your in-laws, your neighbors, even your conscience—you would realize that poor negotiating performance costs you money, time, and perhaps lost chances for happiness.

Most of good negotiating practice is common sense, but unfortunately, common sense is a lot less common than is commonly thought!

Also, the majority of people do not review their everyday negotiations—they are not, in the main, motivated to do so. Therefore, they do not learn to identify their mistakes and correct them for next time.

Negotiations in practice are a messy, almost chaotic, experience. People do not negotiate as if they are playing chess: "First you move, then I move."

Human beings are given to wandering attention, digressions, circular arguments, repetition, interruptions, cross talk, irrelevancies, and a whole range of emotional responses from the passive sulk to the violent outburst.

But in all the chaos there are underlying patterns.

This book identifies the underlying patterns of the negotiating process and presents them in a manageable form.

You will be shown how to improve your judgment in preparing for your negotiations, how to think clearly about the choices you must make as the negotiation unfolds, how to improve your performance while under the stress of negotiating, and how to get better deals *almost* every time (you can't win 'em all—though you won't win any unless you try).

The message of the book is serious—in some negotiations, the stakes are literally life or death—but ten years' experience in negotiating training has convinced me that most people learn more about negotiating lessons when they are relaxed than when they are tense or wearied by the sobriety of the style of presentation. Hence, my presentation style is sometimes a trifle lighthearted.

The book is composed of a central text in chapter form, supported by boxed inserts illustrating the experiences of negotiators in a wide variety of real world settings.

Each chapter begins with a Self-Assessment Test consisting of three or four multiple-choice questions. The negotiating scenarios in the tests are highly simplified, and you are asked to mark the answer you think is the most appropriate one given the information at hand. You should test yourself before reading the chapter that follows.

My answers are given at the end of the chapters, with a suggested score for you to note. As you get into the book, your score should begin to increase, marking your progress as a negotiator.

Don't worry if you disagree strongly with *some* of my answers—negotiating is a question of style, and some styles suit one person but not another—but in the main, the answers given are the ones that will produce, in my opinion, the best results in the long run.

The questions have been tested with hundreds of negotiators, and their comments and suggestions (including the marks) have been taken into account for the versions used in this book.

In this book you can work through the central text independently of the Self-Assessment Tests and the boxed insert examples. Or you can choose any combination of the three elements that suits your particular needs.

How you use the book is entirely up to you, but I believe that you will gain most from it by working diligently through the Self-Assessment

Tests, followed by the relevant chapter. You can look up the answers before or after you have read the chapter.

There is one additional activity that you might find helpful while you are reading the book, and that is to try to think up negotiating scenarios, either from your own experience or from other sources (colleagues, friends, the media), that are relevant to the material in the chapter you are reading.

We learn best by counterposing concepts (new or familiar) with our experience, and this seems to be a productive way to bring out the important, though often subtle, principles of negotiating.

No matter how bad or good you are *now* as a negotiator, you can improve your performance, to your own and your company's benefit, if you apply yourself with an open mind to the methods outlined in this book.

Then, as you secure more confidence as a negotiator—mainly from securing better deals—you will actively seek opportunities to practice negotiating. And like learning to ride a bike, the more practice, the more confidence. Each reinforces the other.

The end result could be a new beginning.

For a start, it could get you through the recession in better shape than you think possible at the moment.

And if you can learn to do well when it's tough going, think what you might achieve when the economy picks up again!

SELF-ASSESSMENT TESTS

We begin with a short and painless Self-Assessment Test.

Read the questions carefully and then mark the answer you consider to be most appropriate, given the information available.

As you read the chapter you may wish to reconsider your answers; you should look through them again before moving on.

My opinions of the answers (with nominal scores) are set out at the end of the chapter.

The opinions I express are my own; you might have cause to differ with them. You are invited to question my opinions, and anybody else's, on negotiating!

I believe the views I have expressed of the answers represent the most regular notions of "best practice" for the majority of occasions but, as every negotiator knows, some people see things differently from the way we do—that is why we need to negotiate—so I am not going to be upset if you decide to differ.

However, the scores you get should give you an indication of your performance as a negotiator *before* each chapter. It is to be expected that as you work through the book your scores will improve, indicating how much you are learning from what you are reading and thinking about.

SELF-ASSESSMENT TEST 1

Q.1: You want to sell your yacht and you know that you would be very fortunate to get as much as $85,000 for it. While you are considering placing the advertisement, a keen yachtsman approaches you and offers $110,000 in cash immediately for your boat. Do you:

a] Accept his offer without further ado?

b] Tell him to wait until the boat is advertised?

c] Haggle?

Score:

Q.2: You are in the market for a yacht and have taken a fancy to the *Isabella,* which is advertised at $85,000. The most that you can raise is $73,000 from selling your own boat and borrowing from the bank. You meet the owner in the clubhouse and casually tell him of your (strong) interest. You mention that you could raise $73,000. He agrees to sell you the *Isabella* for that sum. Is this:

a] An offer you can't refuse?

b] A lousy situation?

c] An occasion to celebrate your bargain?

Score:

Q.3: A young talented actor wants to get into the big time; she meets a television producer who is desirous of securing her services for an important part in a detective film. He tells her that she cannot get top rates until she is known, but if she does this one cheap and gets famous she will see "trainloads of money" coming her way for her future work. Should she:

a] Tell the producer to buzz off?

b] Agree, as she needs to start somewhere?

c] Demand top rates if she is to do a top job?

Score:

1

THE WORST THING
YOU CAN DO
TO A NEGOTIATOR
or How to Avoid
a "Bargain"

What is the worst thing you can do to a negotiator?

At the Negotiators' Clinics we invariably get answers like:

> "Insult him."
> "Get her annoyed."
> "Go over her head to the boss."
> "Make him look stupid."

All or any of these behaviors are to be avoided, perhaps. However, none of these repsonses is the *worst* thing you can do to a negotiator.

The worst thing you can do is:

Accept his first offer!

Why is it so bad to accept a negotiator's first offer, especially if it is one of those offers which is "too good to refuse"?

Junior sales staff are most given to thoughtless dancing to the "offer-I-could-not-refuse" tune. It is partly the fault of their sales training, which turns them into order takers. "The order, any order, and nothing but the order" is drummed into them by trainers who have forgotten to beat the drum as loudly about the equally important business message of profitability.

Graduates of these training programs end up like computer programmed football players who only know about scoring goals because
the programmer forgot to distinguish between the various plays.

Partly also, junior sales staff make the cardinal mistake of first-offer
acceptance as a result of their lack of experience.

WATCH THOSE FIRST OFFERS!

An impatient wholesale watch seller, having experience in negotiating with his
country clients, decided to short-circuit the higgling and haggling and get
straight to a price near where he and the buyers settled last time.

He tried out this plan on his first call at a store right off the highway up
in the Catskills:

"Let's save ourselves a lot of time and sweat," he told the owner, "and
cut out the ritual haggle between my high price and your low one."

The buyer looked suspicious, but said nothing. The seller took this for
agreement with his proposal.

"OK," he said, "I'll give you my absolute best price—no kidding, no padding—and you tell me how many watches you want at that price. Then we can
settle up and both go fishing this sunny afternoon."

He opened with a good price, much lower than he normally started at
and below where they had settled last time. The price was good enough to
warm the buyer slightly.

"How many watches do you want at my absolute best price?" he asked.

"None," replied the buyer. "None?" queried the astonished seller. "That
price is better than last year's and it is my absolute best price. So how many do
you want?"

"You must think we country folks are stupid or something," replied the
buyer. "I learned long ago that any city slicker who tells you he is opening with
his absolute *best* price still has some ways to go before he reaches his absolute
bottom price, and even when we get to that price, I might just tell you I don't
want any watches at all!"

They haggled all that afternoon and long after the sun went down. In the
end they settled below the seller's "absolute best price," giving him a profit
that wouldn't cover his gasoline for the sales trip.

This taught him how to make a negotiator happy: Give him haggling
room. He also learned that country folks never accept a city slicker's (or anybody else's) first offer.

Euphoria is always generated when a difficult task is accomplished,
and those readers who have been baptized in cold canvass selling will
know how difficult it can be to get that first order from a prospective
customer. It is the euphoria (or relief) that somebody wants to buy that
leads junior sales staff to say yes to the first offer. They sign, grab it, and
run.

This is why women often make the best negotiators—they learn at
their mother's knee never to accept a man's first offer!

If this proclivity to first-offer-acceptance was confined to the inexperienced, it would be a minor problem, and self-correcting as time goes by. Sales staff gain experience—if they can't, or don't, they find another career—and experience will teach them never to accept a negotiator's first offer.

However, first-offer-acceptance is widespread among negotiators, some of whom have considerable experience. This presents you with the first challenge, and opportunity, to improve your negotiating performance, because you are bound to find yourself, sometime in the near future, in a situation where first-offer-acceptance is a likely temptation, either for you or for the other guy.

Let me illustrate the traumas that first-offer-acceptance can cause to even the most experienced of negotiators.

In the west of Scotland there are several famous yacht clubs. These clubs are patronized by a fair cross section of the community, but, as with everything in life, there are various layers of affluence between the owners of the most expensive boats and the more modest.

The size and capacity of a boat helps in these circles to distinguish its owner's social position. Such foibles are our ruin but few escape from them, which explains why somebody once described boats as holes in the sea into which the owners pour money.

Some people buy boats for the pleasure of sailing, which in the west of Scotland tends to produce experts in handling boats in force-eight gales, whereas in Bermuda or the Mediterranean it produces people with suntans. Indeed, at St. Tropez, in France, people pay thousands of dollars to hire a boat for a few days, with absolutely no intention of leaving the harbor—the hirers of the most expensive boats sit on deck and sip champagne and watch the crowds on the quayside watch them sit on deck sipping champagne.

The owners of the boats are obviously meeting some deeply felt tribal need among their customers; rightly, they are not ashamed to charge outrageously for meeting it.

Back in Scotland a modestly affluent small businessman (Angus McTavish) was looking for a bigger boat recently; he took a fancy to the boat for sale in his club belonging to the commodore (roughly equivalent to a golf club's captain). The commodore wanted $90,000 for his boat. He too was looking for a bigger boat, being even more affluent than Angus.

The most that Angus could get together to purchase the commodore's boat was about $75,000—the price he could get for his own smaller boat, plus a small loan from his bank.

It happened that Angus was in the club one afternoon and got into a conversation with the commodore. The subject of bigger boats came up, and Angus expressed an interest in the commodore's. The commodore said he would be delighted to sell his boat to Angus, him being "such a good club member" and so on.

Angus decided to go in near his top price and said: "The absolute most I can offer you for your boat is $73,000, but I don't suppose you'll take that for it?"

He was stunned by the commodore's reply: "OK. I'll sell you the boat, Angus, for $73,000."

They shook hands there and then, and each went away to arrange the transaction (both are solicitors, and in Scotland a verbal agreement is a legally binding contract). Literally within minutes, Angus had doubts. In fact, he felt somewhat sick about the whole business. Instead of rushing off to tell Mrs. McTavish the good news that they had acquired the commodore's boat (she being a keen sailor too and not just an indulgent wife), he wondered whether he had done the right thing.

What would Mrs. McTavish say when she found that he had bought a $90,000 boat for only $73,000?

She would ask how long the obviously prolonged negotiations took and what concessions had her husband made to get the boat at that price? If he told her it only took fifteen seconds to clinch the deal, she would be skeptical, either about her husband's truthfulness (was he paying much more than $73,000 and hiding the true price from her?) or about the boat's seaworthiness.

Indeed, Angus himself could think of all sorts of blemishes in the commodore's boat (he had sailed in it several times), and he began to worry about any blemishes he did not know about. Before the deal he was prepared to ignore these blemishes, even excuse them; after the deal they loomed before him.

In fact, the commodore's acceptance of his first offer depressed him no end. Instead of a bargain, he wondered if he had a lemon.

We don't know how the commodore felt, as I got the sorry tale from Angus himself, but I guess that he was in no less of a torment than Angus once he thought about what he had done.

How would "Mrs. Commodore" feel about her husband selling their $90,000 boat for $73,000 in a fifteen-second "negotiation"? She would hardly be impressed with his business acumen—her mother's worst fears were obviously true (behind every successful man stands a surprised mother-in-law).

Angus would forever ponder: What price might the commodore have gone down to, as he had accepted $73,000 without blinking?

Should Angus have opened at $71,000 or $70,000 or—why not?—$51,000? He would never know.

And not knowing worried him. In fact, it worried him so much he derived little pleasure out of the entire transaction.

What had the commodore done to Angus by accepting his first offer? He had made Angus miserable. Instead of a good bargain he had made it into a doubtful deal.

He had undermined Angus's self-confidence as a negotiator. He had also done the same to himself, if he thought about it. Instead of two guys happy with their deal, he had made it likely that neither would be happy with it.

By treating Angus's first offer with due respect as one negotiator to another, the commodore could have made them both happier with the deal, even if Angus had to pay *more* than $73,000 for the boat.

How could the commodore achieve the remarkable situation of an agreement on apparently worse money terms than the fifteen-second deal he arranged in the club?

Think what would have happened if the commodore had haggled with Angus over his first offer of $73,000. How he haggles is not the point here (we look at haggling techniques later), only that he does so in some way.

SEND US YOUR INVOICE!

Recently I was approached by a multinational company with a view to my conducting a two-hour negotiating seminar for their senior managers.

The company president interviewed me before approving the arrangements for the seminar. He asked about the proposed contents and I showed a slide presentation on "the worst thing you can do to a negotiator—accept his first offer!" He expressed strong approval for the topic and wanted it to be included, as "my people could do with that message."

After various other details were agreed, he said I could go ahead. He was about to close the meeting when I suggested we agree on my fee for conducting the seminar.

"How much do you charge?" asked the company president.

"Normally, $1,200 a day," I replied, expecting to have this challenged, especially considering the slide presentation I had just completed.

"Fine," said the company president. "Just send us your invoice."

Exit one much demoralized negotiator, who to this day wonders what fee he should have shot for.

Suppose after due time has elapsed, he gets Angus to raise his offer from $73,000 to his limit of $75,000 (or perhaps even higher by forcing Angus to see his bank manager). If they settle at a higher price than the first offer, will Angus be happier?

Yes!

He would rush home to Mrs. McTavish to tell her what a brilliant negotiator he was. He got them a $90,000 boat for *"only* $75,000: a fraction of the price" (you can bet your last penny that this is exactly how he would have put it).

He would minimize the "very minor" blemishes in the boat ("normal wear and tear; overall, the boat is as sound as a battleship"), and he would promote the family image in owning such a magnificent boat—"That's one in the eye for the folks next door and their holidays at St. Tropez!"

Altogether, he would be feeling very, very pleased with himself. So, too, would the commodore. He had negotiated a better price than he was first offered. He could be $2,000 or more better off. His wife (and her mother) would be duly impressed, or at least less unimpressed as a result. He had proven his ability as a negotiator.

EVEN SMART GUYS GET BARGAINS

A marketing professor at a European business school was asked to team up with an American professor and run a four week top-level marketing course at a U.S. midwestern university during the long vacation.

He was asked to quote his fee for conducting the course. He sat and thought about it for a week, and decided to go in at his very top price of $20,000 (being the equivalent of his annual university salary). He justified this to his family on the grounds that "the Americans must learn that if they want the best, they have to pay for it."

He was a trifle surprised, but nevertheless delighted, when the U.S. university accepted his fee without a quibble, and he duly conducted the course in a euphoric mood at the "price he had forced them to pay."

During the first week he got into conversation on the subject of fees with the U.S. marketing professor (who came from Texas and whose constant refrain was: "you get what you pay for").

He declared his own joy with his fee of $20,000, and how it had enabled him to bring his wife over for the course and for a holiday in New York afterwards.

However, he was mortified to discover that the Texan had gotten his "normal" rate for top-level executive courses: $40,000 plus the family's expenses for accompanying him!

From this moment on the European professor's enthusiasm for the course sank to zero.

All this would remain true even if *the final deal was exactly the some money price as the original one.*

How so?

If the commodore haggles and finds he cannot get the price up, but makes an effort to bargain ("cash deposit now and the rest in two days, bare boat minus all movables and less the radar," for example) he would make Angus *work* for the deal. And a deal somebody works for is a deal they are happier with. I know. I've heard Angus on the subject.

It wasn't the money terms of the deal that were wrong. It was the way they were arrived at. People like to get bargains. Much of the retail trade plays on the desire for bargains in promotion campaigns and so-called sales.

"Save 15 percent by buying now" shouts the advertising. And it works. People who had no intention of buying the item flock in to buy it when it is reduced by 15 percent. In effect, they are not saving 15 percent at all—they are *dis*saving 85 percent!

But they are happy with the deal because they believe they have paid less than they would have done if they had bought the item yesterday.

Negotiators expect to negotiate. They feel cheated if somebody does not recognize this. A first offer accepted without a haggle undermines their confidence in both the deal and themselves.

If the first offer is acceptable, what other offer might have been accepted if it had been tried first?

ANSWERS
SELF-ASSESSMENT TEST 1

Q.1: a] You are thinking only of the profit you might make and not about the problems you might create. *Never* accept a first offer. (− 10)

b] How crazy can you get? His offer is already more than you were hoping for, and to delay a decision by sending him out of your sight is foolhardy—he might see another boat on the way back to his car. (− 10)

c] Absolutely right! No matter how good the first offer, haggle: He might offer even more; anyway, he will be happier with the boat if he thinks he squeezed you. (+ 15)

Q.2: a] Oh dear, you are impetuous, aren't you? (− 15)

b] Because he has accepted your first offer, it must cast doubts in your mind about the *Isabella* and/or what you might have got it for if you had opened lower. (+ 15)

c] How do you know it is a bargain? (− 10)

Q.3: a] Obviously a very determined young woman! But consider the risks that she might blow it by trying to intimidate the producer. He might buzz off and she might never "make it." However, if she thinks she can batter him into a higher price through c], then it is a good move. (+ 5)

b] Terrible! He has pulled the sell cheap/get famous gambit beloved by casting producers the world over. (− 15)

c] Has the implications of a] without its risks. Shows she knows what she is worth. She can come down *a little* without losing out or relying on vague hopes and fantasies as in b]. If you sell yourself/your products cheap then you will get exactly what you show they are worth! (+ 10)

SELF-ASSESSMENT TEST 2

Q.1: You are in dispute with a supplier over items he has charged you for in his monthly account, which in your firm opinion were delivered in a faulty condition. Do you:

a] Stall on payment of the total account?

b] Stall only on that part of the account in dispute?

c] Offer to compromise on the disputed amount?

Score:

Q.2: Your office is due for a rent review and you expect the landlord to demand an increase of 20 percent. Do you:

a] Make a "reasonable" offer of 10 percent?

b] Demand a rent reduction?

c] Offer to go to arbitration?

d] Itemize all the defects that you want rectified?

Score:

Q.3: You are managing an engineering project for the Saudis, who have imposed a time delay penalty clause on you. A subcontractor has missed a delivery of important machinery. Planned start-up times may not be met. Do you:

a] Check through the supply contract to discover his liability?

b] Ask the site agent to list all the failures associated with the defaulting contractor since the job began and telex their head office with your complaints?

c] Telephone their managing director and threaten to sue for any penalty costs imposed on you by the Saudis?

d] Arrange an immediate meeting with the contractor to put into operation an alternative delivery program that your own engineers have drawn up?

Score:

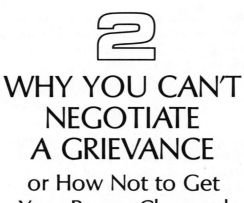

WHY YOU CAN'T NEGOTIATE A GRIEVANCE

or How Not to Get Your Room Changed

Have you ever been on the wrong end of a somebody else's incompetence? Of course you have. People let you down. In fact, the only thing that is certain about some people is that they let you down incessantly.

The divorce courts are full of claims of broken promises, unrealized expectations, and unfulfilled dreams.

And not just the divorce courts. Sit in any court for a few hours and watch the litigants in pursuit of retribution for real or imaginary failings on the part of those they were happy to do business with—until the roof fell in.

The distribution of short straws is random enough for all of us to get one sooner or later, and not just in business. You can draw them at home, in a restaurant, hotel, or bar, at an airline check-in, theater ticket office, passport office, shop counter, taxicab, or even at your local PTA.

Anywhere that Joe Citizen meets Fred Citizen there is a possibility that one or the other, or both of them, will find cause (real or imaginary) to complain about something the other does or does not do that they expected them to do or not do. (Throw in their in-laws and you can have a real bust-up, especially after a breach in the Christmas "cease-fire").

16

Don't just take my word for it! How many hours has it been since you last thought you had cause to complain about something or somebody, either in your professional business or elsewhere? If you answer more than eight you are either of divine origin or you've been asleep (and if you were asleep I bet you *dreamed* you had a complaint).

Complaining is part of the social intercourse of human beings: If only the other guys were perfect. . . .

This chapter is not a plea for moderation in the habit of complaining—far from it. Unless King Canute's humiliation against the waves was in vain, we have no call to struggle against the irresistible tide of human nature!

My purpose here is quite different. It is to improve the effectiveness of your complaining about the failings of others by giving *them* an alternative to merely telling *you* to get stuffed.

Not all negotiating relationships are sweetness and light. Some can get very acrimonious, and I am not just thinking of industrial or international relations. Commercial deals can fall apart when one of the parties believes the other is failing to meet its commitments in some way.

Not only are promises not kept, but deliveries are not always made on schedule, quality controls sometimes fail, performance can fall short of specification, and earnings may be less than expected. Agreeing on a deal is only part of the commercial relationship—keeping the deal implemented is the other part.

In complex production systems there are many opportunities for failings to occur; some way has to be found for resolving the conflicting interests that arise after contracts have been signed.

The problem with most people faced with a business (or domestic!) grievance is that they have a remarkable facility for doing the one thing that is *least* important to them and their grievance, while at the same time they display an astonishing incapacity to do the only thing that *is* important. People, almost without exception, play their strongest suit in the pure mechanics of complaining.

Anybody writing a book called *How to Make Insulting Complaints* would probably find a steady market, though most people—having acquired from middle childhood their repertoire of insults, complete with appropriate sarcastic innuendoes—hardly need to make a publisher richer by handing over cash to read what they are already expert at. On the other hand, it might help a poor writer, so you could regard your purchase as a social service.

People undoubtedly are good at complaining, especially when their grievance is tinged with a perceived slight of some kind or when an element of unfairness is felt to be present.

DON'T RING THEM,
CALL US INSTEAD!

A large property development company, operating in a rapidly changing market, relied heavily on information of its financial status. This was particularly critical during the first hour of business each day.

If their funds ran down overnight, they needed to know *before* they placed deals that day in case they were forced into borrowing short-term "hot" money at high interest rates to bridge gaps of a few days. A firm of their nature going into the market for temporary funds more than a few times a year could start damaging speculation.

However, a problem developed when the accountants found it increasingly difficult to get through to the local bank on the telephones early in the morning. This caused friction between the bank tellers and the firm's accountants.

Relations got so bad that pressure appeared for the account to be moved to another bank on the grounds of the bank's "incompetence," "delay," and "bad faith."

A crisis meeting was arranged with the bank, and the accountants spent a weekend documenting the failings of the bank over the past month, itemizing the alleged costs of telephone delays to the property company's finances.

Before the meeting, the managing director of the property company rejected the entire approach of his accountants and threw their thick report into the wastepaper basket.

Instead, he asked them what arrangement would suit their needs, either with the current bank or a new one. In lieu of an answer, he suggested that they get the bank to ring them each morning at 9:05 on a special line, instead of them fruitlessly ringing the bank. He also noted that this would save them the cost of the phone calls!

The bank willingly agreed to this proposal.

There is no doubt that had the accountant's report been discussed there would have been a bitter row and a breakdown in the relationship.

But they are usually absolutely bereft of ideas about their most important interest, namely, getting their grievance *remedied* in some way.

That's why I urge:

Don't just state a grievance, negotiate a remedy!

Remember, it is not the other guy's failings that need sorting out—it's your *interests* that need attention.

I can illustrate how easy it is to fall into the lack-of-a-remedy trap by recounting an incident from my own experience. (The best lessons are our own mistakes.)

In October 1977 I arrived in Rome late one wet Sunday evening, having driven there by car from sunny Edinburgh (via a North Sea Ferry, of course). I was very tired, to put it mildly.

I had been in service with a United Nations agency for three months and they had reserved me a room in a small hotel on the Aventino. The room I was given had one major failing: It was damp. In fact, it was very damp. It was like a sauna—only a cold one!

It was also late, I was tired and had nowhere else to stay that night, so I remained dressed, put on my overcoat, and spent a very restless night on the damp bed.

By now you have the picture: *I had a grievance.*

In the frequent moments when the dampness woke me I rehearsed the speech I intended to make to the hotel management next morning.

My imaginary agenda began with a description of the lousy room I was in, the management's total lack of consideration of my health, let alone my comfort, and the extortionate price they were charging the United Nations for a cold sauna. My *pièce de résistance* was a sarcastic joke about the ancient Roman proclivity for bathing being taken too far when it was brought into the bedrooms! My imaginary speech ended with an account of the exhausting extent of my car journey and finally what I thought of their Roman welcome to strangers.

Believe me, through the night the agenda was altered several times, and the levels of authority I considered invoking escalated—a telex to the United Nations in New York, perhaps even a meeting of the Security Council (you can see how delirious I was as a result of the dampness).

I had no doubt that the force of my complaint, if not natural justice alone, would immediately provoke the management to apologize profusely and move me to a magnificent room, complete with marbled bathroom and private balcony.

Next morning, I marched to the reception desk ready with my complaints, and spoke to a young man. He had that Roman air of authority and also that charming Italian indifference to anybody other than good-looking women.

So I told him about the dampness in the room, but copped out of the more outrageous aspects of my prepared agenda, including my joke about Roman baths.

What was his reaction? *He suggested that I try shutting the window!* What he did *not* do was offer me another room.

I was flabbergasted, and withdrew a defeated and demoralized complainer.

But reflecting on this episode—as I did later that day from my dry room in *another* hotel, the excellent *S. Anselmo,* Aventino, Roma—I had nobody to blame by myself:

> *As I had not asked for another room,*
> *why on earth should 'he offer me one?*

19

If my remedy was to be given another room—a perfectly reasonable proposal unless the hotel specialized in damp rooms—it was up to me to say so.

By not stating *my* remedy, I left the initiative of suggesting a remedy to the other guy, and one thing you can be certain about—if you leave the initiative to somebody else, it is likely that they will only consider their own interests in framing their remedy rather than yours. Hence his suggestion that I shut the window.

This is all the more certain if, as is usual in situations where you feel aggrieved about something, you colorfully blame the other guy for his failings. Attack people and they will defend themselves. Attack them ferociously and their defense is returned with interest. Impugn their competence and stand back while they dissect yours. Challenge their parentage and they will challenge that of your children.

THE CASE OF MOTHER'S "MILE HIGH" APPLE PIE

A harrassed mother was trying to cope with the tears and tantrums of her younger son, who was loudly complaining that he always got the smaller piece of apple pie because his older brother always took the bigger piece.

She decided not to bore her chidren with another lesson on the morality of sharing in families, but instead asked, "Who cut the pie?"

"I did," said the older boy adding sarcastically, *"he's* too little to be trusted with a knife."

"I agree," the mother replied, "but he is not too little to know which is the bigger slice of my apple pie on the plate. So he chooses first which slice he wants."

The younger son triumphantly chose the bigger slice of apple pie, and the older boy was livid.

"In future," the mother added, "the rule will be clear: One of you will cut the pie and the other will choose which slice he wants."

At this the older boy whispered to his brother that as he always cut the pie, he would get even next time by making sure the two slices were the same size!

The mother returned to her TV show happy to have solved a problem so constructively.

Tempers are never calmed by being tested, and the longer the row goes on the less the likelihood that you will get anything other than a sore throat—and perhaps even a thump on the nose for your trouble.

Try the hopeless tack of making them responsible for the problem and they will deny responsibility.

In Italy, for instance, hotel receptionists, car-rental people, and airline check-ins have a devastating way of shrugging their shoulders and blowing hard through tight mouths when they want to deny either responsibility or concern for your plight. (Though I must say in defense of Italian *waiters*, that they are the best in the world).

The lesson is clear. Time spent preparing for a blazing row about your grievance is totally wasted. So is the nervous energy.

What of the alternative?

To negotiate a remedy, you have to have one. And thinking through what your remedy ought to be requires preparation—another reason for not wasting time thinking up articulate insults about the other guy's incompetence.

The case for your negotiating a remedy is fourfold:

1. You take the initiative in choosing the remedy, and your remedy is more likely to start with your interests in mind than theirs.
2. The negotiation will be on your remedy and not stuck in an argument about the legitimacy of your grievance.
3. By proposing a remedy you provide helpful information to the other guy—he does not have to guess what will assure him of your future business.
4. He may very well be relieved that you want so little and are not demanding, like an attorney, grossly exaggerated recompense for your "losses."

Putting the discussion into a business context, suppose, say, you just complain to a supplier about a missed delivery of components. You can be fairly sure that their shipping department will justify, excuse, explain, blame, or even apologize for the delay. They might just tell you to buzz off—they have bad days too.

But remember, if you have no remedy prepared, you leave it to them to choose whether to do anything or nothing about deliveries in the future. If you attack them, they are unlikely to be motivated to do anything other than defend themselves.

It is not always wtihin your power to withhold business from them —at least in the short run—and if you haven't clout like that you had better be careful that you don't provoke them into turning their system's gremlins loose on your deliveries in the future.

The capacity for people in large organizations to quietly screw up their own systems in pursuit of private revenge on difficult customers is known among the cognoscenti as the "buggeration factor."

Anybody who has ever suffered the runaround in business will recognize the seriousness of my caution.

But even if you have clout, you have no guarantee that pushing them will produce a remedy suitable to your interests. If pushed, they might do something for you, but only the minimum possible. If, however, you state your (reasonable) remedy, you could be halfway to getting them to agree to it.

The greatest source of grievances are the result of vague promises that disappoint when what they promise fails to materialize.

Plumbers and electricians who offer to fix something in your house are notorious for not starting or finishing it when they promised, though car mechanics are by far the worst "liars," and their notoriety is unbounded in the way they calculate the bill.

You must never accept a promise to fix anything that is not supported by an estimate of the likely cost, complete with a breakdown of the individual items, *before* you indicate that they have got the order for the work. Also, get the detailed estimate in writing or write it down in front of them as they quote prices and always record their starting/completion times and any extras they promise.

If you do not agree with their estimate, you can negotiate from strength *before* they start. They might suggest a cheaper way of doing it—ask them—or they might suggest you use stock materials instead of the super-duper stuff that has just arrived in their shop.

Remember, before they get the job they are in the business of selling their services, not collecting "debts," and they are at their keenest to persuade you to give them the order.

In an emergency—a burst pipe, a live electric cable, a storm-damaged roof, a fallen tree across the drive, and so on—your needs are greater than their's. But you can still protect yourself. If you don't even try they must take advantage and quote outrageous prices and terms.

Haggling that might take minutes will tilt the power balance enough to trim their first (high) prices; the alternative of panic demands for their services will inflate even more the first high price they thought of upon seeing your reaction to the emergency. If you act like a damsel in distress in emergencies, you ought to know that the age of chivalry is over.

If, in the course of the work, you want to change something from the original plan, don't ask them how much they will charge you for the change (what an invitation that is!)—tell them the changes you want and leave it to them to raise the issue of extra payment, and if they do—negotiate!

When something goes wrong you should think what (realistic) options you have, and you must concentrate entirely on the issue in dispute and not irrelevant side-issues. If the meal was rotten, make that the issue and not the way they took your coat (that's a separate issue). In the same way, if your spouse is late, that is the issue and not your mother-in-law's views or last year's missed anniversary.

Lastly, look for trade-offs that will meet your interests. Will a refund off the bill make up for the lousy lasagne? How about a free video for the machine that needed repaired within two days of purchase? Why not a free meal in the hotel where the room TV is not working properly, or a free taxi when reception forgot to call you for your flight?

Recently, British Airways mislaid my luggage in Amsterdam and through over-booking shunted me into the Economy cabin from First Class. I was furious with the airline at that moment, and I told the cabin crew that I was not very pleased with their company, but that a free brandy would go a long way to making me smile again. I was instantly given two brandies! Within minutes I was grinning like a Cheshire cat.

ANSWERS
SELF-ASSESSMENT TEST 2

Q.1: a] The first thing you must do. This is also the most commonly chosen response by managers. (+ 15)

b] A move that reduces your bargaining power. (− 10)

c] Never! Let *them* offer to compromise. (− 15)

Q.2: a] You are in danger of implying a 15 percent compromise before you know how strongly he feels about his demands. (− 10)

b] A strong opening—better left as support for d]. (+ 10)

c] Arbitration removes your veto on the decision. (− 15)

d] Open with the defects in order to get something back for what you pay—support it with b] if possible. Could reduce the pressure of his demands. (+ 15)

Q.3: a] It's a bit late to check liability; anyway, this does not resolve your own liability to the Saudis. (− 10)

b] Wasting time and telex money, as it does not move the machinery to your site. (− 15)

c] Threats won't get the machinery to the site. (− 20)

d] Don't just state a grievance, negotiate a remedy! (+ 15)

SELF-ASSESSMENT TEST 3

Q.1: You run a courier business and one of your vehicles breaks down just before a busy weekend. A friend has a spare van and agrees to loan it to you until your own vehicle is back on the road. He asks you to sign a receipt that reads: "One vehicle, $175, one week's rental." Do you:

a] Sign as asked?

b] Insist on a properly drawn up legal contract?

c] Tell him a receipt is not necessary between friends?

d] Ask for more details?

Score:

Q.2: You have been approached by a Saudi Arabian company to handle the management contract of a large civil engineering project. Do you:

a] See this as an opportunity to get into lucrative Middle East business and therefore go in easy on your initial fee?

b] Assume that as the market is strong enough to take a high fee you can go in high?

c] Prefer to wait and see what fee is likely to be acceptable to the Saudi company?

d] Base your fee on what is profitable to you?

Score:

Q.3: You are a manufacturer of engine parts and have been granted an interview, after many last-minute cancellations, with the boss of America's largest car firm, who insists that you meet him at Kennedy Airport a few minutes before he flies off to Europe. This is your big chance! While walking towards customs, he opens with a demand for your best price for a six months' contract to supply fuel injection pumps. Do you:

a] Show him what you can do by quoting the lowest price you can in order to get your foot in the door?

b] Go in slightly above your lowest price?

c] Go in high to leave yourself room to negotiate?

d] Wish him a pleasant flight.

Score:

THE NEGOTIATOR'S
MOST USEFUL
QUESTION
or How to Avoid
a One-Truck Contract

Experience is a great help in dealing with the routine—you know what to expect if you know your line of business and there are few, if any, surprises left. Experience in one field of negotiation can also help in another where you are totally ignorant of what is considered normal and what is out of the question.

But how can you make up for lack of experience other than by taking the time, which you may not have, to get it?

If you have to make a decision, perhaps with a lot of money (or something more important) riding on the outcome, and you have almost no experience to draw upon, you will need more than just luck to help you out.

Fortunately, you can apply the principles of negotiating to give you the elbow room to make your decisions. Recently, for example, three authors were involved in negotiating the sale of the video rights of a book they had written. Now, in the field of negotiating authors' rights they had some experience, but video rights were a new game altogether. The question posed by the video company's offer was whether it was a good or lousy deal?

The three of them spent a not inconsiderable time pondering that question, but none of them had a clue to the right answer. Their problem was that they had no idea what the rights were worth *to* the video company or what to look for—and what to avoid—by way of contractual obligation. The amount of cash they were offered could have been a small fortune in the video business or a mere bagatelle. The proposed contract could have been normal or outrageous.

In other words, they could have been offered a deal that experienced authors would have been delighted with, or they could have been giving away the video rights for next to nothing.

It is important here that you do not concern yourself with the actual amount of cash involved. That is of no relevance to anybody in a *new* market, though it is often the first rationalization made by newcomers for why they accepted the first offer.

If your money flow tends to be stuck in the tens and units range, try not to show you are overly impressed when someone opens their offer with a number followed by several zeros—it weakens your negotiating position.

Likewise, don't fall into the opposite trap of being unable to negotiate seriously for what are trifles compared to your daily business quotas. More than one top negotiator, handling millions of dollars a deal, confesses at the Clinic how they tend to get done in on the little deals worth a few hundred dollars or less.

If anybody offers you what appear to be *big* sums of money for what you value relatively lightly (or its converse, pennies for what you value greatly), remember: *They* may not be nuts—*you* may just be naive!

Therefore, don't sign, grab it, and run. The bargain price for a product in one market can be sheer robbery in another. And there is nothing worse for your ego than finding out later that you cheated yourself. An offer you "can't refuse" is one you ought to think carefully about.

Consider: What is the price for a gallon of water for a thirsty tourist in the middle of New York? Not much, considering the amount of water that falls on New York at any time of the year. Certainly you are unlikely to get mugged for water in New York—though I cannot discount the possibility of you being taken for a half bottle of whiskey! But what of the price for a gallon of water in the middle of the Arabian desert?

In 1980 I was driving a Land Rover around up-country Oman, selling diamonds to expatriate Britons working in oil exploration, and such was the dehydration that I drank a gallon of water every twenty miles just to stop my mouth from cracking like sandpaper.

And that was only part of the discomfort. I was under strict instructions from the old Arabian hands in Muscat not to drink alcohol even if I found an unlocked brewery, not to complain about having sand in every orifice of the body, and under no circumstance was I even to *think* of women—"If you must look at a camel, make sure it's a male one," I was advised!

I can tell you straight, if for any reason I had been cut short of water for any length of time in that climate I would have traded all my diamond samples for a glass of water, and probably thrown in the company's Land Rover as well.

So, a bargain can look different depending on from where you are looking at it, and faced with an offer from the video people the authors needed to know the market price for video rights: should they take the deal or count their fingers?

Therefore, they needed a lot more information about the appropriate money worth and implications of the deal if they were to prepare a negotiating position quickly.

Their efforts were aided by the use of a single question, asked over and over again. In this case, they got the up-front money considerably increased and eventually reached agreement on the wider issues. So they're glad they asked their questions.

It is with these questions, and the wider implications of going into deals where the market is new to you, that this chapter is concerned.

So many deals come undone it is a wonder that any get put together, but the time to concern yourself with the small print of a deal is *before* pen is put to paper, not afterward in your lawyer's office.

And bringing in the lawyers doesn't help too much—they tend to throw monkey wrenches in the works of any deal they are associated with and always deny any responsibility for the deals that get past them.

They act like a wet blanket before a deal and incessantly chant "I told you so" after it.

They are also too damn friendly for my liking with the lawyers from the opposition—after all, they are both making money out of creating problems in a deal that didn't exist until they got involved.

In new business fields, particularly in countries new in your itinerary, you will have to handle the negotiations yourself and hope that you survive long enough to acquire the experience that will protect you from the pitfalls that are obvious to the old hands.

You can start improving your performance in "one-off" negotiations by first of all not trusting to luck to take care of your interests. Look after them yourself, instead. And to look after your interests you have to identify them.

The simple two-word question that was used in the video negotiation can get you started; to this I now turn.

Because hindsight is a cheap forecaster of the deals we should avoid, the bars and dinner parties of the world are full of smart guys willing to give you advice on what you should have done after you have already done it. Foresight, a much scarcer commodity, is all the more valuable for that.

One type of deal we must avoid, though circumstances often conspire against us, is known as the "one-truck" contract.

These are lethal because everything that can go wrong probably will (Murphy's famous law) and anything you insure against only happens after you miss a premium (floor joke at Lloyds).

The time to avoid the disasters of ill-thought deals is when they are being negotiated. This can be illustrated by considering the following contract to hire a truck offered by a "pal" in Muscat:

> "One truck, $500, one month's rental."

What is wrong with a clear and simple "one truck, etc." contract like that? No complications, no red tape, and no hassle, just pay your cash and drive off.

The basic problem with "one-truck" contracts is that they leave almost everything to the mercies of Murphy's law.

And this is true for *both* parties to the deal.

Neither of you is protected in the slightest by the "One-truck" contract you have negotiated: If you sue them you will either lose the case or waste your cash in a deadlock. Either way, the only guys laughing on the way to the court are the lawyers and their bank managers.

If you are the renter, you have no assurance that you will get the truck your "pal" showed you in the compound and not some wreck he keeps out of sight at the back of his lot.

Of course, you may protest: "I trust him, we went to the same school." Indeed, he could be your best friend, and so on.

Fair enough, but many a member of the down-and-out fraternity begins the story of their road to ruin with: "I went into business with my closest friend and a loan from an awfully nice bank manager."

If you are the owner in a "one-truck" contract you have no assurance that it will be returned in the condition that it left you.

When (if?) it comes back it might have to be parked behind your lot because it is too dangerous to park in the compound. Then you will have to off-load it onto the first fool to walk into your office looking for a "one-truck" deal!

There is more than enough room in a "one-truck" contract for disagreement about the condition of the truck, when it is to be returned, who is responsible for insuring it, and who pays the parking tickets it collects while out of your sight.

How, then, do you avoid "one-truck" contracts? Easy. The only thing you have to do is ask lots of questions that begin with two simple words, and to keep asking questions until you are perfectly satisfied that you have covered everything.

The words to put in front of every question are:

What if?

Applying this to the hire of the Land Rover for an up-country mission in the bleak wastes of Oman, you could ask, or need to be ready to answer:

> *What if* the truck breaks down up country for a reason unconnected with my usage or unrelated to parts for which there are spares?

Agree on warranty and responsibility for delivery of replacement parts or a new truck.

> *What if* the truck breaks down after being improperly driven?

Insist on a "no claims for improper usage" condition, and the return of the truck to your premises at the renter's expense.

> *What if* it is stolen and I cannot complete my sales trip within the month?

Agree on an insurance premium that covers immediate replacement of the truck, but avoid any acknowledgment of liability for his estimates of his loss of sales (no salesperson ever reckoned somebody else was responsible for them losing a *small* sale—they're worse than anglers with the fish that got away).

> *What if* your carelessness about parking causes it to be stolen?

Have a waiver clause inserted that absolves you of liability in these cases. Try to get your brother as sole and final arbitrator of any decision about the extent of "carelessness."

> *What if* it is repossessed by one of your creditors and I cannot complete my sales trip?

Get this covered by the insurance premium for immediate replacement and insist that this be paid for by the truck owner.

> *What if* your creditor damages it out of both our sights?

Shove in another waiver claim, but insist that the renter get a signed statement as to the truck's condition before he parts with it.

> *What if* you socially misbehave and the locals smash up the truck in revenge—or shoot at it if a camel is involved?

Insert a high returnable-deposit condition that can be withheld in these cases (again, try to get your brother nominated as arbitrator).

WHAT IF THEY LOSE THEM?

An Irish manufacturer neogtiated a radio-tower deal with a Fiji government department and delivered the tower parts on time by ship to the designated island in the Fiji group.

The erectors had to unload the cargo by lighter to the shore as there were no adequate port facilities on this particular island.

During the transhipment of one load, the lighter partially capsized and much of the cargo went into the sea. Fortunately, everything was believed to be safely recovered. The contractor erecting the pylon did not realize that several angle plates were missing until they found they needed them several weeks later. They telexed Ireland for replacements; these were rushed through the plant in a weekend.

The Fiji government decided that they could not wait for them to be shipped out and insisted that they be air freighted. They also held the Irish manufacturer liable for the cost of air freight as they had no proof that the plates were actually in the capsized lighter (or on board the ship for that matter). Also, they pointed out that the contract required delivery CIF to the construction site *on the island*.

The Irish company's contract did not have any provision for third-party liabilities—in this case, the erector or the lighter company—and was advised to pay up. They did, and their profit on the contract was reduced by 75 percent after the additional production and the air freight charges.

> *What if* you knock down a camel and the locals hold the truck in ransom?

The returnable deposit isn't.

> *What if* the truck is unlicensed for cross-border journeys and I accidentally make one?

Commit the renter to usage within the territory and liable for all breaches of local emigration laws. Charge him a "lieu of export" deposit and also *sell* him a map of the territory.

> *What if* we dispute the amount of damage or the extent of the seriousness of minor scratches?

Clearly covered by the appointment of your brother in the arbitration clause.

What if I find you are not the legal owner of the truck and it is re-possessed by the authorities?

Demand legal proof of ownership or, in the absence of the relevant documents, get a *large* discount off the rental fee and the insurance premium.

What if you fail to return at the end of the rental period on time?

Insert an excess-hire charge at a steeply rising per diem rate and, of course, loss of the returnable deposit.

What if you use the truck for some illegal purpose and it is impounded by the police?

Require legal usage on pain of forfeit of the returnable deposit.

WHAT IF THEY ARE COVERED AGAINST SCREW-UPS?

In a twelve-month period between October 1979 and November 1980 over 400 claims for faulty design, inaccurate calculation, and inadequate checking of work were made against consultant engineers by their clients from all corners of the globe.

The insurers were convinced that the cause was "weak supervision" or "inadequacy of the site engineers."

The insurance association recommended that consultants refrain from "accepting contractual responsibility that performance criteria would be met."

It was also adamant that consultants must not disclose, even casually, that they had professional indemnity coverage for their actions. The most common cause of this disclosure was for the consultant to include in his contract the limitations of his indemnity, which only encouraged the litigious client to try to recoup something from a contract that did not meet his expectations. Apparently they only sued those they knew had some coverage irrespective of the justice of their claims.

The insurers also issued a warning about the modern younger engineer. He was too much given to relying on computer printouts instead of sound engineering sense. They advised young consultants to have their calculations and drawings looked over by a senior engineer with a well-developed eye for what was obviously wrong.

While the insurers were convinced that many, if not most, of the claims they got from clients were spurious try-ons, they were anxious that the consultants get the situation clear from the start with their clients by:

a] disclosing no sources of indemnity funds

and

b] making sure the computer did not spill out garbage because you forgot your basic engineering principles.

(And, *What if* we don't settle the "what ifs" before it is time for me to return to America?)

(Clearly the hustle-close tactic. Tell him if he agrees to your terms he can have the truck now—otherwise, later.)

These 'What ifs' are somewhat tongue in cheek, but they have a serious message for all negotiators.

Look at the following summary of an Oman hire contract and compare it with the "one-truck" contract above:

One 1980 model Land Rover, as new, 12,020 miles certified on the clock, with all parts in working order, serviced at 12,000 miles complete with spare tires, fan belts, exhaust system, plugs, a new battery, a wheel, chain and tackle, and twenty-five gallons of fuel. Delivery to your hotel by 6 A.M. Tuesday next. $500 COD—cash only. Insurance for month's use and all legal penalties for traffic and other offenses to be borne by hirer. Any defects in bodywork to be notified at delivery, otherwise as is. Rental fee covers one month's hire and unlimited mileage from Tuesday next to 2nd of November next only. At the end of the rental period the hirer must return vehicle by 6 A.M., fueled and in sound condition, to the company and pay (cash only) for any damage, defects, or missing parts on return.

Now I freely concede that even this contract is not *legally* cast iron, but it is certainly better than the original "one-truck" deal offered by a "pal" in Muscat.

You can see this by looking at your last car rental form. The big rental companies are experts at avoiding "one-truck" deals—their rivals who didn't are no longer in business.

However, car rental companies are not quite as cautious as the airlines, who have exclusion clauses on their tickets (which by the act of buying you are deemed to agree to) such that even if a 747 knocks you down on the runway and reverses over you twice, you, or more likely your widow, will find that they are absolved from all liability by something called the Warsaw Convention.

That is why people of a nervous disposition about their chances ought *never* to read the small print on their airline tickets—they could die of shock and still not have a claim on the airline!

In a large deal there could be numerous What if? questions that need to be asked and answered if the parties are to protect their interests. In a *new* deal, or strange country, it is even more necessary to do your preparation with a list of "what ifs."

Negotiators face a big problem when a previously prepared contract that suits the interests of the other party is presented to them—that's why its previously prepared!—and do not know where to start opening it up for discussion.

The asking of questions, and particularly the act of thinking them through *before* the negotiation, will suggest terms for negotiation.

In every deal there are dozens of "what ifs" and consideration of them is a useful way of creating negotiable variables for you to trade against the liabilities they are proposing that you accept.

Of course, in some parts of the world in times of disorder a "one-truck" contract is all that you can get. On these thankfully few occasions you just have no choice but to take it.

In the melee for the last plane from Phnom Penh, you are not advised to negotiate a seat using "what if" type questions nor to demand that the "one-truck" liabilities be amended before you remove yourself from the tarmac and get on board.

However, you could still try to negotiate a deal on the price if you've run out of dollars and the pilot is being difficult.

Ask him if he accepts payment by American Express—you never know, he just might have a "pal" in Muscat who has an Amex account (too bad if he only accepts Diners Club), and you *might* be able to negotiate the surcharge!

ANSWERS
SELF-ASSESSMENT TEST 3

Q.1: a] A very risky decision on your part (and his).   (− 10)

b] If you had time, but you haven't.   (0)

c] Oh dear!   (− 15)

d] Yes. Get more details. Ask "What if" questions.   (+ 10)

Q.2: a] "Sell cheap, get famous" is no way to riches.   (− 20)

b] Assumptions are dangerous until tested.   (− 5)

c] This leaves it open for you to go in high.   (+ 10)

d] OK, but it leaves out of account how badly they want your services, nor does it distinguish between high and low profits.
   (+ 5)

Q.3: a] He eats guys like you for breakfast. His intimidation has obviously worked and he knows what you can do!   (− 40)

b] If you concede at your first (short) meeting, what will he achieve at a longer meeting in a month's time?   (− 15)

c] A trifle better—you have resisted his bullying tactic, but still not your best move.   (+ 5)

d] Yes. Tell him to call you when he gets back; say that meanwhile you will talk with his technical people about what exactly it is that they need. They may need your pumps more desperately than he wants you to know about, and he can worry about that all the way to Europe and back!   (+ 30)

SELF-ASSESSMENT TEST 4

Q.1: You are looking at a freezer in a showroom. The price on the ticket is $800. You decide to buy. Do you:
  a] Inform the sales assistant of your decision?
  b] Ask what they charge for delivery?
  c] Insist on a discount for cash?
  d] Ask what special discounts they are offering at present?

  Score:

Q.2: You are looking at a car in a showroom. It is priced at $8,500. You decide to buy. Do you:
  a] Ask what is included in the sales price?
  b] Offer them $7,700?
  c] Tell them you'll think about it?

  Score:

Q.3: You are a management consultant and receive a telex from Sydney asking you to quote for a sales seminar. Do you reply:
  a] Asking how many and who is to be there?
  b] Telling them that your standard daily fee is $1,200 a day plus expenses?
  c] Asking for $1,700 for the seminar plus expenses and $400 per day for travel?

  Score:

Q.4: If after two weeks you have not heard from Sydney, do you:
  a] Telephone or telex them, asking for information?
  b] Wait?

  Score:

Q.5: Suppose they reply to a request for $1,200 a day plus expenses that you are asking too much for the fee, though they agree to meet your expenses. Do you telex back and:
  a] Reduce your price because you want to go on an expense-paid trip to Sydney?
  b] Confirm your price but offer to travel economy class?
  c] Confirm your price but assure them you are worth it?

  Score:

THE NEGOTIATOR'S
DILEMMAS
or How to Stop Worrying
and Love the Haggle

People up to their necks in negotiations every day of their business life don't have a great deal of time to sit about and contemplate what they are doing. They just get on with it and either sink or swim.

Periodically, some people are troubled by having to act without thinking through why they move the way their business nose leads them and occasionally, in retrospect, their bank balance suggests they shouldn't have.

I am referring here, of course, to the very successful, not to nature's natural losers. These guys get where they are going by being good— very good—at what they do, and they are good because they know their business better than their rivals—for if they don't, their rivals surely will teach it to them.

However, no matter how good they are at what they do, as negotiators they still have to face the same problems as everybody else. This is a revelation to junior staff who as yet have little experience in negotiating, *and* to those who think that the problems they face across the table are personal to them.

Not realizing just how common their condition is can make them act like a first-time young mother-to-be who believes *her* pregnancy has the historic significance of the Immaculate Conception.

New guys on the team take what happens in their negotiations very personally and in consequence, get quite emotional when they discuss the perverse pleasure they believe their opponents experience from making life exceedingly difficult for them.

Sadly, a few entrants are soon lost to their company because nobody explained to them the causes of the very real problems of negotiating; eventually, these problems prove overwhelming.

They drop out and join a commune, become radicalized, smoke pot, get into weird religions, and spend the rest of their twenties preaching against the horrors of the rat race (which I have always considered to be a libel on the innocent rat).

In their thirties most turn up again. Some grow up to find a quiet niche for themselves in the suburbs and make the same discoveries in love and business as the rest of us. Others graduate as trendy entrepeneurs, selling organic food kits to dropouts (in the alternative society they note the absence of competition and, like Henry Ford, get going).

A few hang around parties chatting to impressionable young (and not-to-young) women about "one day" writing deeply meaningful poems, plays, books, or film scripts on the "horrors of the rat race" and the "boring meaninglessness of affluence" (the last being a pass).

That we lose such people for a while is perfectly understandable once you contrast the fragility of human nature with the problems of the negotiating process. Identifying the source of these problems is fairly easy. Wishing them away is hopeless.

Every negotiation creates the pressures of its own dilemmas. If you claim that it doesn't, you are either exceedingly thick-skinned (in which case the sex life of a rhinocerous should fascinate you) or you ain't doing much negotiating.

Top negotiators, when questioned about the dilemmas of negotiating, admit to experiencing them. A few confess that they remain baffled by the negotiating process and that thinking about their bafflement worries them, hence they don't. However, if they did, they would soon realize that what they think is a personal problem is in fact the very essence of the process of making decisions by negotiation, and once recognized as such it soon diminishes in importance.

I will illustrate what I mean by reference to the experience of a successful negotiator I know "down under."

In 1981 I was walking along Macquarrie Street, Sydney, looking for a bookshop, and had stopped at the traffic lights for the "Walk-Don't Walk" sign.

I was hailed—yes, hailed—by a man across at the other light. When I got closer I recognized an old friend whom I had not seen for twenty-two years. Being British, I lied and told him he hadn't changed a bit and, being Australian, he confessed he couldn't say the same about me!

Bob, for such is his name, was on his way to eat, and naturally we teamed up. We walked back a few blocks and passed the Wentworth (where I was staying, although I did not disclose this fact in case his destiny had been all it had promised to be when I last saw him). Eventually we found an all-hours diner.

We had been close friends in our teens and had been through several adventures in those halcyon yesterdays that get more halcyon only because time passes. Eventually, Bob went back to Sydney to write the Great Australian Novel, and I went to London to change the world.

Our conversation that afternoon when we met again was intense, as you would expect. Eventually the subject of what we were doing now came up. Blandly, I told him I was in Sydney for a week conducting seminars on negotiating. As blandly, he told me he was into property development. Obviously the Great Australian Novel had been left to be written by somebody else!

Over the next few days I went up the coast to his beach house (magnificent views and privacy), flew over one of his developments in a light aircraft, and sampled suburban affluence with his wife, who was a professor, and his teenage kids.

All this background is by way of ensuring that nobody gets the notion that Bob is one of society's losers when it comes to the negotiating business.

Bob expressed interest in my seminars and asked how much a place cost.

"Two hundred dollars," I told him.

"How much for a friend?"

"Two hundred friendly dollars," I replied.

"Well, how much for a very old friend?" he countered.

"Two hundred very old dollars."

We bantered on a lot, with occasional serious interludes. During one such I asked him about *his* negotiations; to my astonishment he told me that it was one side of his work he did not enjoy.

Now this was curious, because if there is one business that is all negotiating it must be the property business.

"But you negotiate constantly," I said.

He agreed, but insisted that he often hated it when he had to negotiate with anybody. He coped, he said, by gritting his teeth and getting on with it.

"Tell you what," he said, in the manner of someone about to make a proposition, "if you can explain to me how to cope with my aversion to negotiation, I'll come to one of your seminars."

Now there is nothing more dangerous in my field than for a generalist to attempt a specialist's problem: The road to grief among consultants is strewn with "experts" who rush into assignments faster than they can complete them.

"OK," I said, "I'll have a go at your problem if you tell me how you came to be a millionaire from being a broke libertarian, but it will still cost you $200 for a place at my seminar."

The deal being struck, Bob insisted on talking it through at once.

Bob's real problem, it emerged, was that he thought of himself as the only negotiator who experienced his problem. He couldn't talk to his own people about it because such a confidence could undermine his reputation as a hard-nosed negotiator. And losing a reputation for hardness in Australia could be terminal in his business.

What did Bob think was his problem? It was really several closely related dilemmas.

In negotiating, we do not know for sure what the other guy will accept—sometimes we are not too sure about our own limits—and not knowing what the other guy is thinking creates a dilemma.

The three dilemmas raised by Bob were:

1. Where to open?
2. When and how far to move?
3. How long to hang on?

The root problem here is that of *uncertainty,* and decision making under uncertainty is one of the most perplexing of all activities.

A brief summary of the workings of a market economy should enable us to see why the first dilemma arises.

A mass consumer society has the singular advantage over its rivals in that it enables people to make informed judgments about what they want to do with their money.

Their wants lead them to look at the price tags on the abundantly available goods, and they mentally compare the benefits of those goods with the benefits of holding onto their money.

If they prefer the goods more than they prefer to keep their money (bearing in mind how little, or how much, they have), they exchange their money for the goods. If they prefer to keep their money they may do so, but then they must do without the goods.

The problem with this admittedly idealistic picture of consumer markets is that for a very large number of goods and services in our economies there is *no* price tag on them: You can't simply look at a price tag and make a choice.

You and the guy who owns the goods have to fill in the price tag before you can decide whether to buy or he can decide whether to sell.

The process by which the tag is written out is called negotiating.

Now prices in markets for goods without price tags aren't fixed by fiat—they are decided by what somebody is prepared to pay and what the owners will accept.

These two prices—what you are prepared to pay and what they are prepared to accept—need not start out the same or even similiar. Nor need they move closer in the course of the negotiation. They only have to be identical if and when a deal is struck.

If the price has to be settled by negotiation, the first decision "crisis" (as Bob put it) is which price to open our bids at?

WHAT'S IT WORTH?

Australia has a lot of sandy acres. How much an acre? Some of those sandy acres were worth next to nothing until it was discovered they were high-grade bauxite.

A downtown Sydney site with a two-story colonial-style pub on it has one price. Get planning permission to clear the site to build a forty-story office block on it, and the same site has another price.

A film studio's library of thousands of old black-and-white movies cluttered up its warehouses. What were they worth in cash, not sentiment?

The new management sold them for $9 million cash to an agent and then sold off the acres of warehouse land for redevelopment for $15 million, making $24 million in all. Meanwhile, the agent resold the old films individually to the world's television companies and has so far grossed $45 million, over five times what he paid for them. Which was worth more—the films or the land?

If we pitch our opening price too low we could blow the deal, with the owner being insulted at our impertinence.

Alternatively, the other guy could say yes out of relief at the timidity of our offer compared with his expectations of his good's worth (clearly, he hasn't read Chapter One).

Hence, are we too cheap or too expensive?

This is a dilemma felt by all negotiators, including the most experienced; it causes them to hesitate before declaring an opening price, just in case they open too far from where they might be able to settle.

As Bob expressed it, there never is a price he would gladly accept for a building that he wouldn't abandon at the first hint that he might get somebody to give him more for it. Nor, presumably, is there a price for somebody else's property that he wouldn't drop if he thought they would accept less for it.

In the business of buying and selling, where there are no preset price tags, we are torn between our need and our greed, though what appears to be highway robbery at one moment can look cheap at the

next if the buyers know something about the market that we don't—
yet!

WHAT ARE YOU WORTH?

A technical specialist in deep sea engineering at a German university was asked
to tackle a problem that was causing delays on a drilling rig in the North Sea.
The professor worked for two weeks on the project and eventually came up
with a solution that worked.

The oil company concerned asked him to send in his account. He carefully calculated the cost of using his laboratory equipment and the university's
computer, plus a nominal charge for his time; the problem had enthralled him
technically and he was delighted to have had the opportunity of working on it.
He thought his charge was a "bit cheeky" but the oil company could "afford
to pay it."

The oil company were stunned when they were billed the sum of
DM16,000. The problem was costing them at least DM2 million a year before
the professor solved it for them, and they were expecting, and quite happy, to
pay at least DM800,000 for the professor's solution.

When they rang up and queried the bill (in case it was a mistake) the
professor misinterpreted their concern and offered to cut it! He was delighted
when they passed it for payment.

Not knowing for sure where to open in each individual case, we
suffer the mild stress associated with making any decision under uncertainty.

I told Bob that we can never avoid the dilemma of deciding what
price to open at in negotiations. Contrary to some views, experience does
not totally eliminate the problem.

Experience helps, though, to reduce the stress of uncertainty. Also,
the existence of competition acts as a restraint on wildly erratic pricing
behavior. But reduction in stress and restraints on behavior are not
enough to *eliminate* the dilemma.

Why?

Because as we become more conscious of the consequences of missed
opportunities, experience only pushes this knowledge into the background, while in the foreground we reflect privately that we do not like
the ritual tensions of negotiating.

This leads us to ask: When and how far should we move in a
negotiation?

Inside every negotiator there is a guy wanting to make a deal.

We just don't like losing an order, nor do we like starting over
after we've lost.

HOW NOT TO PROTECT
A BOTTOM LINE

A big-league European company has a firm policy against concessions when the package price is on the bottom line. It also has another policy that permits the sales force to make concessions below that bottom line!

Each sales negotiator is issued with a pad of Customer Concession Forms to itemize any concessions they make in excess of company policy. These forms must be sent to the highest levels of the company—each level requiring a signature of approval by the responsible person—and are allegedly treated very seriously by all concerned.

If you talk to the sales negotiators about the deterrence value of the CCFs, they are less than intimidated by them. How often are the CCFs used? Regularly! They are treated by the negotiators as a license to concede, if that is the only way they can get the business.

If you have gone into a negotiation wrong-footed, you search for a means of getting back from the dead, *if you can.*

If your company policy does not allow an adjustment in price below the bottom line, you will try to invent an exception that covers your retreat from the high ground. You know you shouldn't, but you do anyway. Salespeople the world over are always inclined to cross a bottom line price in hot pursuit of an order.

In the cases cited by Bob it was not the bottom line price that he was concerned with. He wanted to know how to handle a situation when the deal he was offering was unacceptable to the other side and he did not know how far he might have to go to get an agreement. He need not be anywhere near his bottom price when this happens.

That precisely is the dilemma: We do not know for certain what the other guy is up to when he refuses our offers. Is he laying it on thick just to get us to concede more, or is he testing our resolve to stick to our offer as it stands?

If we make a movement—because we believe that it is necessary to do so to save the deal—we could incite them to continue haggling. If we don't respond, or respond too late with too little, we might provoke a deadlock. Getting it right and minimizing the chances of our movement —or lack of movement—being misunderstood by the other guy is by no means easy. They face the same dilemma as we do (this at least is of some comfort). They don't know whether we are bluffing or being candid when we resist their pressures to move from our positions.

Some negotiators have tried to resolve the movement dilemma by making a unilateral preemptive offer and refusing to budge from it, come what may.

This tactic has the singular advantage that it removes the indecision about how far to move: You don't! However, it has a number of draw-backs that make it unsuitable as a negotiating policy on most occasions. Not the least is the necessity that you have overwhelming bargaining power and a credible willingness to use it. Among the consequences of using naked power is the retaliation it provokes among its victims. No-body likes to be pushed around.

EDWARDES'S LAW

At British Leyland in 1980, the managing director, Michael Edwardes (brought in to turn the company round from bankruptcy), forced through a single-offer wage award with credible threats to close the business down if it was resisted by strike action.

The credibility of Edwardes's threat was founded on both the absolutely serious nature of Leyland's finances and his personal style of always doing exactly what he says he will do. In a word, he is not given to bluffing.

In 1981 he tried the same tactic, once again threatening to close the com-pany if strikes occurred. This time it almost backfired, as the resentment of the workers boiled over and the management was very lucky to get away with only a minor amendment to their offer in exchange for peace.

The Longbridge factory, which had grumbled the most and had gone out on unofficial strike, accepted the offer reluctantly on the votes of the other plants and returned to work in a bitter mood.

Within a week of accepting Edwardes's imposed pay settlement, the men at Longbridge were out on strike over "tea breaks"; they stayed out for three weeks.

Edwardes got the strike his ultimatum tactics were designed to avoid, and the company lost both cars and face in the process.

Desperate situations (such as Leyland's) sometimes merit desperate reme-dies. However, no negotiator should underestimate the longer-term influences of "desperate" behavior, nor ignore the fact that people can be driven only so far and no further. Also, there are always those around (political agitators, the competition, opportunistic politicians, and so on) ready to put your behavior in the worst possible light.

Normally, movement is required in negotiation, but there is no pre-determined rule that can tell you how far you may have to move or if you have to move at all. Would that there was! We could then compare the extent of the move we have to make and decide whether we prefer to move that far or deadlock.

Where does this leave the negotiations? One thing is certain: The dilemmas cannot be avoided. Every negotiator faces them; realizing this alone should help you cope.

"Well," asked Bob, "how long should I hang on for a better price?"

"We are back with another dilemma," I told him.

As we don't know for certain what is going on in his mind, we do not know whether his reluctance to settle on our by now amended terms is not just another test of our resolve to stick to them.

Remember, it is his job to keep pushing us on the current offer. He must try to nibble away at the edges or try to take us with a frontal assault on some core principle. He wouldn't be worth a plugged nickel if he didn't. Nor are you if you don't resist every step of the way.

The problem this causes us is to think about the time spent on the negotiation with one guy that might be better spent in negotiation with another guy.

Negotiations take time which has valuable alternative uses.

Instead of chasing a better deal with Fred by holding out for more, we might be able, by settling for the terms that are on offer (or breaking off at a deadlock), to get over to Bill's office to spend the time negotiating an even better deal with him.

Alternatively, we can hang on at Fred's and perhaps secure a deal that justifies our forgoing the opportunity to open up a negotiation with Bill.

How much time to spend on a particular negotiation is never obvious until after the time has been spent. But it's not hindsight we are short of!

Every man knows that feeling when they are trying to read a woman's mind: Is she saying no to test our devotion and our intentions, or are we wasting our time trying to change what is for her (and there-fore for us) an irreversible decision to have nothing to do with us?

Eventually, we get the message and perhaps look elsewhere—though she can never be sure that this is not a ruse on *our* part to test her resolve!

Time puts a great pressure on negotiations. It is always the case that there is no point spending time negotiating if it doesn't matter *when* we reach agreement, for if it doesn't matter when we agree we might as well do something else meantime.

Though time pressure is present in every negotiation, it is not necessary that every negotiation reach a decision within its alloted time —deadlines, like the seasons, come and go.

Judging whether to hang on for a better deal or to try elsewhere is the inescapable dilemma for every negotiator.

Some people can never reconcile themselves to the negotiator's dilemmas, and they avoid wherever possible overt negotiating situations. Upon such people every fixed-price store builds its business.

Others face up to the dilemmas and make the best deals they can.

If the dilemmas are difficult when you are dealing with money prices for goods that you are familiar with, it is a great deal more complicated when you are confronted with barter-deals, and these have been getting a lot more common in international trade recently.

Barter was the norm in trade negotiations about four centuries ago and it was replaced by cash deals only as the international trading system accepted gold as a common currency. When paper currencies became "as good as gold" (i.e. they could purchase real goods when presented to the country concerned), international trade moved over from barter to cash transactions.

Today the world is divided into those countries that have "hard" currencies, that are instantly accepted as payment for goods, and those that have "soft" currencies, which nobody will accept in payment for anything. Communist and some less developed countries are soft currency traders, while all the capitalist countries and some oil suppliers have hard currencies.

When negotiators attempt to trade with "soft" currency countries they will be faced with the demand that payment for their goods are made in the buyer's products rather than in the seller's hard cash. This creates all kinds of problems for the negotiator.

Because the negotiators are completely sure of the monetary value of the goods they are selling, it does not follow that they have the slightest idea of the eventual monetary value of the goods offered in exchange by the buyer.

Some surprises can be experienced in this business. A Swedish office equipment firm agreed to sell typewriters to the Soviet Union and got in exchange ladies watches. Upon inspection these were found to have a Western market value (because of their quality) greatly in excess of the nominal "price" of the typewriters. Indeed, the Swedish firm disposed of them to a Dutch importer at a considerable premium and were most happy with the barter deal.

However, not all barter deals are as successful. In order to dispose of the barter goods, the negotiator may have to sell them to a third party. In one such deal, a Belgian exporter of chemicals swapped them for Polish cement which it sold on to an African country (of "Marxist" persuasion). The Belgian negotiator told me that the cement was of such low quality that water mixed with corn flakes was a safer material than the cement, and he considered himself lucky to have got out from under the disastrous deal (he got cocoa for his "cement" which he sold for US dollars).

In barter deals, the negotiator does not know the value of the goods that are offered, and he must remain perpetually vigilant about quality—at least until he has off-loaded whatever he has been lumbered with. He still does not know where to open or whether to reject the barter deal altogether and risk the collapse of the deal.

As is usual in these negotiations, Communist officials do not announce their demands for a barter deal until late into the negotiations, when a great deal of time, and not a little expense, has been undertaken by the Western negotiator, who is then faced with losing the entire deal or hanging on in case something can be rescued from it.

Should the negotiator settle for his losses or press for better terms and a larger proportion of the payment in hard currency? How hard and how long should he push for a better deal? At what point does he conclude that the deal on offer is the only one likely to be offered? If so, does he take it or shove it?

The dilemmas are worse in these negotiations than in cash deals. In this case, it is the reverse of the problem of settling on terms that are far short of the best opportunities that are possible—the negotiator in a barter deal does not know for sure whether the deal he agrees to is going to lead to substantial losses in the third party trade-offs he must make, given the (generally) poor quality products he is offered. Instead of missing the prospect of a small fortune by settling too low, he risks the prospect of a large loss by settling at all.

That is a brief summary of my discussion with Bob in the wee hours of the morning. He ran me out to the airport later that week and bought me a few beers (and toy koala bears for my kids). Just before I left him to get on the plane for Hawaii, I asked him about the secret of his phenomenal success from the old days. He said it would have to wait, as it was "a long story of hard work and good judgment." I asked him for a short version.

"Well," he said, "the short version is I guess quite simple: An aunt died in 1965 and left me her business and $95,000 in cash."

With that he smiled broadly and said: "See ya."

ANSWERS
SELF-ASSESSMENT TEST 4

Q.1: a]   If you do you will certainly pay $800.   (− 15)

    b]   If you do they will certainly charge you for it.   (− 10)

    c]   Not bad. A step in the right direction.   (+ 5)

    d]   Better. The assistant will know he has a possible sale and he might just need your order more than he needs the ticket price.   (+ 10)

Q.2: a]   A good move with cars, as the window price is usually the base line upon which they build lots of extras (delivery, number plates, etc.).   (+ 10) b] Much better if this move folows a], as they might agree and then build the price back towards $8,500. (+ 5)

c] Car salespeople hear this several times a day; generally, it means a polite withdrawal. How do you get back into a good position when you return? (− 5)

Q.3: a] Always a good move as it gives you information. (+ 10)

b] Pricing depends on how badly you want to make a twenty-nine-hour air flight to Sydney and how much you think they will pay. You certainly must not go for less and you have an opening to add on a premium if they accept the standard rate. (+ 5)

c] A much more impressive move, but as you don't know what they have in mind you may be pricing yourself out of the running. It's the opening dilemma! (+ 10)

Q.4: a] No. This weakens your negotiating position. If you are really good at your job and worth your fee you should be so busy with other clients that you haven't noticed their delay in replying! (− 15)

b] Yes. (+ 15)

Q.5: a] You probably will if you are more interested in long-distance travel than in making profits. However, they ought to worry whether you are worth *any* fee if you drop your price so easily. What exactly are you going to teach their negotiators if this is how you behave? (− 20)

b] Not as bad as a], but still subject to the same criticism that it undermines your credibility. If you are earning $1,200 a day in Europe, why suffer the trauma of a twenty-nine-hour flight to Sydney for the same money? (− 10)

c] Much better. You may not get the job (this time), but you are obviously setting high standards as a negotiator, which shows you are worth your fee. If they agree to the fee it will be because they realize you are more likely to make an impact on the conference participants than your rival cheapies. (You could put it that way in your reply!) (+ 15)

SELF-ASSESSMENT TEST 5

Q.1: You are in Tokyo negotiating for a long-term contract with a Japanese producer of conduit pipe, and the negotiations have stalled for several days. It feels like you are going round in circles. Do you:

a] Wait for them to make the first move?

b] Make a small concession to shove the boat out?

c] Change the subject entirely?

d] Adjourn?

Score:

Q.2: You are negotiating with a video publisher who has offered to market your series on management education. They offer you an advance against royalties of $50,000—$25,000 on signature of contract and $25,000 on delivery of the videotapes. They rejected your demand for $60,000 split similarly. Do you:

a] Accept their offer?

b] Tell them it is not good enough?

c] Offer them a repackaged proposal?

d] Walk out?

Score:

Q.3: The buyer for a large chemical company responds to your price for naphtha by telling you: "The competition is very strong and you'll have to do better than that?" Do you:

a] Offer to cut your price in exchange for the order?

b] Ask him by how much your price is above the others'?

c] Suggest that he accept the other offers?

d] Ask to see the other offers?

e] Ask him what he likes about your proposal?

Score:

THE MYTH OF
GOODWILL CONCEDING
or How to Teach Wolves
to Chase Sledges

It is paradoxical that the handling of concessions is probably the most difficult task facing the negotiator, despite the fact that the rule for above-average performance is fairly simple:

> In negotiating, be more like Scrooge than St. Francis of Assisi.

Why should you accept this somewhat uncharitable advice? Because in negotiating, generosity is *not* contagious. Indeed, experience suggests that liberality in concession making is the worst thing you can do if you want to get concessions from the other guy.

If you concede, why should he do likewise? Surely by remaining where he is he might induce you to concede yet more?

In this chapter I discuss the goodwill theory of concession making, hopefully to eradicate it from your repertoire.

Where does this goodwill concession theory come from?

Its origins are obscure, but I have traced it back as far as the unlikely named Bjorn McKenzie, who was a traveling salesman for a short while in the 1890s in the Hudson Bay area of northern Canada.

Whether further research could throw new light on the origins of goodwill conceding is, perhaps, less important than the fact that it appears now to have a widespread grip in all walks of business. You have only to ask negotiators if they practice goodwill conceding to realize just how prevalent it is.

Strange as it may seem, those people who wax lyrical about goodwill conceding cannot understand criticism of it.

This had led to some stormy sessions at the Negotiating Clinic.

Two of the most common defenses of goodwill conceding take the form of:

"I concede a couple of little things early on, just to soften them up"

and

"Somebody has to push the boat out or we'd never get the negotiations underway."

Both of these defenses, in a triumph of delusion over experience, indicate utter confusion as to the tactics that produce better deals.

Naturally, at the Clinic, when I put it so bluntly, I do so in order to ruffle the feathers of the afflicted negotiators and to get them thinking about the consequences of their beliefs.

Consider the first defense:

Goodwill concessions soften them up.

What is the evidence for this?

I won't go so far as to say *all* research findings—in case I have missed some—but certainly all I have seen suggest that the opposite is the case:

Goodwill concessions by one party do not soften up the other side, they make them *tougher!*

True, the research I referred to is mainly conducted in the hallowed halls of academe and therefore is vulnerable to being loudly dismissed to the sound of raspberries by "practical" people.

I too have laughed loud and long at some of the research projects conducted in our universities: Not so long ago, someone was researching the phenomenon of deviance (i.e., criminality) among *left-handed* immigrants into the Orkney Islands; another, this time an anthropologist from the London School of Economics, was studying gossip in a Highland village.

But these are totally atypical of the serious academic research into negotiating behavior conducted all over the world during the past forty years. Incidentally, much of this research is also largely confirmed by the practical experience of those negotiators who are free from the curse of goodwill conceding. You have only to consider what the goodwill believer is suggesting to see that they must be wrong.

The idea that concessions soften up opponents suggests that negotiators are provoked by evidence of your generosity into being generous themselves. Now why should your early concessions have that effect? Consider it from your opponent's point of view. In seeing you make a concession, he can interpret what you are doing in one of two ways. Either you are displaying goodwill, or you are displaying your weakness.

Even if he accepted the first interpretation, there is no compelling need for him to react with reciprocated goodwill and be generous in return. He still has the tempting option of taking a tougher stance himself.

And if he makes the second interpretation of your conceding behavior, he will be even more inclined to take a tougher stance. Certainly, the likelihood of him reacting with goodwill must be very small, unless both of you are imbued with an overwhelming desire to be generous despite your perceptions of the relative strengths of each other.

If both of you are compulsive goodwill negotiators, may you always *only* negotiate with each other!

But what happens if your next negotiation is with an opponent who is not a believer in goodwill conceding, either by conviction from practical experience or the evidence of the academic research? Your goodwill strategy then relies entirely on him being converted to goodwill conceding by your example.

How do you convert him? Do you tell him that the purpose of your concession is to soften him up (that will go down like a lead balloon, won't it?), or are you going to be less than candid (farewell, St. Francis!) about your motives and merely hope that his defenses are down?

GOODWILL IS A PRECEDENT

A supplier of electrical-switch gear was asked to quote a contractor for a job in the Middle East. They went in with their list price and ran into serious resistance from the contractor, who flatly refused to pay the list price for anything.

An exasperated sales negotiator eventually pressed the question: "Why are you so adamant about getting a reduction from our list prices?"

"Because you gave a subsidiary of ours a ten percent discount off your prices last year."

"But that was a once-only introductory discount for a special job in anticipation of future work," the negotiator replied.

"Well, this contract I am offering you is part of the 'other work,' and as far as I am concerned I want to be 'introduced' to your below-list prices too!"

What is the most likely consequence of your attempt to soften him up? You don't need a Ph.D. in human nature to suppose that he is most likely to read your concession as a sign of weakness and act accordingly by getting tougher.

Turning to the second defense of goodwill conceding, this time "to push the boat out" and "get things underway," you should note the sense of desperation in the tone of this line of defense.

As a tactic, it is vulnerable to the same response as the other one: It is more likely to provoke a tougher stance in your opponent rather than an outbreak of goodwill, because he will interpret your concession as a sign of your weakness.

But there is a more fundamental criticism of it.

Presumably, if you are feeling a need to get the negotiation underway, so is the other guy. If this is the case, why is a goodwill concession your best move? Far from getting the negotiation underway, you only succeed in moving your own negotiating position toward the other guy's. In effect, you have moved onto the slippery slope to surrender.

If you concede when I press you, my best bet is to keep pressing until I am convinced that you are not going to move any further.

Up in the northern tundra, the people are smarter than your average goodwill conceder. They know about the fallacies of conceding as a negotiating style. They learned it the hard way.

Indeed, drop into any little town inside the Arctic Circle, up in northern Norway, or Canada, or Alaska, and announce over your beer that you are a devotee of goodwill conceding—they will throw you out into the snow, even at forty below.

Some trading posts have local ordinances against the practice of goodwill conceding, and sheriff courts up there show no mercy to city folks brought before them charged with the offense. In fact, goodwill conceding in the tundra is positively antisocial.

Why?

Well, years ago when the first traveling salesmen went up there to sell them the benefits of civilization—refrigerators, suntan lotion, and ice cold beer—they were welcomed in the warm and generous spirit that snow people are renowned for the world over.

The salesmen went from outpost to outpost carrying their wares on sledges pulled by dogs. (I refer to sales*men* rather than sales*persons* because the disaster was entirely the fault of smart-assed males from down south, and in those days the only women in the tundra were born there and were too sensible to ride around on sledges selling suntan lotion).

The trouble was that some of these salesmen brought with them their "civilized" vices, one of which was the filthy practice of goodwill conceding.

At first, the locals didn't realize the poison that had been brought into their midst by their new friends, and life carried on as normal. The trouble began when the locals taught the salesmen how to hunt for meat to eat on the long sledge journeys between outposts.

The practice that led to disaster was slow to gather momentum, but once it got going drastic measures were needed to stop it.

It seems that Bjorn McKenzie, a cold beer salesman, presumably of Swedish and Scottish extraction (the accounts vary and are probably mixed up anyway), found himself one afternoon being stalked by a wolf some miles up the track. He had just shot a large elk and had struggled might and main to get it onto his jumbo-sized sledge.

The piercing howl of the wolf made Bjorn jump, as it seemed to be very near. Fear forced him quickly to evacuate his camp and he set off, as fast as the dogs could pull him, down the track to the nearest outpost.

The wolf followed, just out of rifle range. Bjorn increased the dogs' pace and the sledge lurched forward, groaning with the heavy weight of him, his cold beer samples, and the dead elk.

As the wolf closed in—he swore he could hear it panting behind him—he searched desperately for a solution to his predicament.

It was then that Bjorn had a blinding flash: Of course! The wolf was hungry and wanted some of his elk!

"What better way to get the sledge moving faster than to cut off some of the elk meat and throw it behind to the wolf?" Bjorn asked himself, and immediately congratulated his mother for having such a brilliant son.

The hungry wolf, Bjorn reasoned, would be satisfied and would stop hounding him if he was given *some* meat to eat; meanwhile, Bjorn could give it the slip and reach the safety of the outpost.

Hence, Bjorn cut off a small slice of meat—a difficult task, as the sledge was moving fairly fast at the time—and threw it behind him. He had plenty of meat left and he knew that a small slice would not matter much to himself but would likely help to lower the wolf's hostility toward him.

Everything went according to plan for the next two miles. The dogs strained away and the sledge fairly skidded along over the icy track. Bjorn was already composing the story of his brilliant escape for his pals at the outpost. But suddenly he heard the howl of the wolf again. And this time he thought he could hear two of them—perhaps three!

Bjorn's heart thumped away, and it was all he could do to remain in a state one degree short of panic. Thinking quickly, he concluded that he had not given the wolf enough meat—he did not bother to ask himself where the other two wolves had come from—so he cut off some more meat and threw it behind him. This time he threw out three portions, just in case one wasn't enough, which still left Bjorn with lots more for himself.

He swore later to his pals that he had only gone a few hundred yards when he heard the howl of wolves again. There must have been more than three behind him this time, and he could see several more coming through the trees alongside the track, all racing like crazy for the sledge.

Bjorn whipped the dogs harder, and croaked out "Mush! mush!" (as they do in the movies), and also began to cut meat off the elk at a furious rate, throwing out great chunks of it in all directions.

And still the wolves came on. Dozens of them. From every direction they raced after the sledge, yelping for more.

And more.

And yet more.

They howled in what Bjorn was convinced at the time sounded like derision when they got a chunk of his meat at their feet. Nothing, apparently, would satisfy the wolves. They appeared to have gone crazy (they were already wild, of course, but now they were furious, too).

Bjorn started throwing meat to specific wolves, hoping that by pleasing them they would recognize a friend if it came to the final supper with him as the main dish.

Before long Bjorn was running out of elk, but he didn't run out of wolves: Now there were hundreds of them!

He threw the last of the elk to the wolves just as he reached the safety of the outpost.

It was a close-run thing. Bjorn felt lucky to escape with his life. True, he had thrown away all of the elk, though he had intended only to throw a few small bits away. But he was alive and able to tell the locals and his fellow salesmen of his brilliant ploy to get the better of the wolves.

The locals had never heard the like of his tale in all the years they had run sledges in the tundra. No wolves ever came near their sledges and certainly no packs of wolves ever bothered them in the slightest. They shook their heads and put it down to the city slicker's imagination.

In contrast, the salesmen, who had no experience with wolves or what they were really like, immediately made preparations to load up their sledges with elk steaks; they were not going to be caught in the tundra without a defense against ravenous wolves!

And that was the source of the disaster. For the next six months Bjorn and the other salesmen raced around the tundra, plying their refrigerators, suntan lotion, and cold beer, and throwing meat to any wolves that chased after them.

They considered Bjorn's discovery of how to handle wolves the most brilliant idea they had heard since their companies had sent them to the tundra to make their fortunes.

True, none of them had made a fortune yet, but neither were any of them eaten by a wolf.

They were absolutely shocked beyond belief when the local people ganged together and sent them packing down river at gunpoint.

"Haven't we brought you the prizes of civilization?" they asked as the locals herded them with menacing looks into makeshift canoes.

"Yes," the suntanned locals replied as they distributed more cold beer from the outpost's refrigerators to the armed guards. "But what about the wolves?" they demanded, much to the astonishment of Bjorn and his pals.

"Wolves? What about the wolves?" Bjorn asked. "My fellow salesmen and I have done nothing to any wolves. In fact," he added, "we've been following my infallible system for keeping ravenous wolves at bay."

At this, the locals almost lynched Bjorn on the spot.

"You haven't kept the ravenous wolves at bay, you idiot," shouted the locals. "You've simply taught wolves that if they want to be fed they should chase sledges!"

Now what happened to the good folks of the tundra is a poignant lesson for the rest of us. They managed to eradicate the source of their trouble—wolves being taught to chase sledges to get fed—by deporting the salesmen who introduced the practice of goodwill conceding into their territory. Eventually, as the wolves tired of chasing sledges, getting nothing but empty cold beer cans thrown at them, they went back to getting fed nature's way and left the sledges alone.

Unfortunately, though Bjorn and his pals are long gone from this life, and the tundra is free of the filthy practice of goodwill conceding, no such remedial action was taken in the big cities of the world.

Negotiators still go around throwing out concessions to their opponents, sometimes out of fear of not getting the negotiations started and sometimes in the hope that the other guy will recognize a friend and be nice to them.

The disease is widespread, and for those afflicted with it for more than a short time, it can become terminal—they get done in so often by other (tougher) negotiators that they are fit only for a job in sales training, where they will teach tomorrow's bright young salespersons Bjorn's infallible system for dealing with ravenous wolves.

Q.1: a] With the Japanese you could wait a long time! (− 5)

b] Free gift concessions do not push the boat out, they encourage the opposition to sit tight and wait for your next free gift. (− 15)

c] Yes. The Japanese will get the message. (+ 10)

d] Weak. It shows your impatience. (− 10)

Q.2: a] Not if it's their first one! (− 40)

b] Invites them to bid blind. They won't. (− 15)

c] Much better. You could try an offer such as: either a two-thirds advance of their $50,000 (i.e., $33,000) or a half advance of your $60,000 (i.e., $30,000). This gives you more of the money they are offering sooner. (+ 10)

d] Almost always a foolish move, unless other video companies are fighting for an appointment! (− 10)

Q.3: a] You are bidding blind and he will tell you your cut is not enough. (− 15)

b] He might bluff you on the difference. (− 10)

c] A risky call of his bluff. (+ 5)

d] Good, if you believe there are other bids, but could be bad if you catch him out in a bluff. (+ 5)

e] This is a positive move and could lead to a discussion of the differences between your offer and the others. Price is not the only determining variable in a buying decision. (+ 10)

SELF-ASSESSMENT TEST 6

Q.1: You want to buy a house that has an asking price of $160,000. Which opening offer would you consider making to the owner:

a] $156,000?

b] $160,000?

c] $142,000?

d] $146,000?

e] $163,000 with one hour to accept or reject?

Score:

Q.2: You have decided to replace your word processor with a more powerful model and have been quoted a list price of $25,000 by a supplier. What size discount do you expect?

a] 5%?

b] none?

c] 15%?

d] 7.5%?

e] 20%?

Score:

Q.3: You see a used Jaguar for sale and have seen similar makes and models advertised recently for $2,500. Somebody suggests that you make a once-only cash offer in the amount of $1,400. Do you expect the owner to:

a] Haggle but take it?

b] Haggle but refuse it?

c] Refuse to consider it?

Score:

Q.4: You are a copier machine sales representative and make an invited sales call at the local home for unmarried mothers. The social worker in charge indicates that she wants to purchase one of your machines which has a list price of $3,700. However, her budget fixes an absolute ceiling of $3,000. Do you:

a] Regretfully decline to do business?

b] Use your pricing discretion and make a sale?

c] Suggest that she consider a cheaper model?

Score:

IN PRAISE OF
MOTHER HUBBARD
or How to Make Them
Cut Their Prices

Jack lives in California. He is an economist and, as a hobby, collects old model (circa 1960s) Jaguar cars.

Every couple of years he decamps from Berkeley to visit his wife's family in Edinburgh. While in Scotland he tries to buy old Jaguars, or bits of them, for export to the United States.

Apparently old Jaguars, or their parts, feature in the life-styles of some of the affluent folk in California, who, having everything, also want the best—when, that is, they are not after the weirdest.

On his return to Berkeley, Jack lovingly refurbishes his own collection of vintage cars with the worn-out parts from the assorted stock he brings back with him.

Occasionally, out of neighborly compassion—rather than vulgar avarice—he sells a car (or just some bits of one) from his personal collection to desperate Jaguar fanatics (who "crowd his space" when news gets round that he's back), providing that his beloved Jaguars go to a "good home."

I have been able to watch him negotiating the purchase of a Jaguar, mainly from his habit of requiring me to pull over and stop if he sees a Jaguar of early vintage parked on the road. This habit of Jack's makes no concessions to where we are heading or what time we are supposed to be there. And unlike Bob in Sydney, Jack loves every minute of a negotiation.

If you're there to listen to him on his way back from a deal, he relives the moves with you (and if you're not, I'm sure he recounts them aloud to himself). And when he gets back to Mrs. Professor, his enjoyment is by no means diminished, for he tells her in detail how he got the deal.

I have never seen anybody so wrapped up in his negotiations and so good-tempered about them. If a deal doesn't come off, it joins the list of amusing anecdotes he has on buying used cars. Jack insists that a deal that failed did so almost always because he didn't use his cardinal rule for negotiating:

Shock 'em with your opening offer.

Jack swears that this principle has served him well over the years. How does it work? Simple. When you open, make sure it is very low (if you're buying), or very high (if you're selling).

Jack doesn't believe in opening with a price close to where he might be prepared to settle. He likes to leave himself lots of negotiating room.

If you do choose to open close to your expected settlement price, Jack argues, you might indeed settle at it (in which case you are no better off), or you might have to go above/below it considerably (in which case you could be worse off).

Opening is a risky business, and if you open modestly you give the other guy false ideas about how much room there is to for you to move.

If he believes you have a lot of room to move he must follow his best interests and haggle hard, perhaps forcing you to move a lot. As he does not know what your best price (for him) is, he need not accept your protestations nor treat them other than as a bluff.

Whichever way you look at it, a deal on terms considerably worse than your intended terms is not a good way to do business. You might be able to convince yourself that you are happy with the deal "under the circumstances," and the contribution of such delusions to your self-esteem ought not to be discounted, but if by your opening behavior you can avoid the need for rationalizing your defeats it seems sensible for you to do so.

This has all the more relevance when you observe that by using his shock opening tactics, Jack finds that he settles many of his deals a long way short (on the better side) of his best price.

Why is this so?

Because his shock opening price compels the other guy to reconsider his expectations about the current value of his property.

Jack loses some deals because his offer is too far away from the other guy's basement price, but Jack claims that on average he will get most of his deals closer to his opening price than to his rooftop best price. And even if he has to go up close to his top price, he is no worse off than if he had opened close to it in the first place, except that by opening low, Jack increases the distance he would have to travel if the other guy's expectations are for a price above Jack's undisclosed top price.

OUT OF THE MOUTHS OF CHILDREN

A used-car dealer in Aberdeen had a 1962 Jaguar for sale, priced at $1,400. Jack saw it in the lot and went in to have a look. The owner handled the negotiations personally and after discussion, Jack said he would give him $950 for it.

The negotiations stalled, but they kept talking about this and that for a while. Clearly, the dealer knew he wasn't going to get $1,400, but didn't know how serious Jack was. While they were talking, another Jaguar pulled into the lot, driven by the owner's son.

Jack eyed the car and they moved over to look at it. It was slightly newer than the other model and it was in much better bodily condition. Obviously, it had been looked after.

The son said the car wasn't for sale, as it was his. The owner contradicted him by saying that the car belonged to his company and if he wanted to sell it he would.

Jack smelled a sale here. He offered $850 for it.

The dealer haggled a little and then asked how Jack intended to pay.

"Cash," was the reply.

Jack had enough cash, mainly in U.S. dollars, but since the oil boom they know about dollars in Aberdeen.

The deal was struck at $975 and the son was told to get his things out of the car, which he did with a face as long as transatlantic cable. Jack drove off quickly.

Afterward I asked Jack why he had gone in lower for the obviously better car. He said he originally intended to get the other car back into contention, but the old man was so determined to show his son who was boss of the business that he accepted a deal close to Jack's low opening offer. "This was a slight pity as the other car had genuine leather seats in it, which are worth a small fortune back home." However, the car he had bought was worth at least double what he paid for it in Scotland, let alone its value in the U.S.

In other words, getting a high price out of Jack is hard work.

Not surprisingly, what the other guy has to work hard for, he values far more than something that comes easy—*even if he settles at a lower price than he expected.*

The art of making somebody happy by disappointing him with a price lower than he was originally looking for is not a mystery. It lies in your ability to make him negotiate every cent of the way.

Negotiators are always unhappy if you agree too easily with their opening prices, so make them happy by haggling!

Why does the shock opening tactic work for Jack?

First, consider the position at the start of a negotiation. When you are considering negotiating for something—be it cash, a Jaguar, a million tons of Albanian cement, a Norwegian container ship, or a straw hat in a Mexican tourist shop—you have in mind a target price, that is, what you expect to pay for whatever you are buying, or get for whatever you are selling, assuming that you know something about your business. Call this your *expectation*.

How expectations form in your mind *before* the negotiation is less relevant for this discussion than the fact that they change during the negotiation.

If you arrive at the negotiation with predetermined views as to the appropriate settlement, it does not follow that you will stick to them irrespective of events; they may be changed, for instance, by what you come to believe about your prospects of achieving your expectations once the negotiation is underway.

Alternatively, if your views as to what is attainable are formed during the negotiation (you having no predetermined views before you find out what is in the other guy's mind), these views can also be re-shaped by subsequent events in the negotiation, or, more correctly, can be changed by your interpretations of those events.

In these cases, you have the choice of reducing your expectations or seeking a deal elsewhere. It could also be the case that you have the choice of sticking to your expectations or revising them upward if the negotiations reveal encouraging aspects of your opponent's intentions or perceptions.

Expectations in negotiation are entirely *subjective*. They do not have a life of their own independent of how you (and the other guy) read the situation once you are in contact with each other.

It is Jack's belief that the most decisive moment in the negotiation to influence expectations is at the opening contact, when neither of you are too sure of what can be achieved.

Hence, his belief that it pays to go in hard with a tough opening stance. This move has the immediate effect of undermining the original confidence of the other guy in any high expectations he has formed, or, if he has not yet formed his views, it severely limits the price he can realistically hope for from Jack.

In Jack's view, the greater the shock of the opening price the more effective the tactic.

If you are buying, go in low—really low—*if your opening is credible in some way,* and you will undermine even the toughest negotiator's confidence in his starting position.

The same is true for going in high—really high—if you are selling.

Now neither I nor Jack claim that this move will *automatically* assure you of a successful deal. Audacity is essential, but it is not enough.

The main target of the shocking opening move is your opponent's beliefs about his position. You are trying to structure his expectations of the likely outcome of the negotiation. To the extent that you reduce his expectations—even by a little amount—it has to be good for you as a negotiator.

If he arrives thinking he is going to buy your business for $15 million and you open with a demand for $30 million, he is bound to have some problems with your opening: Do you really mean what you say, is *your* price realistic, is *his* price realistic, has *he* done *his* sums correctly, are *you* in as weak a bargaining position as *his* accountants reported, and so on? He may not roll over and play dead, but it will certainly stop him in his tracks while he thinks it over.

You walk into a store to get a discount of 15 percent and the clerk tells you that the company only makes 7 percent gross.

What do you do?

If you even half believe him you know you have no chance of getting 15 percent. So either you lower your expectation or try another store.

You decide to get your company products advertised on television and allocate a budget of $10,000 to the project. At your first meeting with the producer he tells you it costs $3,000 a minute to shoot twenty minutes of film, which will be cut down to a forty-second commercial. Anything cheaper would get you a wooden Oscar.

What do you do?

Either you increase your budget or you forget about TV.

Your pitch for a 20 percent share of the gross income and your partners show you that they only make 10 percent net and then only if they sell 1,000 sets a month.

What do you do?

Give up dreams of a Hollywood life-style or get new partners?

You ask her to accompany you to a convention in Acapulco and she tells you she might consider a dinner date in a month's time.

What do you do?

Lower your sights or try dating her sister?

These cameos illustrate the impact that a shocking opening can have on the negotiators. Whatever else they do, (such as try their luck elsewhere), their sights must be lowered in the negotiation.

Moving someone from an opening that is a long way from your original expectation is like climbing Mt. Everest in the nude.

If you aim for the stars and the other guy intends to start with the trees, you have a long way to go to get him airborne.

It is a fact of negotiating life that the majority of us will not persist with what we come to believe are unrealistic demands. We will sooner back off than persist.

Generalizing from Jack's insight into negotiating behavior, we can see that the best opening is the toughest opening. All else weakens your influence on the eventual outcome.

The tough opening has, however, to be *credible* in some way. What do I mean by it being *credible*?

The shock opening tactic is of little use (in the sense of getting a good deal) if you believe that *any* crazy price will do.

There is no point in trying to buy the Empire State Building with an opening bid of $200—though if you wait long enough the city might pay you one day to demolish it.

A SHOCKING BID

A city council called for bids to demolish an old slaughterhouse and clear the site. Several demolition firms submitted bids ranging from $17,000 to $40,000. One company sent in a $2 bid. This was accepted (after checking that it was not an unfortunate typing error).

Why did they want only $2 to do such a large job?

Because their survey showed them that there was about 2,500 tons of iron girders and iron piping in the building plus several hundred tons of other metals, with a scrap value in excess of $120,000.

A SHOCKING TYPING ERROR

A union official submitted a written pay claim for his distillery members and a week later met the management to negotiate the new contract.

He was surprised to be given details of company sales and costs. He also listened to a long presentation from the management on the financial prospects for the next year.

Perplexed by this unusual behavior, the official scanned the papers across the table. On top of them he could see his written claim, and he read it upside down.

He spotted the cause of the problem. His secretary had typed the figures incorrectly: Instead of a claim for a 12 percent wage rise (with an expectation of settling at about 7 percent) she had typed "21 percent." No wonder the company was making such an extraordinary fuss!

He said nothing and waited to hear what they would offer after their heartrending presentation of how poor the company was at present. They opened with an offer of 12 percent and eventually they settled at 15 percent. This was 8 percent more than he expected to settle at before the meeting, which taught him something about the modesty of his previous claims.

The difference between a shock opening and a silly one is not easy to define, because the boundary between a negotiating move that pays off and one that doesn't is not always obvious. The only important difference between one and the other is that the shock opening is *credible* and the silly one is not.

62

If you can credibly defend your opening, you can make what in some circumstances would plainly be a silly opening into a winning one.

Credible reasons for an opening position give it a lot of mileage. And remember the reasons you give for your opening only have to be credible to the guy listening, not to a panel of neutral judges.

Jack, for instance, has one disadvantage when he opens his mouth to negotiate in Scotland: He sounds just like what he is—an American, and, as every canny Scot knows, Americans abroad (unless they are in the Navy) have more money than sense.

Jack would be stretching credulity if he was to plead poverty as a reason for his low offer. So naturally he doesn't bother.

However, he does have a credible line: He has to ship the vehicle all the way to California. This, he tells the sellers, "doubles" his costs.

He always adds that his deal is a cash deal, the mention of which is often a strong incentive to settle where a used-car negotiation is concerned.

Also, the fact that Jack is taking the car to California does not escape the seller. This removes him from the vicinity where the seller lives and therefore from comebacks if the car is not all it is cracked up to be by the seller's pitch. These circumstances make Jack's negotiating position fairly strong.

Of course, the real issue that ought to concern the sellers is not what the car is worth to them in Scotland, or what it costs Jack to ship it home, but what the car is worth to Jack in California when he gets it there. And by all accounts, the value of the Jaguars in Berkeley exceeds by a long way the price Jack pays for them in Scotland.

In general, if your shocking or tough opening is credible, it has a good chance of forming the basis of the negotiation, so open with the toughest credible opening you can think of.

One way to give you confidence in using the tough opening is to use the Mother Hubbard (of "the cupboard is bare" fame).

In this tactic you must convince the seller of two interconnected points:

1. That you genuinely want to buy the seller's product.
2. That you do not have the resources to reach the seller's opening price.

In effect, you tell the seller that the cupboard is bare.

How close you pitch your Mother Hubbard to the seller's opening price is a matter of judgment. Perhaps it will be best if you try it out first on prices close to the seller's, then gradually widen the gap in subsequent negotiations as you gain confidence in its use.

You must decide just how bare you are going to make your cupboard and which stance is credible in the circumstances.

The seller is bound to ask you (if he has bitten the bait): "How much can you afford to pay?"

At this point you must be wary of being sidetracked into a deposit-with-a-loan deal or some such way of undermining your play (including the "running two budgets together" move). You must establish that the *total* amount you have available for the purchase is *all* that will ever be available.

AT THAT PRICE,
I'D RATHER SCRAP IT

Getting mechanical things repaired can cost a small fortune. This is especially true of cars, boat engines and light aircraft.

Harry Smith had engine trouble with his small week-end boat. He took it to the repair yard and asked them to diagnose the trouble. A week later the yard rang Harry and told him that he needed a new engine as the shaft had gone on his old one and it would not last another twenty hours use. A new engine would cost him $1,800, which the yard was willing to fit for another $300.

There was no way that Harry was prepared to fork out $2,100 for a new engine on a boat he used only occasionally.

He tried a version of the Mother Hubbard.

He told the yard that he had decided to sell the boat for "whatever it would bring" (probably about $400 in its current condition) and that he would "collect it next Tuesday."

On Monday, Harry turned up at the yard to collect his boat, implying that he had found a customer. He told the manager that the money he got from selling the boat and the money he saved by not buying an engine would go towards his holidays.

The manager was not keen to see a lost engine sale but could also see that Harry was determined to sell his boat. He asked Harry how much he was able to pay to replace his engine. Harry (springing the Mother Hubbard) told him that he was only prepared to stay with power boating if it cost him no more than $750, but that he was quite happy to quit sailing as engines "cost money to fit, to maintain and to fuel."

The manager went for the $750 ceiling.

He told Harry that if he was interested, he could trade-in his old engine for a reconditioned engine from stock for $800 net—"a customer had left it three years ago and had not been heard of since"—plus $165 for fitting.

Harry agreed (eventually) after getting a warranty on the "new" engine and a free fitting, all for $690.

Let me illustrate the use of the Mother Hubbard by a barrister friend in London.

We were having lunch in a busy trattoria in Dean Street, Soho, in 1979, when he asked my advice about the purchase of a computer that he had been put in charge of by his partners. At the time I was working as a sales consultant to a computer company and was familiar with the market.

My friend's problem was that he knew which machine he wanted but was $7,000 short of the total price the computer sales negotiator had quoted him. There was also the important question of doing well in this negotiation. As he had only just joined the practice as a partner and as their first black barrister, he wanted to do well.

I suggested that he raise more cash, but he explained he could not do this as he was already running two office equipment budgets together by making the purchase at the end of one financial year and the beginning of the other.

So I suggested he use the Mother Hubbard technique, and was persuaded to explain it in detail for the price of the lunch and a bottle of chianti classico. After the lunch Nelson (for such is his name—as exotic as the beautiful island of Barbados, where he hails from) returned to his office to meet with the computer negotiator. Incidentlly, they were rivals of my client, so I was delighted to put them under the squeeze.

Being imaginative (and slightly inebriated, for the chianti was followed by several Sambucas) he contrived a very convincing script and used it at the negotiation.

Nelson started correctly by making the computer seller go over the machine's virtues once again. He also booked a demonstration of the machine for his partners in the office later that week.

The seller really got to work on what he now considered to be a prospect and (correctly) he kept plugging away at the deal. However, he also disclosed (incorrectly) that he was anxious to get the machine into a legal practice as a basis for making sales to other partnerships nearby.

Nelson did not pretend to have the gift of those sales at his disposal, but he hinted vaguely (correctly) that if the machine was as good as it was claimed it was bound to have some effect on sales in the profession.

A week later, after the office demonstration, the Mother Hubbard was sprung.

The seller was told that the partners had approved the purchase of *a* computer in principle, but they had imposed a budget ceiling on the acquisition of $18,000.

"Not a penny more is to be spent," Nelson reported, and to underline this point he read the decision out from the minutes of the weekly partnership meeting. He placed the minutes across the desk in full view of the seller.

This was a correct (almost inspired) move on Nelson's part.

Why?

Because, since Moses brought the tablets down from the mountain, the written word has an authority over the mere spoken word.

People appear to accept almost anything as true if it is written rather than spoken, which is why sellers have their prices printed in lists to give them an altogether undeserved authority!

You will hear people cautioning you not to believe what you read in the papers, but you will seldom hear anybody say the same about what you see or hear on television, it supposedly being unnecessary.

Regretfully, Nelson told the seller that as his machine was priced at $18,000, to which was added an $800 training charge, an annual maintenance fee of $3,000 and a tax of $3,200, giving a gross price of $25,000, the partners had instructed him to look elsewhere for a more realistically priced machine.

He regretted this move, as he thought the machine on offer would meet their needs, and he pointed out that the partners were less keen on modernizing than he was, but wanted to see some more demonstrations of other machines in the coming week.

The seller was visibly put out by this news (though it was a mistake to display his emotions) and, predictably, he tried several lines of attack on the ceiling price of $18,000.

He offered (incorrectly) several concessions in the form of additional software free of charge, a reduced training package, and an extended payment period.

His mistake was that none of these tackled the central problem of the $18,000 budget ceiling, though Nelson (correctly) made a note of the concessions for later use.

But on the gross price of $18,000 Nelson could not budge. As his shocking opening was credible—the written minutes "proved" it—his regret was genuine. He accepted that searching for a cheaper machine was a drag, but he would have to do this as the price of $25,000 was way above his budget.

The seller was boxed in; he knew that if he wanted to make this sale he would have to come down in price. But $7,000 was some drop, and he needed a good reason for arranging anything like that.

As he didn't have a good reason at hand, he agreed to get back to Nelson after he had "consulted his head office."

It would have been better for him to have said he would get back after he had thought it over and if he had not disclosed his lack of authority in the negotiation. Also, it was a risky decision to leave his prospect in case the competition came in while he was away and introduced Nelson to a cheaper machine (in computers there is always a cheaper machine available or on its way).

Three days later Nelson received a call saying that the computer company would make a "special offer" of a machine at $15,800, which would reduce the tax bill considerably.

There was more, too!

The seller announced that his company would show their faith in their computer by postponing for twelve months the annual maintenance fee of $3,000.

This "never to be repeated" offer, plus the training charge, gave a gross purchase price of $17,850, "which is $150 inside your budget" (confirming the credibility of Nelson's Mother Hubbard).

The offer was conditional on the partners being willing to allow the computer company to quote them as clients to other partnerships, but "for obvious reasons" the special price they had been given was to remain confidential.

I congratulated Nelson on his success and remarked that his deal might have been improved if he had tried to press them on the training charge—a wholly ludicrous proposition, in my view, that requires the customer to pay a computer firm for training its people how to use their machines. It is regarded as a giveaway by many computer negotiators, but you have to press them.

However, Nelson's first attempt at the Mother Hubbard saved his partnership slightly over $7,000—less the cost of lunch, chianti, and Sambucca at the trattoria!

ANSWERS
SELF-ASSESSMENT TEST 6

Q.1: a] This is so close to his asking price that he must conclude he has a chance of getting $160,000. (− 5)

b] You are not trying very hard, are you? (− 10)

c] A tough opening indeed—you risk not getting the house, but if you do you're going to get it cheap. (+ 10)

d] Still a tough opening and sufficiently far away from his price that he must reconsider his expectations. (+ 7)

e] You have been hustled or have more money than sense and know something about the house that I don't! (− 15)

Q.2: a] A modest expectation. (+ 5)

b] Oh dear! (− 15)

c] Good. (+ 10)

d] Not so good. (+ 7.5)

e] Very good. (+ 12)

Q.3: a] You're optimistic. (+ 5)

b] You're pessimistic. (0)

c] You're selling yourself short. (− 5)

Q.4: a] A close-out move; try c] first. (+ 3)

b] She's done the Mother Hubbard on you. (− 10)

c] Correct. (+ 7)

Q.1: You want to sell your car privately to finance a new car purchase. You think it is worth $4,300 and you know of its (to you) minor defects. Do you:

a] Advertise it at $4,300 ONO (or near offer)?

b] Advertise it at $4,500?

c] Advertise it at $5,000?

d] Advertise it without a price?

e] Advertise it at $4,300?

Score:

Q.2: You are quoting for the installation of a heating system in a factory. Do you:

a] Give a detailed cost breakdown of every item in the quotation?

b] Give a rough breakdown of the costing?

c] Avoid giving a cost breakdown, only the total figure?

Score:

Q.3: Your spouse complains loudly to you that the old trailer you no longer use is blocking the side drive of the house, and you must get rid of it. As the weeks go by the complaints get more strident, and eventually you sit down to compose an advertisement to sell it. You think it is worth about $175, given its condition and the likely market for used trailers. What do you say about price in your advertisement:

a] $190?

b] $225?

c] $175 ONO?

d] Make me an offer?

e] First offer of $190 gets it?

f] Nothing?

Score:

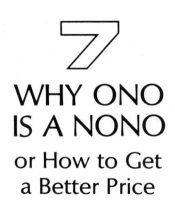

WHY ONO
IS A NONO

or How to Get
a Better Price

The used household goods market is peanuts compared to the world of multinational business, but it has some potent lessons for negotiators. This chapter is about some of them.

In America, schoolboys sell knives and horror comics to each other; all children, everywhere, soon learn to trade with their pals.

Their parents are no different. Alongside the official markets of everyday business and commerce, there is a flourishing, almost underground, market for household goods.

In Communist countries too, the ordinary people engage in trade, whatever the official laws say to the contrary. Walk down any main street in a Communist country and somebody is bound furtively to offer to buy something from you—even your clothes!

In 1965, at the main rail station in Warsaw, for instance, the government money changer in his office offered me one zloty rate for my money, which I refused, and a totally different rate—much more favorable to me—five minutes later as I walked through the tunnel to the train track (apparently he had closed his office for a few minutes in the interests of a little private enterprise).

My faith in moral man was slightly reduced by this incident. After all, Christ had driven the money changers out of the Temple courtyard, and here was one of them "polluting the glorious Soviet Socialist victories of the masses." This did not prevent me from doing business with him, as my faith in the power of free markets to overcome the idiocy of dictatorship was refreshed by it!

Hungary too, was run by economic lunatics in the 1960s. At Budapest airport, no money changer would give you Polish zloty for Hungarian dinars, even though both were "brother Socialist" economies (and each presumably had plenty of zlotys or dinars). They would, however, give you *unlimited* amounts of U.S. dollars (which officially they were desperately short of) for your dinars!

However, I don't want to give the impression that private deals are confined to those living in the "workers' paradises."

In Washington, D.C., in 1978, I was caught off balance in a bookstore by the clerk offering to buy the red striped shirt I was wearing for twenty dollars cash. I admired his taste almost as much as I regretted his timing, as I was on my way to lunch at the International Monetary Fund two blocks along, and the thought of appearing there shirtless ruined the deal. (Of course, it would have been different if I had been going to a welfare office instead).

In fact, everybody at some time or another has sold something—a used car, some furniture, a box of old books, or such like. The deal could have been made with a friend, a neighbor, a member of the family, or a complete stranger. They hear of our intentions of selling by word of mouth or from an advertisement of some kind.

For example, many people sell their cars by placing a notice in a window, along with a telephone number. Often they include the price they are looking for:

> For Sale
> This Car
> $5,500

As often, almost by the compulsion of convention, they also include the message:

> ONO

meaning "or near offer." Why do they add "ONO" after their price? Answers vary. Some say it stops a potential customer being put off by the price: If they believe the price is negotiable they are more likely to ask to see the car. Others say they do it because they do not want to lose the chance of a sale even if they must drop their price a little. Still others do it because they have seen other people's ads use "ONO" in them and they presume that it is part of the "rules" for selling used goods.

70

In my view, writing ONO is a mistake. In fact, I believe that ONO is a No-No.

Why?

Ask yourself what a buyer thinks when he sees ONO.

It tells him that you are willing to accept *less* than $5,500 *before even hearing what he has got to say*. This weakens your position.

How?

Well, instead of the buyer thinking he has to compete against others for the right to buy at a price *above* $5,500, he starts off knowing that the seller is worried about the possibility that he will not get a sale. And who does that help? The potential buyer, of course!

It is generally true that in writing ONO you almost always weaken your bargaining position by disclosing your keenness to sell. You open the negotiations at an implied price below your opening $5,500, without having found out anything about the extent of the buyer's keenness to buy. That way, you start off with a handicap—like opening at love–forty in tennis.

For all you know, the buyer, because of a family commitment, may desperately need to purchase a car that very day. Yours may be the fifth car he has looked at, and he has run out of time. This could make $5,500, or even more, for your car a bargain for him (and for you).

In negotiating, you don't know what is in the other guy's mind or the extent of the pressures upon him—and you certainly don't know anything about this before you meet him.

Once you are in contact with him you *might* get a clearer picture of his real position by what he says, but by using ONO, you forgo that opportunity to find out his real position. Meanwhile, he knows something about your position as soon as he reads your sale notice—that is, before he has met you. There exists an asymmetry in bargaining information—in his favor!

If he knows something about your attitude to the asking price—namely, that you have so little confidence in it that you are willing to accept less before the negotiating begins—and you do not know anything about his attitude—namely, whether he thinks $5,500 a good or a lousy price—it follows that to the extent that bargaining strength may be determined by relative keenness to trade, the eventual price must be more to the buyer's advantage than to yours.

IS IT NEGOTIABLE?

A consultant had just completed a ten-minute presentation on how he thought he could solve the client's distribution problems for a fee of $35,000.

The company president leaned over the table and asked: "Is that fee negotiable?"

The consultant knew that if he answered "yes" he would be pushed downward on the fee and if he answered "no" he might box himself into a corner on a price objection.

He thought for a second and replied: "I am always prepared to listen to any constructive suggestions that will improve the acceptability of my proposals."

The client noted his response and said nothing.

A week later he received the go-ahead to start the project. Nothing more was said about his fee.

I believe that the use of ONO-type messages is a mistake on the seller's part, *and* that a failure to take advantage of them on the buyer's part is a mistake of equal seriousness. Experience shows that buyers often ignore the ONO invitation to make a "near offer" and actually pay the asking price!

In other words, buyers do not always get the message implied by ONO, and they let the seller off the hook he put himself on in the first place.

Unfortunately, we cannot rely on our errors always being rectified by the errors of others, useful as they are as an excuse for our behavior!

Why buyers fail to take advantage of the seller's ONO-type invitation could be a source of employment for an out-of-work sociologist or student of abnormal behavior; it ought not to be the kind of mistake you make in future.

If you see something for sale with an ONO price tag you must assume immediately that the *maximum* price the seller is expecting is certainly *less* than the asking ONO price. And you also know that his rock bottom price will be lower still, because the *minimum* price he will accept will be *lower* than his maximum expectation.

You don't know what he will take until you try him out with some low (and I mean *low*) opening offers. Follow Jack's rule!

You might be the fifth potential buyer he has seen and he may be desperate not to lose you like he lost the others. Sooner or later, time runs out in every deal, and time may have run out for him. The fact that he has used an ONO price indicates an amateur approach to selling, and you need not be shy about taking advantage of this. Indeed, you do him and the wider community a great service by teaching him how to conduct his business. The extra discount on the price is your reward and the gratuitous experience is his.

Could there be a fairer way of educating the ONO seller?

If you ask people (as I do at the Negotiating Clinics) why they include ONO in their advertisements (not just for cars), they often rationalize it by claiming that their prime aim is to sell the used item because:

"I needed the space and it was in the way."

"I needed the money for a trade-in deal."

"I just wanted rid of it and any price was a bonus."

In other words, they felt under pressure of some kind to make the sale. The money was a secondary consideration as long as it was somewhere around the asking price.

But remember, being under pressure to make a deal is not unique to you. Nor should you assume that the other guy is not under even greater pressure. To do so is to make concessions before the negotiations begin, and in making opening concessions without receiving anything in return, you are in danger of sliding down the slippery slope to surrender.

Self-induced delusions that the other guy has all the power (commonly heard from trade union negotiators about the management, and from the management about the union men, and from buyers about sellers and vice versa) can be a costly mistake.

The price you set for your surplus household items is often purely arbitrary. It represents the price you would *like* to get, rather than the price you know for certain it will fetch.

Fortunately, you will soon learn if the market thinks your price is totally unrealistic. The notion that the world will beat a path to your door to negotiate a deal for a pile of old junk dies rapidly with every outbreak of seller's naiveté in the suburbs.

It is not altogether different in business, despite treatises written by economists to show that price setting is a science rather than a hunch. You are unlikely to know what the market value of used personal property is at any one moment; anyway, you are likely to be prejudiced about its value. You might think the old table is worth a small fortune just because your granny got it as a wedding present; the market may see it as more fit for firewood. But good luck to you—at least you are not underselling yourself.

Recently, I raced across Boston to see what was described in the advertisement as an "antique desk," priced at $125. (At that price I should have known better, but you never know what a fool might be throwing away for next to nothing).

The desk in question was clerical-grade (i.e., the very bottom) civil service, circa 1950. It had been bought by its redundant owner out of his own office when the government had a clearance sale. For some reason he thought it antique because he had sat at it for twenty years!

You know what you paid for your household property, perhaps, but you cannot know what other people are prepared to pay for it today until you attempt to sell it.

Not knowing what the price should be, you are tempted to use an ONO price tag as an encouragement to potential buyers to come and look at the item. But it is also an invitation to them to correct your assessment of what it is worth and, having taken the trouble to oblige you on the former, they are more than likely to help you with the latter.

Naturally, getting someone to your front door to look at your car, or old washing machine, or box of books, is an essential first step to selling them. If nobody calls to see what you are selling, then certainly nobody is going to buy these items. Hence the temptation to set a price low enough to attract customers but high enough to make it worthwhile for your trouble.

Choosing the right price is a difficult task—how high is high and how low is low? But having set a price, why choose to qualify it with ONO? By doing so, you undermine your decision on the price. You know that anybody taking the trouble to see your goods is halfway to buying them—searching around the secondhand market for a sofa can be a time-consuming business.

After a while the buyer is inclined to lower his sights if the price for something—not quite what he is looking for—appears to look like a bargain.

You can define a bargain any way you want to. You can compare it with what you expected to pay, or with the price a friend paid the week before. The range is limitless—which is why we can rationalize our "bargains" at least to our own satisfaction.

The buyer's strength is that he knows that the cost of newspaper advertising for low-priced household items can be a relatively high proportion of the selling price, particularly if the advertisements have to be repeated several times before a sale is made.

THERE'S A RIGHT TIME
AND A WRONG TIME

Graham is a farmer and he knows about the importance of the seasons. He also knows that there is a right and a wrong time to buy or sell almost anything.

He argues that most people forget the elementary rule of business: if you want to sell, avoid a buyer's market (and vice versa).

How do you avoid a market when the advantage is with the other guy? For one thing, Graham argues, you can deliberately choose not to enter a negotiation when a moment's thought should warn you off.

He gives the following advice for timing negotiations:
- The best time to buy a boat (Graham has two) is at the end of the season when the owner faces marina fees for the winter if he doesn't sell; conversely, the best time to sell is at the start of the season when the buyer is itching to sail his new boat.

- The best time to buy a house (Graham has three) is when the owner has to sell it irrespective of the season, hence enter the market in the winter if you're buying, avoid it if you are selling.
- The best time to get cash, use of the car, and a late night at a party is when father/husband is about to watch the big match on TV, or mother/wife is talking avidly to a girl friend.
- The worst time to negotiate about anything is when you are in a hurry, you're tired, you're emotional, you've just been fighting, you're sexually aroused, you've something important on your mind, or you want to be somewhere else.
- The best time to buy Christmas presents is right after Christmas in the New Year Sales, buy your Christmas cards in the Spring, Mother's Day cards near Father's Day, winter coats in the summer, summer clothes in the winter (especially if it is snowing), holidays off-season, logs and coal in the summer, vegetables near closing time in the street market, travel at off-peak hours, booze during "happy hour," hotel rooms at the week-end or near midnight, and property during a war (or revolution).

You must consider the consequences of a prospective customer hesitating over buying your car. This automatically produces prospects of additional costs (such as advertising *and* waiting) to attract alternative buyers.

If you are tempted to avoid these costs, you can only do so by being prepared to reduce the asking price from $5,500 to something near it. Hence, the mistaken reason for ONO: You want to make it clear that a near offer will be accepted.

My point is that you ought to bear in mind that the buyer also faces search costs and that he can only avoid these if he settles with you on your offer. The pressure on him to settle is just as relentless as the pressure on you, but he has no way of knowing what pressure you are under unless you tell him or indicate it to him in some other way (e.g., appearing very anxious to close the deal).

If a reduction in your asking price is necessary to clinch the deal, it is up to you to decide how far to move downward, if at all (but make sure that any such moves are small and infrequent).

But what is not necessary at all is for you to signal at the *start* that the price is negotiable.

If he wants to haggle, he will. You are no worse off by leaving that opening move to him; indeed, you are better off, because if you leave it to him to open the haggling with you, he has to overcome any inhibitions he has about haggling in order to do so.

And lots of people find it very difficult to open up a haggle. They cannot bring themselves to do so without a great deal of stress and effort.

They are inclined either to accept the deal as it stands or back off. If they accept the deal because of their shyness about haggling then you are home free.

If they need encouragement to negotiate, you might have to provide that—*but only in the negotiation.*

Ask questions such as what they like about the item, is it what they were looking for, in what way does it suit their needs, and so on. The answers will reveal their inhibitions about price. If you can coax an offer out of them, you can decide how you want to handle it—offer them a deal or go to deadlock.

This is by far a much stronger line to follow than ONO.

ANSWERS
SELF-ASSESSMENT TEST 7

Q.1: a] ONO is a *no-no!* You are telling the buyer that your price of $4,300 will be reduced. (− 15)

b] A strong move, as it gives you room to come down if you need to and is in touch with your target price. (+ 15)

c] Out of touch with your target and weakened by ONO. (− 20)

d] Could be OK depending on the state of the market. (+ 10)

e] Not good—any concessions bring you below target. (− 10)

Q.2: a] Never offer to give breakdowns (always ask for them!) as they encourage buyers to squeeze your price. (− 20)

b] Ditto—don't even give rough ones! (− 15)

c] Correct: A total figure helps repackaging. (+ 15)

Q.3: a] Competent buyers offer less than what you ask for, so you leave yourself some negotiating room. (+ 5)

b] Good. This leaves you room to move and scope to argue about the trailer's worth and condition. (+ 10)

c] No, because you encourage a buyer to expect to pay less than $175 *before* he sees the trailer. (− 10)

d] A sure hostage to fortune—what happens if he opens at $100 and your spouse is glaring at you? (− 15)

e] Firmer than a] and better than c], *if you mean it.* (+ 7)

f] *If* anybody turns up you will be too euphoric to hold your price, especially when they note the trailer's defects. (− 5)

SELF-ASSESSMENT TEST 8

Q.1: You are the key account negotiator for a soft-drink firm and have just been told by the chief buyer of the country's largest supermarket chain that you must cut your prices by a penny a case or they will drop your brand. They sell a million dozen cans of your Cola Pop a year. Do you:
a] Smile and say no?
b] Agree?
c] Suggest a compromise?

Q.2: Your next negotiation is with the rival supermarket chain, whose chief buyer expresses his delight at seeing you, as your main rival has stopped deliveries because of a strike. He asks if you can fill the gap with an emergency order of 50,000 dozen cans of Cola Pop, with immediate delivery. Do you:
a] Smile and say yes?
b] Say yes, but offer a reduced discount because of the additional costs of emergency delivery?
c] Smile and say it isn't possible at such short notice?
d] Tell him it's his lucky day, because not only can you deliver what he needs, but you can also give him the bulk purchase discount that is being offered this month?

Q.3: You have been working only three weeks in a new job in a shipping agent's firm in Baltimore. You plan to get married on Friday, August 18 (which you did not disclose at the job interview). Your intended has demanded a proper honeymoon of at least a week in Miami. It's now August 1 and you ask your boss for leave both for the wedding day and for the honeymoon. He is visibly put out by the request and asks stiffly how long you are thinking of being absent. Do you say:
a] The wedding day only?
b] Two weeks?
c] Three days?
d] One week?

THE LAW
OF THE YUKON
or How to Toughen Up
Your Negotiating Style

Toughness in negotiating, in my view, does not attract enough attention from practitioners. As with the great classics of literature, which are more often quoted than read, toughness as a negotiating style is more often spoken of than practiced.

In this chapter a case is made for toughness in your negotiating behavior which, it is hoped, will succeed in moving you along the tough–soft spectrum *toward* the toughness end.

Toughness is not a simple concept. There are many facets to toughness, and it takes as many forms as there are people willing to use it as a negotiating style.

A *tough* negotiator generally:

- Opens with a very high demand.
- Sticks to (or close to) his demand.
- Makes a few small concessions, but no large ones.
- Makes smaller concessions as the negotiations continue.
- Is undisturbed by threats of deadlock.

In contrast, a *soft* negotiator generally:

- Opens modestly.
- Moves considerably away from his opening position.
- Frequently makes large concessions.
- Is terrified by the prospect of deadlock.

Which are you at the moment?

Consider Joe, a key account manager for a firm of soft-drink manufacturers. He negotiates with major food store chains and has the authority to close his deals on whatever he judges to be the best price.

He sells cans of soda in quantities of up to a million dozen at a time. His company is in heavy competition with others and he is under constant pressure from the buyers he deals with to shave a penny off here and a penny off there. He is constantly told that his rivals are making these concessions and that if he doesn't match them his products will disappear from prime shelf positions.

Watching him negotiate under these conditions is an education in professionalism. He never betrays the slightest reaction to bad news of any kind, or to threats, or to shock-horror tales about what his clients have done or might do about his product lines.

He speaks very softly and manages to combine a nodding head at what he hears from the buyer with a smile as he says a clear "no" to the latest outrageous proposal.

Obviously, for the buyers, the tactic of squeezing until the pips squeak must work against the majority of sellers they see. They don't hold their jobs at the top of the buying tree by failing to get it right more often than they get it wrong. It's just that with Joe they get it wrong when they try the squeeze on him.

Joe knows that once he starts competing with his rivals to shave his prices he will be as ordinary as they are, and, perhaps more serious, he and they will start a slide downward to the extinction of some of them.

Fortunately, Joe's company believes in sustaining a high-profile advertising presence in the media; they are not dependent on the goodwill of particular food store chains. In this way they maintain public demand for their products, and where there is demand there has to be supply. If one chain does not stock these goods, others will—moreover, the local store managers don't like losing sales of popular products that the head office refuses to stock to their rivals who are not so inhibited, and they are easily encouraged to put pressure on the head office to ensure them of supplies.

ROOMS TO LET, FIFTY CENTS!

There is one good thing about the luxury hotel trade in the 1980s for the business negotiator—it's a highly competitive business and there are some great deals waiting for you out there.

The hotel business relies about 70 percent on business travel—I am not including the holiday hotels along the beaches of the world, which are in an entirely different business from the airport and downtown hotels used by negotiators.

The early 1980s recession hit the business hotels in two ways. It cut down corporate budgets (less use of hotels for strategy and sales conferences) and it hit air travel (less use of airport hotels for one-night stopovers).

What did this do to hotel tariffs? They got more negotiable than they have been in years. Many hotel chains froze their corporate rates and froze price hikes. Most upped the commission to travel agents for placing travelers in their hotels. This commission can be as high as 15 percent, which suggests that if you book through a travel agent you can negotiate a share of that 15 percent with them!

Some hotels even offered (only if asked—so ask!) 2 percent off the bill if you paid immediately rather than had them bill you or the credit card company. (Speak to the manager, not to the front desk).

If you are a regular traveler, a discount of 2 percent could give you a couple of nights free over the year, so don't turn your nose up at what you might consider peanuts.

The airport hotels are in the weakest negotiating position because they suffer from the recession *and* the cut in air travel, hence you can squeeze them harder or stay downtown.

If you plan to run a conference you can really get tough. The hotels in the exotic resorts are down to 20 percent and even 10 percent in occupancy.

Can you get yourself a deal in these circumstances? Put it this way: if you can't you're either not trying or you're in the wrong business!

You see, Joe does not act as if he is at the mercy of the buyers. He may be alone in the buyer's office for a negotiation, but he does not forget that he represents a large operation and that his products have a loyal support among the customers in the buyer's stores.

When buyers try to hustle him into thinking that pennies off his price are absolutely critical (after all, that's their job, isn't it?) he does not forget that the customer who buys a can of soda for thirsty kids to drink is not aiming to save a fraction of a penny per can (assuming the store passes on the discount instead of banking it as a profit, which is more likely in the retail grocery business). The truth is that kids like his company's product enough to badger their moms into buying it.

While Joe's perception of the realities of why customers purchase his company's soda gives him enough confidence not to crumble at the bark of the buyers, it is in no way sufficient to permit him to dictate terms. However, it is just enough not to lead him into the negotiations entirely naked.

Hence, Joe adopts a tough position on his prices, and his concessions are miserly. If a buyer wants a penny off a case he is going to have to work hard to get it. Joe has established his style over the years, and most of his buyers know he doesn't frighten easily—not that this stops them from trying every now and again. What do you do when the buyer hits you with "You'll have to do better than that!" Do you cave in and wish you could beam up to the Starship *Enterprise,* or do you refuse to panic?

The answer is to some extent a matter of personal concern to you alone—on it may depend your career progress, your material affluence, and, indeed, your personal happiness.

It is also of interest to your company, because a lot of other people in the organization—whose welfare is every bit as important to them as your welfare is to you—depend on the negotiating abilities of you guys in the front seats.

No matter what else those back at the office think of you as a person, you can bet your last paycheck that they prefer you to get big orders for the company's products rather than small ones, and they also prefer you to be tough rather than soft with your concessions.

Every penny off the case you give away too easily is money taken away from their next pay increase—perhaps even from what is available to keep them on the payroll.

Nobody profits from a company that makes losses, and every step you take down in price is a step nearer to bankruptcy. It is no comfort to argue that a penny cut by you is trivial. Dispatch may concede a penny on vehicle repairs, the works may concede a penny or more on the wages, accounts a penny on bad debts, and administration a penny on carbon paper. And so it goes on. Nobody thinks their behavior counts because on its own it doesn't. But taken together, this habit of cutting and running could put your company out of business.

Well, what of the evidence on toughness? Surprisingly, it is extremely consistent. Briefly, it pays!

Negotiators form their opinions about the realism of their expectations in contact with their opponents. They cannot act in this matter independent of the other party. What is or is not realistic is not decided by a court of Socratean sages who sit in judgment and pass the results of their deliberations to we mortals below. It is decided by our beliefs about what is possible, and those beliefs are influenced by what the other guy says and does. If the other guys act contrary to the way we expect, this must influence our judgment about the likely outcome of the negotiation.

For instance, in the unlikely event that a buyer greeted Joe with: "Am I glad to see you!" and then pleaded with him for an emergency delivery of a million dozen cans of soda pop that night (when Joe was expecting a big fight to get a small order), it is unlikely that Joe would respond by offering a discount and free delivery. The buyer's disclosure of his predicament is Joe's opportunity. Would Joe take it? You bet he would!

If the other guy goes in real hard on you, how do you rate the chances of an order? High, middling, low, or none at all? You would be less than real if you associated a tough stance in an opponent as an indication of his generosity. You would be an eternal optimist to conclude that it is going to be easy to settle on your best terms in such circumstances.

What is true for you is true for them.

Ironically, most negotiators react to the appearance of a tough stance and the absence of generosity by playing the role they sought for the other guy: They go soft and (good grief!) demonstrate their own generosity.

In effect, they reward the tough stance with softness on their part, for observation shows that toughness generates the opposite response from an opponent.

If you take a tough stance, he is *more likely* (and the evidence is that he is *much* more likely) to take a soft stance than a tough one, either by modifying his prepared tougher opening position or by cranking down his tough position to a much softer plateau.

The converse is probably more obvious: If an opponent opens up with an unexpectedly soft demand, it is most likely that you will revise your expectations upward rather than downward. If you don't, then you are in the wrong business!

This is precisely the basic weakness of the theory and practice of goodwill conceding—if you are soft, he responds by being tough. If he doesn't, you're dealing with as dangerous a threat to his company as you are to yours.

Negotiators, in between drinks at Thank-God-It's-Friday "seminars," will warn you that taking a tough stance increases the chance of a deadlock. That this may be true appeals to intuition.

The question that ought to be put is this: Just *how much* more likely is it that a deal will fold because I take a tougher stance?

It would take a very wise negotiator to answer that question with any confidence, because nobody knows before an event what is the precise likelihood of a deal folding for a given degree of toughness. (If you think you can predict this likelihood accurately there is a Nobel Price—worth $186,000—waiting for you!).

In the real world, it is impossible to be certain about the likelihood

82

of a deadlock in a negotiation because you take a specific stance in it. That deadlock is more likely is not disputed, but if the likelihood of deadlock is only *marginally* more likely if you take a tough stance, and the rewards of doing so are much higher if you are successful, then clearly it might pay you to be tougher rather than softer.

REMEMBER, THEY HAVE A CHOICE!

The gambling boom in the United States led New Jersey to attempt to skim off some of the glittering prizes flowing to Las Vegas. They invited casino operators to set up shop in the state.

Some of the locals thought this a heaven-sent opportunity to cash in on the bonanza, but one home owner went too far. His little two-story brick house occupied a part of the site where the *Penthouse* group wanted to build their casino. He asked them for $2.5 million for his house and refused all entreaties to budge his price.

Negotiators always have a choice of saying no, and this is what happened here. The casino group gave up negotiating and built their casino right up to the house property boundary. The casino now rises seven stories above the house on three sides, completely blocking the view except at the roadside.

Whatever the house was worth to the owner before the negotiations ($70,000?), it is now worth much less, except perhaps as a curiosity!

Observation and experimental evidence around the world suggest that the likelihood of deadlock is only *slightly* greater if a tough stance is taken. You may achieve slightly fewer deals, but the ones you do get are so much better in value that the gross result is a much higher income stream flowing to your company.

What happens all too frequently is that young negotiators listen intently to what old hands tell them at the weekly TGIF and react out of all proportion. They reason that if what the old hands say is true, and that it is more likely that a deal will deadlock with a tough stance than a soft stance, it follows that a soft stance will be more likely to lead to a deal than a tough one.

Also, their experience before hardened buyers convinces them that the only way they will get the buyer to recognize them as part of the human race, let alone like them just a little, is to please them in some way, such as by giving them concessions. It takes a heavy investment in training to eradicate this nonsense.

As to the wisdom of a TGIF seminar, new hands should make an allowance for the old hands' natural desire for a quiet life. They should also study the arithmetic: Seven negotiations that result in five deals at $10,000 are better than seven deals at $7,000.

It could be that the number of "hits" will be higher than five out of seven, making the arithmetic even better. It all depends on how big a difference in the *likelihood of settling* there is between a tough stance and a soft one in your product line and the price difference between the two stances. Certainly, you will never know until you start trying a tougher stance, as nothing much was ever proven over a few beers at a TGIF seminar, except perhaps that the old negotiators pass on the bad habits of each to everybody else.

The adoption of a soft stance is wrong because it starts a process of creeping limpness in the people who operate it.

First, they convince themselves that by being softer (read cheaper) they get business that would otherwise go to the competition. Then, as the habit of softness gets a grip on them, their outlook, and their behavior, they develop a cringe and even palpitations every time they see signs of the other guy teetering on the brink of deadlock.

Naturally, they convey this attitude unintentionally to the other guy, and he soon learns—as if programmed—to exploit their insipient fears of not getting a deal. He lays it on and before long all their deals are at or below the bottom line of profitability to their company.

Soft negotiators seek out soft buyers and never find them. Like opposite poles of a magnet, the soft negotiator attracts tough negotiators only.

If a buyer goes soft, the response borders on the paranormal: Hordes of tough sellers gravitate to the buyer's office carrying hard deals by the bundleload. You see, the word soon gets around.

Why?

What you are you don't beget: You create your opposite type.

How does toughness manifest itself in negotiating tests where the "beam me up Scotty" option is not available?

Tough negotiators have high expectations. They use shock openings and stick to them. If they meet a tough opponent they either face it out or end up at deadlock. They don't give into toughness by becoming soft. In the game of chicken they jam the accelerator and lock the steering wheel at straight ahead.

The pressure on them to modify their stance is exactly the same as on the other guy, and experience shows that most people respond to toughness in negotiating by becoming soft. The tough guy doesn't.

If he modifies at all it is slowly and in small, infrequent, and irregular steps that get smaller, not bigger. Tough negotiators always make smaller concessions than their opponents—they take more than they give. If they are offered a horse, they respond with an egg.

Tough negotiators are less concerned with deadlock than soft negotiators. Their main concern is with the deal being close to their expectations rather than with making a deal just for the sake of it.

If you are worried about the order, your opponent will sense it, like a dog always knows who it is safe to bark at and who it is prudent to slink away from.

If you can't walk away from a deal that is stuck on unsatisfactory terms you are psychologically halfway to rationalizing any terms you can get. Remember, in negotiating you must act more like Scrooge and less like St. Francis of Assisi.

In other spheres of human contact perhaps the exact opposite should apply. But negotiating is unique—it is a remarkable fact that negotiators who set out to achieve high goals end up enriching a far wider set of people than themselves. Those who aim for the trees never get off the ground, and they drag more than themselves down with them.

Years ago, when I was a boy, my grandfather entertained me with stories about his days as a gold miner in Canada before the First World War. He told plain, unsophisticated stories, for his was a hard, laboring life.

There was a proud fatalism about the North American miners in those days, and he often recited a few lines of verse that captured their spirit (apologies and appreciation to their anonymous author). They are an apt inclusion in this chapter:

> This is the law of the Yukon:
> that the strong shall thrive.
> For surely the weak shall perish
> and only the fit survive.

Remember the *Law of the Yukon* as you prepare for a negotiation, because it can call for great toughness of spirit to hold out for your target while looking into the cold, steely eyes of an opponent who thinks he has got your measure.

ANSWERS
SELF-ASSESSMENT TEST 8

Q.1: a] Definitely your best first move. A million dozen cans suggest a lot of happy customers the chain would not want to disappoint. (+ 10)

b] Not unless you want price pressure on every call. (− 10)

c] A sign of weakness. Make him work for his cuts. (− 5)

Q.2: a] No. Are you an order taker or a negotiator? (− 10)

b] Much better. A plausible opening counter. (+ 10)

c] Surely not if your company is a serious rival. Anything is possible if the price is right. (− 10) d] You are obviously an out-of-work kamikaze pilot. If you avoid taking advantage—even mildly—of a buyer's predicament, you'll never survive when he doesn't need you. (− 15)

Q.3: a] No. An abject surrender which you will spend the rest of your married life explaining to your spouse (and your mother-in-law). (− 15)

b] Good. Start high and work down if you have to. Your boss will respect your courage—eventually. (+ 15)

c] Weak. He'll squeeze you to a weekend in Newark. (− 10)

d] Not as good as b], but showing some signs of negotiator's grit, hopefully with future potential! (+ 10)

SELF-ASSESSMENT TEST 9

Q.1: You are a package-tour operator negotiating with a Spanish hotel chain on the terms for next season's bookings. The price they are asking per person for a week in their hotels is nine dollars higher than your current offer. They offer to split the difference fifty-fifty. Do you:

a] Suggest, say, 60–40 in your favor?

b] Say you can't afford to split the difference?

c] Agree to their offer?

d] Agree, if it is a 75–25 split in your favor?

Score:

Q.2: Do you see negotiating as being about:

a] A fair and equal transaction?

b] Finding the most acceptable compromise?

c] Making a joint decision with the other guy that meets as much and as many of *your* interests as possible?

d] Give-and-take?

Score:

Q.3: You are engaged in extremely difficult negotiations with a Lebanese-based construction consortium. After much haggling over finance for a road project, they make a small unilateral concession on their demand for irrevocable lines of credit. Do you:

a] Note the concession but otherwise ignore it?

b] Reciprocate with a concession of your own?

Score:

THE NEGOTIATOR'S MOST USEFUL TWO-LETTER WORD
or How to Make Your Offers Count

When asked what they think is their most useful two-letter word, many negotiators suggest:

No

This answer is not surprising if the question is posed *after* they have heard the story of Bjorn McKenzie's infallible system for coping with wolves or about the Law of the Yukon, as these tend to leave a somewhat negative impression of good negotiating behavior.

However, while *no* isn't the right answer, it isn't entirely wrong.

The question asks for the negotiator's *most useful* two-letter word; *no* merely qualifies for the status of being *useful*.

The most useful two-letter word in the negotiator's vocabulary is:

If

Why is *if* such an important word to a negotiator?

The answer lies at the heart of the negotiating process itself and fully explains my unrelenting hostility to unilateral conceding under any pretext whatsoever or for any purpose.

The *Oxford English Dictionary*—that final arbiter of literacy—defines conceding as, among other things, "to *grant, yield,* or *surrender."*

For this reason I begin this chapter with the quiet but firm statement that readers are not reading this book to improve their skills in commercial *conceding.* Your only interest is to improve your performance as a *negotiator,* which has nothing to do with surrendering.

If you have to surrender, there is no need for the other guy to negotiate: You will be told what to do by the guy with the whip.

On the other hand, if you choose to surrender by unilaterally conceding *when you don't have to,* you are obviously an out-of-work kamikaze pilot, and are less than suitable to be in charge of protecting anybody's interests (including your own).

How do you know when you're in a negotiation and when not? It isn't always obvious to begin with! It is possible for a negotiation to be almost over before you realize you're in one (that's when you'll regret those early free-gift goodwill concessions), just as it is possible to abandon hope of negotiating about something too soon (that's when you start cringing instead of cold-eyeing them).

You will find out sooner or later, of course, whether you can or should negotiate your way to a better deal. One thing for certain, though —always test the situation at the outset before you assume anything about the relative power of the other party.

We will discuss this in more detail later, but for the moment do not assume that the sound of a whiplash is proof positive that they have the power and you don't. They may just be good at sound effects.

If you identify the elements that make negotiating different from the alternative means of making a decision, you can use that knowledge to see if the conditions for negotiation are present.

Essentially, negotiation can be defined as a transaction in which both parties have a *veto* on the final outcome. If you don't have a veto (which includes the right to walk away and do business with somebody else), then you will have to accept whatever is being offered.

Each party in a negotiation has to consent to the outcome if it is to be implemented, and each has an interest (not necessarily an equal one) in the other agreeing to it.

Thus, by negotiating we make a *joint decision.*

If you don't like the other guy's proposal as to what the joint decision should be, and are unable to agree on an alternative, you have the option of *not* agreeing to what he proposes, because:

> Negotiation involves the *voluntary* consent of both sides to the decision.

If you are compelled to agree *against* your will, it's *not* a negotiation (the sharp sting on your back is the whiplash).

What does this view of negotiating imply?

First, that the parties can have different preferences for which of the available outcomes is suitable as a joint decision. Naturally, you prefer the joint decision to be more rather than less favorable to yourself. If you don't, you've no business negotiating, because if you negotiate, you'll soon have no business.

> If you are selling, you prefer high prices; if buying, low prices.
>
> You prefer longer time to pay back than you do to get paid.
>
> You prefer large simple orders to small ones with precise specifications.
>
> You prefer less up-front money if you're buying than you do if you're selling.
>
> You prefer sale or return if you're buying and no returns if you're selling.
>
> If he wants delivery everywhere in awkward loads, you'd prefer he paid extra for it.

And so on.

It's not simply a matter that you gain what he loses.

If you've negotiated successfully, the total package gives you more on the swings than you lose on the roundabouts. That is what is meant by it being more favorable to you.

A trade-off in one area for something in another may give a differential advantage to you, but this in no way implies that he directly loses what you gain. His swings may be your roundabouts: His willingness to give on price may be tempered by your willingness to accelerate on payment.

On the other hand, if you lose more on the swings than you get back on the roundabouts, your negotiating moves ought to have ensured that the final package isn't even less favorable to you than it might have been if you had been less skillful.

Second, this view of negotiating implies that your most favorable outcomes (the ones you would choose in the absence of having to consider the other guy's interests) are not often available to you because he can veto any and all of your propositions.

Nor are his most favorable outcomes available to him by virtue of your veto.

Hence, you both have to choose a joint decision, from among the many that may be attainable, that meets sufficient of the interests and expectations of both sides not to provoke a veto by one of you.

If you cannot reach a settlement by joint decision, you must deadlock and, excluding the possibility of arbitration, take your business elsewhere.

Part of the work of negotiating consists of the careful search for outcomes that are veto-free or can be made veto-free by one means or another (of which more later).

Some of the proposals for a joint decision or settlement are more favorable to both of you, some less, and some others may not have been considered during the negotiation.

Which outcome is finally chosen depends on a lot of factors, not the least of which is your view of the prospects (including the cost in time and energy) of negotiating a better outcome than the one presently on offer and the consequences to both of you of deadlock.

If you view negotiating as surrendering—in whatever form your surrender takes, including a proclivity for unilaterally conceding in the futile search for goodwill—then it is predictable that the deal will be less favorable to you and more favorable to them.

This is not to say that poor negotiators can't get deals. They can, but they tend to get lousier deals than good negotiators.

How, then, is a negotiation to progress if there is a prohibition on surrender? Surely, if we merely stick where we start we will never get a deal?

This is a case where we must not assume that the alternative to "no surrender" is a fight to the death.

It is not the necessity for movement that is denied here. What is most emphatically denied is that movement must take the form of unilateral concessions.

Negotiating is about *trading*. It is when you view negotiation as a process of *exchange* that you see the importance of *never* conceding anything without getting something (preferably more) back for it.

In effect, as a negotiator, if you have to walk toward the other guy, you *must* ensure that he walks toward you as well. Better still, your aim is to get him to walk faster toward you than you do toward him!

Is negotiation a matter of give-and-take?

Not quite.

The idea of give-and-take is acceptable as a broad-brush concept of negotiating only as long as you do not make the mistake *of giving as much as you take!*

There are no rules that say you have to make *equal* moves toward each other—the idea ought to be anathema to negotiators—nor is there anything that says you have to move at all just because he moves.

This leads us to the most important single principle of negotiating:

Nothing, absolutely nothing, is given away free.

I know of *no* exceptions to this principle.

This principle is the foundation of effective negotiating behavior. The fact that it may not be guiding the other guy's moves is not relevant to your behavior—if he wants to give you things for nothing that is his private business and you should accept them without a quibble. You are under no obligation to look after his best interests!

CONCEDING AIN'T NEGOTIATING

A package-tour operator in London (Costalot Travel, Ltd.) had occasion to meet the sales manager of a Spanish hotel chain to discuss next year's terms for block-booking the resorts. The meeting opened with a long list of changes that Costalot wanted following widespread complaints from their clients about the hotels and also several lapses in service contrary to what the hotels had agreed to provide.

The Spanish manager (Señor Paco Eminos) started through the list item by item and agreed to most of them as they stood or in a slightly modified form. Eventually, he stopped his progress through the list with the exclamation:

"Señor, I thought this was a negotiation, but I am making all the concessions."

"True," replied Mr. Costalot, "and when you stop conceding I will start negotiating!"

Thus, if you are negotiating with a unilateral conceder (should you be so lucky!) your best response to his conceding is to sit tight where you are.

And when the other guy requires you to move, you must insist that he move too, preferably by much more than you do.

This might be considered to be unfair (why it should be considered so is one of life's minor mysteries), for you might think that in negotiating we ought to aim to make equal moves and sacrifices from our opening positions.

To my mind that is a mistaken view of negotiating. Just because you reduce your demands, it does not follow that I must improve my offer by the same amount. Perhaps you can afford a 20 percent cut in your price—which shows just how much you padded your opening position. I can't afford to reciprocate, and that's that!

You see, I don't subscribe to the "equity theory" of negotiating, and neither should you. Fair exchange is no robbery, but that says nothing about a fair exchange being equal in some way. In fact, no trading exchange is an equal transaction.

When you buy a Mars bar at a newsstand for thirty-five cents, there is no question of an equal transaction between you and the newsstand owner. The Mars bar is not equal to the thirty-five cents. If you believe that it is, try eating the thirty-five cents! When you hand over your money to the guy in the newsstand for the Mars bar, it is a *fair* transaction. If you believe that it isn't, take your business elsewhere. Nobody in a free society compels you to eat Mars bars—indeed, you have the choice of selecting a Hershey bar or the product of any other excellent chocolate company.

At the moment of purchase you need the Mars bar more than you need your thirty-five cents—you have money, but no Mars bars.

For the newsstand, they need your 35 cents more than they need the Mars bar—they have a warehouse full of Mars bars.

For the soundest of motives (i.e., profit) they prefer to fill their tills with cash and empty their warehouses of Mars bars.

Hence, the trade can be fair without necessarily being equal.

If the best way to conduct a negotiation is to make absolutely no concessions without getting something in return (though we can accept concessions if they are offered for nothing), then how do we avoid deadlock?

This is where the power of the negotiator's most useful two-letter word—*if*—comes into its own.

The most important guiding principle of negotiating, even if you forget everything else, is to preface *all* your propositions and concessions with the word *if*:

> "*If* you drop twenty percent on price,
> I can sign an order."
> "*If* you accept liability,
> we will release your shipment."
> "*If* you waive on-site inspection,
> we can meet your schedules."
> "*If* you pay the courier,
> I will dispatch the plans tonight."
> "*If* you place an order immediately,
> I can meet your price."

IMPULSIVE CONCEDERS

The worst thing about unilateral concessions is that they weaken a negotiating position much more than the amount of the concession.

Consider the following cases:
"How much for the video player?"
"$600."
"As much as that?"
"I could let it go for $550."

"I see you have requested a starting salary of $28,000."
"Yes."
"This operation cannot afford to pay that amount—in fact it would make you the highest paid accountant in credit control. Would you consider less?"
"I'm willing to be flexible, but I must get at least $25,000."

These concessions were got for practically no effort at all—a single question in fact. The drop of $50 in the video negotiation after a single question tells the buyer that the owner has plucked his price out of thin air. He should (and did) push on price even harder (it eventually went for $425). The unemployed accountant dropped her price by $3,000 almost without a whimper, and also demonstrated her total unsuitability to be employed (she wasn't) in a credit control operation—she will never get money out of debtors if she is an impulsive conceder.

In both cases, the use of conditions on the concessions would have protected the negotiating position:

"You can have it for $585 without the spare tapes."

"If you pay me a commission on the debts I collect and you pay my gasoline account I will accept a salary of $26,750."

By using the word *if* you protect the integrity of your proposals. They cannot regard a movement as a unilateral concession on your part precisely because you have tied it to your conditions. As they say, you can't have one without the other.

Get into the habit of using *if every time* you make a proposal, and the other guy will get the message:

> The *if* part tells him the *price* of the offer.
> The offer part tells him what he is *getting* for the price.

Do this in negotiating and you will also help educate your opponents (you are doing the community a social service once again, for if you didn't help educate those guys, who would?). Even the dumbest opponent will get the message eventually.

In one of the university campuses here in the United States, a psychology professor taught a pigeon to pick out the ace of spades in a deck of cards. Now your opponents are always going to have bigger brains than those belonging to pigeons—even Texan pigeons—and you can stake your last dime on the prediction that your opponents will eventually get the message: If they want something from you it is going to cost them.

Perhaps in future they will ask for less?

ANSWERS
SELF-ASSESSMENT TEST 9

Q.1: a] Better than c] but suggests you are in a hurry to compromise.
(+ 5)

b] By far a negotiator's best immediate move. Why should you split 50–50 whether you can afford it or not? By making such an offer they expose that their price is padded by at least

$4.50, probably more. A concession of $4.50 on ten thousand holiday weeks costs you $45,000—does their compromise look so fair when grossed up? (+ 10)

c] Never. If you show negotiators that you practice "split the difference" compromises, they will give you bigger and bigger differences to split! (− 15)

d] Better than c] and tougher than a]. A possible move for later (much later, when you have tested the padding in their $4.50). (+ 7)

Q.2: a] Negotiating is always fair but seldom equal. (− 10)

b] Depends on who it is most acceptable to. If there are echoes of splitting the difference and equal gains, then absolutely not. (0)

c] Yes. It's your interests you are negotiating for—the other guy is the best judge of his interests. Confusing these roles can lead to poorer deals. The fact that it is a joint decision assures that it is at least satisfactory to you both; hopefully, it is more satisfactory to you than the available alternatives. (+ 10)

d] Not if you give as much as you take. (− 5)

Q.3: a] Yes. If they make free-gift unilateral concessions you are not obliged to respond. (+ 5)

b] No. (− 10)

SELF-ASSESSMENT TEST 10

Q.1: You are looking for a job and see an advertisement for out-of-work truck drivers to attend an interview at 2 P.M. on Friday at the personnel office of a local haulage company. When you get there at 1:55 P.M. you join a long line six deep outside of the office. Do you think your chances of getting the job are:

a] Diminished?

b] Not affected?

c] Better?

Score:

Q.2: You are in Accra (Ghana) and are looking for a "mammy truck" that is going to Kumasi. You find one and the mammy tells you it will leave as soon as it is full. You note that there is only one seat left vacant on the truck and decide to take it. When will the truck leave:

a] Immediately?

94

b] Later?

c] When it's full?

Score:

Q.3: You act as a go-between in the sale of a light aircraft. The buyer pays by check; the owner is willing to accept this and release the aircraft once the check is cleared by the bank. When settling up your fee, do you:

a] Press for payment in cash?

b] Send in an invoice?

c] Accept a check?

Score:

Q.4: An Arab with six camels approaches an oasis in search of water. Standing by the spring there is another Arab and a sign (in Arabic): "Water: all you can drink—price, one camel." Who has the power:

a] The Arab with the camels?

b] The Arab with the water?

c] Impossible to say.

Score:

10

WHO HAS THE POWER?
or How to Get Leverage

A thousand or more years ago Viking raiders regularly slipped out of the beautiful fjords of Norway in magnificent sailing ships bound for the coastal settlements of Europe. Today, from those same fjords, their descendants use nothing more lethal than the telex to run highly efficient worldwide shipping operations.

Lars is the vice-president of a shipping company operating out of Bergen. He does scores of deals a year, buying or selling ships, negotiating contracts for newly built ships in Europe and the Far East, handling repair contracts (one of the toughest sides of a tough business), bunkers, freight and charter rates, crew wages, and agency fees. He's a busy man, and after forty years in the business he still has a romantic attitude toward "his" ships.

In the matter of negotiation, Lars is anything but romantic. In fact, he is downright single-minded when it comes to handling his company's business.

Some of the managers—they range from clerks who learned the hard way, through graduates who learned it the smart way, to 'retired' masters who learned it any way—occasionally discuss their negotiating problems between telex messages.

If Lars happens to overhear such a conversation while passing through the open-plan offices, he is likely to proffer the summation of his negotiating wisdom:

> "In any deal, ask who is buying and who is selling."

To Lars, the answer tells him who has *the power,* and as far as he is concerned, having power is an asset, not having it a handicap, which is a pretty sound approach to this aspect of negotiating.

It follows that Lars believes that his managers should seek power *before* a deal in order to exercise it *during* the negotiation.

What does power consist of? If we haven't got it, how do we get it and from where?

First you must rid yourself of any lingering illusions that power doesn't matter. It does. The quaint view that power doesn't matter is often expressed in the belief that the act of negotiating somehow shelters the parties from the crudities of power.

This is altogether wrong. Negotiating merely expresses the power balance in a different form!

The understandable preference for "Jaw-Jaw" rather than "War-War" has nothing to do with the excision of power from the relationship between the two contestants; it merely expresses a preference for one form of the power balance rather than another.

Lars is absolutely right in one thing:

> Power is the very essence of the negotiating process.

It is through our perceptions of power—ours *and* theirs—that we conduct ourselves as negotiators.

This leads us to the most important single characteristic of power in a negotiation: It is entirely *subjective.* In short, power is in the head. And remember, in negotiating there are two heads—yours and the other guy's—not one!

Hence, it is what happens in the heads of the parties that determines how power impacts on the outcome of their negotiation.

"How so?" you might ask. "Surely power has an objective dimension too."

"Explain what you mean," I reply.

Assume that you respond with a good example: "If the market is flooded with unchartered tankers, owners are in a weak position compared to hirers."

If you had weakened your case by suggesting that the owners were weak irrespective of their negotiating skills, I would have had an easy ride home, but as you didn't (despite my writing your dialogue!), I shall tackle your objection the hard way.

I am compelled to agree, of course, that a world surplus of tanker capacity is an objective circumstance of some relevance to the power relationship between a tanker owner and a chartering agency. That cannot be denied.

But what can be, and is, asserted here is that the negotiator's subjective perception is *more important* than the objective circumstances in themselves.

It is what the negotiators believe is true that counts, not what a panel of independent assessors could tell them if they sat long enough and reviewed in minute detail all the so-called objective evidence. (And note that their review of that evidence is itself subjective, as is your interpretation of their assessment).

Negotiators instinctively understand the importance of subjective belief—that's why they spend so much time trying to convince us that their perceptions are so much more credible than ours.

If a shipowner sees a fleet of unchartered tankers riding at anchor in the bay, it does not follow that he rolls over and plays dead when he gets to bid for a time charter.

He will attempt to convince the charterer that the vessel he has for hire is somehow different from the others in the bay (it may be the only one with an inert gas system—those without an IGS are disqualified by international regulations as of 1982).

If they believe what they hear and persist with the negotiations this will reduce the apparent negotiating advantage you credited the hirer with in your example.

Alternatively, suppose your business requires additional computer programming staff. What will they cost you?

"That depends," you answer, "on how many computer programmers are in the market looking for a job."

Now, in an economics class you would get a bonus point for such a brilliantly obvious conclusion—though, not surprisingly, what you have alluded to is of little consequence in the real world.

How many job seekers make it a hirer's market? We could as productively ask, how long is a piece of string? Moreover, we don't negotiate with markets. We negotiate with people. You cannot *safely* assume that the people you negotiate with are as well informed about the market as you are, or think you are.

Nor can you assume that what you know about the market is correct.

Even majority opinion of the state of a market is a notoriously poor guide to its actual state, as you will find if you ask anybody who has been caught short when they played the market.

REMEMBER, WE HAVE AN ALTERNATIVE.

A major European car manufacturer exports its vehicles all over the world in specially designed ships owned by independent shipping companies.

There is a delicate power balance in the annual negotiations over freight prices. If the manufacturer squeezed the shipping companies too hard on price, one or more of them would go out of business or shift their activities elsewhere.

This would reduce the number of shippers and place the surviving companies in a more powerful negotiating position.

On the other hand, if the shipping companies push their prices too high—by overt or covert collusion—this will encourage the other shippers to join in the trade, or perhaps encourage the manufacturer to purchase its own vessels.

A clear understanding of the need to contain the power conflict within "reasonable" bounds is implicit in their negotiating relationship.

FLY ME

An oil company that operates several rigs in the Mexican Gulf hires $70 million worth of helicopter services a year. Most of the business is placed with one of the largest helicopter operators in the world. It is highly efficient, is competitive in price, and has an excellent safety record. However, the oil company does not place all its business with this operator, and about 20 percent of it goes to three other, much smaller companies.

They are run by "two men" outfits (mainly ex-pilots for the major company who branched out on their own) and are slightly more expensive than the corporate giant.

Why does the hirer do this if it costs more? Because the oil company does not want to drive out of business the smaller suppliers in case this should give its largest supplier ideas about the power balance.

In fact, the way to wealth in the stock market is to know better than the market about its prospects: When the market believes shares will go up and you think you know better, you sell out and take your profit; when the market believes shares will fall and you think you know better, you buy in and wait for your profit. If you wait for the market to form an opinion, you could be buying when you should be selling and selling when you should be buying.

Setting aside how you know at any moment that the market has got it wrong and you've got it right, it is certainly true that if you get it right more often, and for bigger stakes, than you get it wrong, you might retire owning a fortune, and if you don't, you won't!

All economists (and I confess I mix with more than my share) assume that something called *the* market makes decisions about prices and quantities and that they (and their students) have a bird's-eye view of the entire market mechanism.

But in a negotiation you don't have a bird's-eye view because you are not a bird—you're part of the mechanism!

Suppose, as an out-of-work computer programmer, you walk into the personnel department of a company that has advertised a vacancy in its computer department and the waiting room is crammed full with other guys.

Are you stronger or weaker as a result? Your natural reaction would be to feel less confident of your chances—clearly, there is a lot of competition for the job.

Or is there? The answer is, and ought to be, How do you know? How do you know what they are waiting for? How do you know that you're not the only computer programmer they have seen all week?

You may be weaker with competition around, but on the other hand, it may not be competition at all. They could be waiting to be interviewed for a receptionist's job in the word processing department. How they are dressed might give you a clue. If they are all wearing neatly pressed dark suits and polished shoes, you know they are unlikely to be computer programmers, who, as everybody knows, are always in denim, tend to beards, and are afflicted with jargonitis. (If the room is full of scruffy guys suffering from *galloping* jargonitis, they are obviously out-of-work CB operators). But if you believe they are computer programmers you will feel weaker and are likely to end up a *cheap* programmer.

THE MARKET MAMMIES OF MAKOLA

When Ernst Weinbanger went to Ghana in 1975 as the marketing manager for a large Dutch oil company, his first assignment was to visit dealers, many of whom lived up-country.

He wanted to see as much as he could of Ghana and meet as many people as possible, and he was advised by colleagues that there was no better way to learn about the real Ghana than to travel by "bus," which in Ghana means the back of an open truck.

Ernst's colleagues did not warn him about the business standards of the "bus companies," and he made the mistake of assuming that Ghana ran its public transport with the same attention to timetables as the honest burghers of his native Amsterdam.

He innocently believed a mammy in the Makola market who said her truck's departure for Kumasi was imminent and that as soon as the truck was full it would depart.

Ernst could see that every seat in the truck was full except for one, and concluded that he would soon be on his way to Kumasi. So, as it was his first visit to Ghana, he paid his fare and got on board—only to see the person next to him get off!

That is how the market mammies use Rent-a-Crowd to fill their trucks with cash customers.

Eventually it dawned on Ernst from the number of times the mammy repeated her sales routine that he was not the *last* but the *first* fare-paying passenger to get onto her truck that morning.

If it happens to you, it's no good trying to get your money back—when a market mammy says no in matters relating to business, you had better believe that she means it!

Ernst Weinbanger learned a lot on his first tour. So much, in fact, that for years he sent newly arrived managers, without a briefing, to see Ghana by "bus."

"Nobody," he is wont to say over drinks in the bar of the Ambassador Hotel in Accra, "warned me, so I didn't warn them, but what they learned in a month about how they do business in West Africa was worth a year at Harvard."

It could be that the employer has hired a group of actors from Rent-a-Crowd to intimidate you into accepting $7,000 less per year.

In general, then, we cannot be sure that what we think is how the situation actually pertains in practice.

If our opponents persist in seeing the situation differently, we have the classic negotiator's dilemma: We can't be sure that our opponent's apparent position reflects the true power relationship between us and is not just a tactical stance on his part to convince us to change our perceptions.

Indeed, we can conceive of all negotiating moves and tactics as attempts in one degree or another to structure how the other party views the power relationship.

The more skillfully we structure our opponent's subjective views of the power relationship in our favor, the less relevant to the outcome of the negotiation is the objective power balance of the market. In other words, if you believe *they* have power then nothing more need be said; they have it (and they have you, too).

For this reason, I tend to disagree respectfully with Lars on the importance of who is the buyer and who is the seller, if by the answer he implies an *automatic* conclusion that buying puts us in a more powerful position than selling. It does not matter whether we are buying or selling if we get the power dimension to work for us rather than against us.

Consider the Arab oil states—the sellers—and the world's consumers of oil—the buyers. Up to 1971–1973 the oil companies believed they had the power and the Arab negotiators agreed. Then they changed their minds, and it's never been the same since.

It all boils down to how you and the other guy see your relationship. If you can influence his perception, you get a better deal.

What factors influence our perception of the power relationship?

The answer could open up that most complex of subjects, what makes people think the way they do, and would fill volumes rather than close off this chapter.

For the moment, let us confine our discussion to the perceptions we form before we meet the other guy, for these are often the most influential on our approach, our manner, our demeanor, our confidence, and eventually, our deal.

Almost all sellers suffer from a twin obsession: the power of the buyers and the extent of the competition. Given the slightest encouragement, a seller will catalog the atrocities committed by buyers or the competition on his good self. Any five guys from sales mixing socially regale each other with ever more incredible tales of perfidy among buyers and "the dirty tricks of the contemptible competition." In short, they psych themselves into believing in their own weakness by assuming the buyers' strengths.

Yet buyers can see things differently. For instance, I know a buyer for a large mainframe computer company who buys millions of dollars worth of components for his company's assembly plants each quarter, and who firmly believes that sellers have the power.

How did he draw that conclusion?

There was a time when he knew his company's computers inside out (he used to make them), but the technology has moved so fast in the

---

CROOKS, CHEATS, AND CONTRACTORS

Sub-contractors in the construction industry are vulnerable to pressure by the main contractor if he negotiates extra-stringent conditions on them. He can do this if he knows they are desperate for work.

The fact that this may drive them into bankruptcy is not a consideration, because once they have done the work on the site it does not matter to the main contractor whether he pays his bills (eventually) to them as a going concern or their creditors after they go broke.

Sub-contractors try to impose standard terms in their negotiations with main contractors but when the winds of recession blow hardest, the weakest (financially) concede in areas where they shouldn't, given their vulnerability.

For instance, the contractor can force the sub-contractor to waive the requirement that he is paid monthly for his work (which forces him to borrow to pay his men their wages) and to accept that he only gets paid upon receipt of the site agents' certificate that the work has been completed. In practice, it is not difficult to delay that certificate for months, which may be too long for his creditors.

A tough contractor can make them totally responsible for the loss or damage to goods on site until the completion of the main contract, even if the sub-contractor leaves the site months, or indeed years, beforehand!

The more unscrupulous contractors also reserve the power to deduct monies from the sub-contractor's account against monies he may (or may not, if there is a dispute) owe to another department of the main contractor on an entirely different site. As there is no appeal, the sub-contractor is left defenceless against phoney claims raised on one site against his money due from another.

The construction industry is a *tough* business and it carries nobody who can't fight their way up a greasy pole, which is also decorated with rusty razor blades!

---

past ten years that he feels at a disadvantage because ten years out of computer engineering is two generations too long.

He buys thousands of different components in large and small lots for the entire range of his company's computers, and he claims that the manufacturers' representatives have an advantage over him as they are specialists in their own components, while he, as a buyer, knows little about any specific item. He must rely on the seller to guide him on technical matters regarding their products.

It all comes down to perception. If you are selling and believe that the buyer has the power, you could be filling your head with the buyer's ammunition.

How do you know whether a specific buyer has more power in a negotiation than you do? Do you believe what he is saying about the competition just because he says it, or worse, do you believe you are up against tough competition before you have even met him and found out what it is he wants?

Think less about the buyer for a moment and think more about the alleged competition.

In the ordinary run of events in business, people deal with more than one company. Their experience with a particular company can vary from satisfactory to absolutely hopeless. It is just not true that every other company that sells similar products or services to you is set to get the order you seek from a buyer.

The buyer may have dealt with your competitor before and been given cause to weigh his products or service in the balance and find them wanting, in which case, you are stronger than you think.

Competition is only strong if every firm that is knocking at the buyer's door is equally competent in providing what the buyer wants. Experience in business suggests that it is very unusual to find firms competing on exactly the same terms (it's so unusual that in most countries they get very suspicious if it happens).

The buyer may prefer to deal with firms that are close to his own plants or are owned by fellow Bostonians. This reduces his power if you're local or from Boston, but enhances it if you're not.

The buyer may operate a company policy that excludes certain firms—perhaps they didn't deliver what they promised or chased too hard for their money or antagonized the staff in some way—and this, too, weakens the buyer's power as long as you are not one of them.

The buyer may be buying to a departmental specification that reflects the preferences or training of the guys who will operate the machinery. This also weakens the buyer's power.

You can bet your last ten cents that if the programmers were trained by IBM, they will tend to specify IBM plug-compatible products. If that is what you are selling, you need not collapse your margins *just because* the buyer has a Wang catalog on his desk. (The first car that people buy tends to be the same make as the one they learned to drive on, which must give a lot of negotiating leverage to driving schools when they buy their fleets).

Conversely, if you're selling non-IBM products, you ought not to feel weak just because the users have specified IBM, providing you sell products as good as or better than IBM.

Also, the buyer may be willing to look elsewhere for other reasons and override the preferences of his engineers. The buyer's choices can be constrained by all kinds of things. He often works to a policy set by other people (not always considerate of the economics of their decisions) and he is often at the mercy of his company's specialists, who seldom consider his problems with suppliers.

He may be under instructions not to give all the business to a single firm in case he gets too dependent on it—that could be your chance to get in—or he could have instructions to always buy bulk—hence you're chasing a big order.

Therefore, don't forget that buyers do not automatically have the power . . . unless you give it to them.

And what of sellers? Do they have the power?

Not necessarily. It depends on what they choose to believe. If the buyer convinces them that the competition really is strong, this must weaken the seller's power. For this reason, a caution is appropriate: Learn to recognize the buyer's theater props (for that is what they are) as he performs his version of the long-running off-Broadway play, *Oh, What a Lot of Competition There Is Today.*

Among the props that alter your power perception are:

- Catalogs from your competitors, preferably with page markers sticking out of them.
- A pile of papers on his desk showing their letterheads (but not their contents), handy to tap when he utters the well-worn (but still devastatingly effective) seven-word killer line: "You'll have to do better than that."

Buyers use these props because they work: The League of Gullible Sellers has always had a mass membership!

Sellers can fight back against these tactics. If your price is challenged, you ought at least to work hard at defending it.

One thing you can do is to ask, "Why must I do better than I have proposed?" The reply can give you information about whether it is a bluff or not—the vaguer or the more heated the response, the more likely it is a bluff.

If you have insufficient confidence in your price, so that your first thought when it is challenged is to think how you can drop it without starting a rout, then there is no reason why the buyer should have any confidence in your price either.

Buyers always challenge prices—it's in the nature of the beast! Many sellers always back off from a price challenge, hence it pays buyers to challenge their proposals with the killer line.

Buyers are not entirely defenseless against sellers who are in, or feel that they are in, a strong position. Nor do they always need to stoop to deceit to alter the seller's perception of his power. They can adopt tactics to convince the seller that they do not need his product, perhaps by showing that there are other suppliers eager to do business with them, or that they have large stocks, or that they might set up their own production facility to make the item. If this is credible, the seller will lower his perception of his own power.

Buyers can hint about the longer-run benefits of the seller going easy on price just now—"sell cheap, get famous"—and the longer-run consequences of exploiting negotiating power—"screw us now and we'll screw you later."

This can curb the seller's use of his power. It is not always in the long-term interest of a business for it to screw the other guy to the floor with stiff demands.

Sellers know that high prices (and high profits) attract competition, and that the One Great Law of the Market is that if you want to sell more, you have to reduce your price or raise your marketing costs, or both. This puts pressure on the seller's power.

You can strengthen your power by persuading him that there is a lot of competition for your business—certainly you will never strengthen your power if you tell him otherwise. Don't confide that your warehouse is full and the alternative to his placing an order is for your plant to cut back on staff.

If he feels there is competitive pressure upon him even when none is being directly exerted, that is bound to reduce his power and increase yours.

Hence, as a buyer you can let him see that you are aware of his competitors' products and know their special features and benefits. Show that you are in regular contact with them.

You should never explain *why* you are not doing business with the seller's competitors or *why* you want to switch from them—and above all, avoid the temptation to knock those who have let you down, as it merely strengthens the seller's power.

WHO'S LAUGHING NOW?

A cabaret comedian had just finished his first act for a far-off-the-strip Las Vegas nightclub and the owner came up to him backstage with tears running down his cheeks—he had started laughing at the first joke and didn't stop for twenty minutes.

He told the comedian, "You're the best act I've seen this year. They're still rolling in the aisles back there. You were fantastic!"

The comedian told the owner he was glad he liked the act.

The owner said, "I'm gonna show you how grateful I am. Just name it, and you've got it. The tab is on the house."

The comedian, who had a fine sense of timing, replied:

"Well, the first thing I want is a raise to $550 a show."

The owner agreed, still laughing—at least until he got back to his office.

If the owner had been less enthusiastic about telling the comedian what a great act he had, he would probably have kept him working for a month for three shows a night at $100 a throw.

By exuberantly praising the comedian's performance he changed the power balance between himself—a hardened nightclub boss giving an untried comedian a break—into a more-than-satisfied customer vulnerable to a soft touch.

Moral: Don't praise your suppliers unless you want to be charged more for the same service!

Conversely, avoid telling him how much you love his products—it might be just enough to give him the courage to raise his price!

Even if your business relationship with a seller is secure, you should keep him unsure of it by showing interest in switching your buying policy to rivals on any credible grounds such as:

- Price ("They're cheaper.")
- Delivery ("They're offering CIF against your FOB.")
- Quantity ("They are offering bigger discounts.")
- Patriotism ("The boss wants to buy home produce only.")
- New features ("Their machine bags the cement too.")
- Security of supply ("They guarantee all the cocoa we can take for three years.")
- Credit terms ("They offer ninety days interest-free.")

This will reduce his power over you, or at least keep him from getting big ideas about his relationship with you.

Who then, has the power?

You do, if your opponent believes you have it. And if he believes that you have the power, you can extract a premium from him for your services.

On the other hand, he has the power if you believe he has it. You can be sure that your perception of the power balance will cost you something extra above what you would have paid if you had been less influenced by what you thought you knew about the other guy's position.

If you need the deal more than you can cope with the prospect of not getting it, you will be less powerful in the negotiation. The con-

106

verse is true for him—if he needs to settle more than he can face a deadlock, you have power over him.

The main point to remember is that who has the power is not decided by the calculation of a formula of relative ability to do without the deal. It is your *perception* of the pressures on him to settle compared to the pressures you feel upon yourself that will influence your reading of the power balance.

If you get this wrong because you are misled by your assumptions, you will award him with a greater power than he might have in fact. That could cost you something on the final price that you needn't concede. And this is true whether you are buying or selling.

ANSWERS
SELF-ASSESSMENT TEST 10

Q.1: a] How do you know they are out-of-work truck drivers?   (− 5)

    b] You are not influenced by what you think you see.   (+ 5)

    c] Obviously "competition" inspires you.   (0)

Q.2: a] You have a tendency to believe what a seller tells you, and in some markets that is a class A mistake. Whether the truck leaves immediately depends on whether you are the last passenger or somebody duped by Rent-a-Crowd.   (− 5)

    b] Again, it depends on whether the other people are on the truck as Rent-a-Crowd or genuine passengers.   (− 5)

    c] Right!   (+ 5)

Q.3: a] Sound advice when involved in these dealings. Until the check is cleared the deal could fall through. Get paid while you have some influence on the seller.   (+ 10)

    b] A risky decision in the go-between business. Sellers value your service less after you have clinched their deal for them—every hooker knows it best to collect before rather than after.   (− 10)

    c] Only if it is certified and he gives it to you in his bank for immediate payment!   (0)

Q.4: a] How many camels has the guy with the water got?   (− 5)

    b] Suppose the guy with the camels is the only one with a loaded rifle?   (− 5)

    c] Correct. There is no way of knowing who has the power without more information, and even that information may be incorrect.   (+ 5)

SELF-ASSESSMENT TEST 11

Q.1: You are a real estate agent and have been assigned by its owner to sell a downtown property. Your instructions are to get the best price you can. Do you:

a] Get on with the search for a buyer?

b] Insist on more specific instructions?

c] Decline the assignment?

Score:

Q.2: You are selling a piano that has cluttered up your garage for several years. A prospect appears to be interested in purchasing it and asks how much you want for it. Do you:

a] Give him a figure at the top end of your expectations?

b] Ask him what will he offer for it?

c] Tell him the amount your spouse told you to get?

d] Go in lower in case he backs off?

Score:

Q.3: You are interested in buying a used twelve-foot dinghy and ask the seller how much she wants for it. She tells you that her boyfriend told her to get at least $650 for it. You find that she is reluctant to budge from her price. Do you:

a] Give her your phone number in case she changes her mind?

b] Take the deal after a haggle?

c] Ask to see her boyfriend?

Score:

Q.4: You respond to an advertisement in the trade press offering a salmon fishing estate for sale. The advertisement insists on principals only. You find in discussion with the other side that you are dealing with an agent of the owner. Do you:

a] Insist on dealing direct with the other principal?

b] Ask if the agent has power to settle without reference back to the owner?

c] Carry on negotiations on a wait-and-see basis?

Score:

11

IF YOU HAVEN'T GOT A PRINCIPAL, INVENT ONE

or How Not to Have Negotiating Authority

Millions of people all over the world read the want ads in their local papers to see what is for sale or what is wanted. To indulge in this constant search you needn't have anything other than curiosity in mind. If something strikes your fancy you can try to buy it, or, seeing the prices offered for certain items, you might be induced if you have similar items to try to sell them yourself.

Some papers actually draw the attention of prospective sellers to the market prospects of goods they may possess but no longer have a need for. A paper could carry a notice like the following:

"Twenty Commode Purchasers Inconvenienced"

The gist of the pitch is that an advertisement to sell an antique commode attracted twenty-one buyers willing to buy at the asking price of $300, and presumably this left twenty buyers without one!

Clearly, by implication, any reader of the paper with a spare commode could contact the twenty disappointed buyers by paying for a similar advertisement.

Whichever way you make known your desire to sell an item, you still face the problem of actually negotiating a price for it.

Getting a prospect to look at your article is a big step toward a sale, but it is only a first step to actually negotiating the price.

Prices in the household goods market are not always specified in the advertisements, which is one way of avoiding the ONO mistake. This creates for both the buyer and the seller the problem of what price to open at.

Alternatively, if a price is mentioned, the buyer can decide to ignore it and see what concessions he gets when the seller believes he will lose the sale if his price does not come down.

It is typical in these types of informal transactions for the buyer, with disarming innocence, to ask; "How much do you want for it?"

This can embarrass a seller who has no recent experience of haggling and is unprepared for the question. The most common counter is to reply, "How much will you offer for it?"

More than likely, both parties avoid eye contact during the exchange of questioning, and each desperately examines the sale item as if it might give them a clue as to what to say next.

This behavior is a natural product of unfamiliarity with the market for used household goods. Only professional dealers conduct similar transactions every day of every week and, consequently, have the confidence to quote a tough opening price.

Unfamiliarity wtih the market comes from a lack of information about the "proper" price for a used car, a desk, a plant pot, a wheelbarrow, a commode, or whatever.

The seller wants to sell but does not know what to ask for; the buyer wants to buy but does not know what to offer; and each tries to pass responsibility for the first move onto the other.

The ritual sword fencing of what-do-you-want/what-will-you-offer is as spontaneously discovered by people as it is inevitable, because essentially, haggling consists off:

> *the seller trying to ascertain the maximum that the buyer is willing to pay without disclosing the minimum that the seller is prepared to accept.*

All negotiating problems involve this perplexity: how to uncover the other party's upper boundary while keeping one's own well and truly camouflaged.

This chapter discusses one common solution to the problem, namely, the tactic of the mandate.

It is stumbled upon by gifted amateurs, as well as being the basis of a lucrative career for some professionals. After discussing its help to the former, we will look briefly at its role with the latter.

Negotiators use the mandate tactic in an attempt to build a negotiating position. It requires only that the parties refer to some absent principal as the person who allegedly has determined the terms they must stick to in the negotiation. By implication, these terms are mandatory.

The negotiator will say something like, "My brother says I must not accept less than $250," which can be countered by, "My husband told me not to pay more than $200." Clearly, if a deal is to be agreed upon, one or both of the often fictitious mandates has to be ignored.

An entire conversation between two would-be traders could be constructed, in which the actual principal parties to the transaction shelter under alleged mandates from their relatives who, conveniently, are not present.

You should be wary of an absolute inflexibility when using the mandate tactic—after all, it is a negotiation—because you could provoke the "organ grinder" sneer: "If you can't make your own decisions, I prefer to speak to the organ grinder and not his monkey." [You should only tease him with the organ grinder sneer when a) you are in a very strong position, that is, he needs your business, or b) you don't care about deadlock, that is, you don't need his].

But if you are not sure what to do next when asked about your price, and don't have enough confidence to go in tough, try the mandate tactic.

In the case of used household goods, it is not normally worth hiring agents to negotiate the sale of, say, a used washing machine (though the author on occasion has done so for friends).

You can use the mandate of a principal not present in the negotiations as long as his or her influence on the outcome is credible. I was once floored by another guy who exclaimed, "What will my mother-in-law think of me if I sell to you at *that* price?"

Managers, of course, use the mandate of their absent bosses all the time: "If I shave any more off the price, *they* will go bananas upstairs." Or, in a slightly different version, "It's simply against company policy to agree to those terms."

Selling a house clearly requires the consent of your spouse to the terms, as does the sale of most household items. So use their mandate in the negotiations, which effectively turns you from a principal into an agent of the "absent principal!"

An invented mandate could give you that margin of confidence you need for the moment you seek eye contact just before the other guy responds—a most off-putting behavior if he is under pressure.

The mandate tactic can be used:

1. To support your demands that the quality of the good is of a certain standard (enabling you to draw attention to flawed features of his product).
2. To demand that the deal must include, say, the cables and spares (enabling you to back off from the sale if these are not included or to demand that the price be discounted in lieu of them).
3. To insist that it must be *demonstrated* to be in working order (creat-

ing the prospect of a discount for anything less—given the "time and trouble, not to mention expense, of putting things right"), and so on.

There is almost no end to the issues that you can confidently raise under the protection of a real or imaginary mandate.

Of course, in return, the seller can quote his brother's opinion that he must get cash only (suggestions of a discount for cash, or, perhaps, a premium for a check?), and that if you want spares you must pay for them separately ("it being normal in these cases").

By displacing the source of our demands onto others, it is easier (in the sense of being less embarrassing) to introduce them into the negotiation, and easier to back away from buying/selling on this occasion if the terms are not right.

In this respect, never underestimate the unwillingness of non-professionals to tell you that they don't want to buy an item: "I didn't want to tell him his car was no good, so I told him I would think about it, which got me out of the house." Professionals are no less coy about saying no, as in the classic "Don't call us, we'll call you."

With an invented mandate we act *as if* we are *agents* in the transaction when, in fact, we are *principals* and, by distancing ourselves from the issues, we achieve a kind of neutrality about them. This makes us very difficult targets if things get tough.

Of course, in used household goods markets we are the principals, and the other party knows this, but the fiction that we are only an agent of our spouse is often credible enough for it to be accepted, so:

If you haven't got a principal—invent one!

Thus, we get a line of retreat if we need it, a bolster to our price defenses if they are under pressure, and less chance of tension if deadlock threatens; after all, "It is not *me* you have to convince, but my wife."

Mandates (real or imaginary) protect the negotiator from taking personal responsibility—and thereby personal hostility from the other party—for the demands they make.

Union leaders are adept at using the mandate demand, as are all negotiators who are representatives of absent principals (such as lawyers who insist on referring everything back to their clients).

For instance, union officials often preface their claims with remarks to the effect that "the members have instructed me to demand" whatever it is they are formally asking for.

Mandates also give those who use them a means to limit the number and size of concessions they can make: "It's not up to me, it's in the hands of my members," or, "My client will never accept less than a full rebate," and so on.

112

A mandate can also give you a first look at their price, particularly for large-value items like houses and cars, and also a note of any concessions that the other party prematurely offers.

You can see a house alone and ascertain what is in the mind of the seller and then escape politely to consult your spouse.

You might be able to finesse the seller's best price and also get an idea of the extra items they might include in the purchase (fittings, carpets, kitchen furniture, etc.).

This leaves the way open for a joint visit, if you decide that the house is potentially suitable, and gives you an opportunity to assess the available extras you want included in the deal.

Finally, you can go to a *third* round by shunting the negotiations, *plus the early concessions,* onto your real estate agent!

Husbands and wives going around houses oohing and aahing together demonstrate no way to buy a house. (I once got priced out of a house sale because my mother-in-law told the owner on the first visit that it was the most beautiful house she had ever been in, which certainly firmed up his soggy ideas about price, because three weeks later he was still quoting her statements to me in the negotiations—after that she went under a strict gagging rule).

Another class A mistake is to be hurried into house purchase by real estate brokers who are more concerned with their take from the deal than with saving you money. (I am often asked how to tell the good guys from the bad guys in brokerage. Well, one thing for sure, the bad guys don't all wear black hats!)

In general, rushing into deals is bad news for your bank balance.

One reason why house owners use agents to conduct the sale is precisely because they can shelter behind the mandate.

When asked, "What price would you accept for the house?" you can neatly sidestep with the reply, "All that is handled by my agent."

The mandate tactic is not just used in negotiations for household items. Some of the world's biggest deals are negotiated using a sophisticated version of the mandate tactic.

Professional agents often negotiate the outline of the deal subject to the approval of the principals, *who are not present.*

It is common in business for advertisements to include the phrase:

Principals Only

This is sometimes an attempt to save time and money.

However, giving an agent a mandate is likely to strengthen his negotiating position. He is arm's length from the deal, and you, as principal, can accept or reject what may have been put together by much haggling with the seller: You were not party to the pressures and compromises of the negotiating process and thereby can reject out of hand elements of the deal you don't like.

In other words, you can repudiate a deal through an agent at no emotional cost, and, perhaps as a result, get it improved as well.

Naturally, the greater the distance between you and the negotiation the easier it is for you to say no. That is why if you want to say no, use the telephone or a letter and avoid personal contact, as it is fatal to maintaining a tough posture.

The other party has no way of knowing the extent of your agent's authority; consequently, he has no way of knowing whether a little more conceded here or there will secure the deal. This might produce bigger concessions in your favor than otherwise.

The mandate can be used by agents to secure better terms: "If it was up to me, I might agree with you, but my client insists on a full penalty clause for late delivery," or, "I'm sorry, but there is no way my client will accept that proposal."

ASK NO QUESTIONS

An agent can have an important role as a facilitator, such as when, for political reasons, two parties cannot negotiate openly together.

For instance, a small Communist country had to purchase grain to supplement its own supplies. For political reasons it would not deal directly with the U.S. government, so it used an agent.

The agent arranged the purchase of U.S. grain FOB and shipped it to Belgium. It then transhipped it CIF across Europe to the client's frontier, showing Belgium as the country of origin.

This met the political needs of the regime—even its own customs people remained ignorant of the origin of the grain—and the agent earned a good commission on the deal.

ONE BY ONE

Another Communist country—less worried about the ideological delicacies of dealing with capitalists—is required to ship grain from all over the world.

Its officials knew enough about market economics to know that if they simply chartered 150 ships in one go, there would be a price explosion at their expense.

Hence, they negotiated a deal with a broker that enabled him to charter the ships individually from a hundred other brokers, each deal to be conducted without publicity.

The main broker knew the market for ships and asked individual brokers for specific ships that were within their areas. This prevented them from racing into the world market and forcing the price up.

The successful use of the brokers saved the Communist country millions of dollars in hard currency. Long after the charters were settled, the world chartering market was still unaware of the bonanza it missed.

Both these types of statements can be very difficult barriers to get around.

If you are negotiating with an agent, you have no control over how he reports the proceedings to his principal, or even whether he reports anything at all.

This is the greatest weakness of negotiating through agents (though I strongly recommend their use when the stakes are high and the market is unfamiliar to you). The agent, for all you know, might be working to bump up the price in order to increase his fee, while the other principal might be quite willing to settle if he only knew about the offer you'd made. Again, you just don't know.

Hence, in seeking to bar agents from the negotiation, the advertisers are trying to meet face to face with the person who has full authority to settle and who, by his physical presence in the negotiations, must perforce be directly subject to their pressures.

However, professional agents at the Negotiating Clinics often wax eloquently on an apparently common complaint among their number.

In real estate, for instance, an agent can be undermined by a principal who instructs him to accept the other party's last offer even though the agent advises him, on the basis of his experience, that the other party can be pushed to a better price.

In fact, the worst instruction an agent can get is to be told, "Get the best price you can, but above all get a price."

This complaint is the reverse of the suspicions voiced by some principals about agents: "I believe that agents always hold out for a higher price from the other party merely to get a bigger fee."

This suspicion can be fed when the negotiations are conducted in semi-public. Competitive business takes place in a relatively small community in any one place. To lose one's commercial reputation in the City of London is as devastating as it is to lose it in Edinburgh, Hong Kong, Bahrain, Sydney, or Los Angeles.

In all serious competing businesses everybody knows everybody worth knowing in the rival companies, and (nudge-nudge-wink-wink) "confidential" whispers travel round the trade like a prairie on fire; there is nothing closer to greased lightning than the tittle-tattle of business (with the possible exception of politics).

Nothing is more deserving of being true than a good piece of the in-the-know scandal—and, anyway, if it isn't true, it's almost certain to be funny!

In negotiating through agents, the other party can seek to undermine your position by trying to contact your principal. Of course, this could be construed to be unethical (indeed, most professional bodies frown at such conduct), but there is more than one way to achieve this end without becoming an outcast.

The other party can leak news to the trade press, such as by asserting that only your personal intransigence on "minor" points is preventing the deal from going through.

GET YOURSELF AN AGENT

In some cases you are better off with an agent, especially if the stakes are high and the market is unknown to you. Your first problem is to get a good agent and this is a lot harder than you might imagine. True, almost anybody can get *any* old agent—there are plenty of people willing to do precious little for "clients."

What you need is an agent who will work for you and not somebody who expects you to do the work for them. If they never return your calls within a reasonable time (though you can't expect them to be in their offices *and* selling your film script), do not keep you informed of progress, and show no evidence of making any, constantly argue with you when you ask reasonable questions, are totally conservative about what they should go for on your behalf, and prefer to haggle with you than haggle with whomever they are supposed to be dealing with, you ought to get out of the relationship. (Just write and close the account—and make sure that your contract allows you to do this!)

The best agents are always in demand—I know one in New York who only has *five* clients at a time, and if you want her, you have to wait until one of them dies or otherwise goes off her books.

Agents cannot produce miracles—at least not on a regular basis! Nor can they be left to get on with it without help from you.

My own rule for judging the worth of an agent is simple: I know I need her only as long as she suggests that we go for a deal way beyond the very best I had hoped for. If the time arrives when she doesn't then I know as much about the business as she does and would be better off holding on to my ten percent!

If your clients read these press reports (and copies can be brought to their attention), they might be conned into believing them, particularly if they already half believe you are holding out for an extra commission.

This causes them to insist on an early settlement, which presumably is why some negotiators go semi-public in this way, hoping that it will sow doubts in the sometimes-anonymous principal's mind about the probity of his agents.

Apart from trying to avoid time wasting and the possibility that overzealous (or greedy) agents are manipulating the settlement terms by provoking an unnecessary deadlock, the demand for principals only can increase the bargaining advantage to the parties.

Suppose the property for sale is a large company, and the seller ends up face to face with a prospect who has authority to settle—it's his own money—but has little experience in handling transactions of this

116

size. If the seller has been the owner of similar properties for long enough to be less than intimidated by them, he must have an advantage over a keen and vulnerable buyer moving into the big league for the first time.

It is also possible that the advertiser is himself an agent for the real owner and is fishing for principals only precisely in order to smoke out would-be entrepreneurs with little professional experience in what they are doing.

More than one hotel has changed hands in recent years on terms less than favorable to the first-time buyer, who arrives at the negotiation clutching a recent legacy or a large severance check. For these reasons, reputable agents are a good protection for an unsure and inexperienced buyer.

What constitutes a good agent is another story. In real estate there is some safeguard in the professional status of licensed brokers, and in other commercial sectors many people make a honest living by acting as agents between principals (but watch out for "Jaws"—he and his cousins swim in the smallest ponds and strike without warning).

But in the absence of an agent, or where the value of the transaction does not justify an agent's expense, your best bet is to become one!

ANSWERS
SELF-ASSESSMENT TEST 11

Q.1: a] If you're new and hungry, you will. But such an instruction is nothing but trouble, because whatever you get, the owner is bound to protest that it is not enough. (− 10)

b] Correct. Get the bottom limit clearly fixed. (+ 5)

c] A trifle hasty. Try b] first. (0)

Q.2: a] A toss-up with b]. If you're confident of your price or just anxious to clear the garage, give him your figure without hesitation. (+ 5)

b] A good protective ploy if you're not sure, but you will need to work hard to raise the offer if it is low. (+ 5)

c] The mandate demand has credibility. It is often a good lead into b] or a]. (+ 8)

d] Never make a prejudgment of his price, otherwise you will always cut yours. (− 10)

Q.3: a] Possibly, if she refuses c]. (+ 3)

b] Not unless you're desperate for her dinghy. (0)

c] Correct. (+ 5)

Q.4: a] Surely a proper first demand if it's 'principals only'? (+ 10)

b] A sound lead-in move for a]. (+ 5)

c] Risky, because he will constantly insist on consulting the organ grinder—at your expense. (− 10)

SELF-ASSESSMENT TEST 12

Q.1: You are in Bergen (Norway) and want to buy toy trolls for your children. You enter a *very* expensive souvenir shop which sells trolls. The ones you want are priced at sixty-five kroner each. You want three. Do you ask the clerk:

a] How much for two trolls?

b] How much for three trolls?

c] What special offers are they offering on trolls?

Score:

Q.2: You are in a bookshop looking for a paperback thriller to read on your vacation. There are several copies of the title you want, but one of them is a damaged book. Do you:

a] Select a clean mint copy?

b] Take the damaged copy to the cash desk?

c] Take a mint copy and the damaged copy to the cash desk?

Score:

Q.3: You are in a store buying a freezer and the one you want is marked at $875. You ask for a discount and the clerk tells you that it is company policy not to give discounts off the goods as they are already marked down to the lowest possible price. Do you:

a] Ask to see the manger?

b] Accept what he says as being plausible?

c] Press your case for a discount with the clerk?

Score:

Q.4: In a survey of buying behavior of customers over three months in a major European store chain, what percentage of people do you think paid the price shown on the tag:

a] 53%?

b] 97%?

c] 37%?

d] 78%?

e] 11%?

Score:

THERE AIN'T
NO SUCH THING
AS A FIXED PRICE
or How to Haggle
for a Lower Price

Why do shops have price tags on their goods?

I have heard many explanations for this phenomenon:

- To save everybody from asking the price of every product.
- To save time in the onerous task of shopping.
- To speed up the buying decision.
- To avoid mistakes at the cash desk.
- To help the consumer make choices.
- To treat all customers the same with the same price.
- To avoid making losses on small-margin goods.

Most of them sound plausible, but all miss the point.

The real reason is much more subtle: The overwhelming majority of consumers are brought up from an early age believing in fairy stories, Santa Claus, and fixed prices.

The first two are quite harmless and, sadly, pass with the age of innocence. But once the belief in fixed prices gets its barnacle-like grip on your brain, it hardly ever lets go. It manifests itself in the enslavement of the consumer to the price tag.

And the stores know this, which is why they use them.

119

In other words, they know that customers, almost totally without exception, will part with their cash for the printed price.

And what a power this gives the owners of stores! They know that most consumers would never dream of questioning a price tag—far from it, because most consumers believe that if it's on the tag, then its *gospel* —and so the stores can choose the price to put on it.

If events prove them wrong, and not enough consumers jump at the chance to buy whatever the store is selling, they hold a sale and mark *another* price on the tag.

One would expect consumers to be outraged at so-called sales where the evidence is as plain as can be that the stores have been padding their prices. But no! The belief in fixed prices appears by some weird logic to be *reinforced,* not shaken, by the visible drop in prices!

Stores even leave both prices on the tag to make you think they are doing you a big favor. Instead, you ought to realize what a sucker they were taking you for before the sale.

Ironically, the greater the drop in price, the greater the bargain consumers feel they have achieved. But the bigger the bargain the more unchallengeable is the evidence of the humbuggery of fixed prices.

P. T. Barnum, of Barnum & Bailey circus fame, confessed that he made his wholly deserved fortune on the willingness—nay, insistence— of the great American public to pay to see his totally improbable spectacles.

They were humbugged—and loved him for it. Yet Barnum only reversed the humbuggery of business life. He sold tickets to dreams that could never be fulfilled—his "products" were always a fantasy.

In retail stores the products are real, many of them are excellent, and there is little or no humbuggery in the claims that are made for them (give or take the occasional exaggeration). The humbug lies in the price. It claims to be real, and you believe it is real—but it is only a childhood fantasy that was reinforced with every transaction you made since you bought your first stick of candy in the corner shop.

That is why the message of this chapter is:

There ain't no such thing as a fixed price!

A LITTLE LESS
FOR A CAR WITH A LITTLE MORE

An Irish luxury car manufacturer ran into liquidity problems, although their cars were technically well received. The problem was that not enough were being sold to justify continuing production.

Stocks of unsold cars began to pile up at the Irish plant, and the company went into receivership.

A leading U.S. car rental firm approached the manufacturer with an offer to take one thousand cars immediately and another one thousand over a twelve-month period.

The car sold at $26,000 in the U.S., which the car rental firm said was overpriced.

They told the manufacturer that if they could let the cars go for a little less, then they should have a deal.

A LOT LESS FOR THE SAME CAR

All U.K. car manufacturers maintained differential pricing policies for cars sold in the U.K. and cars sold on the European continent. Exactly the same cars could cost as much as 40 percent less in Belgium than they were sold for in Britain.

Some people spotted the price differential and refused to buy their British cars from local dealers. Instead, they crossed over to Belgium and bought a British right-hand-drive car there. They brought it back by ferry and saved themselves a couple of thousand pounds.

Eventually, dealers got in on the act. Instead of ordering their cars from the British plants direct, they ordered them from the Belgian dealers, who shipped them over from Britain first!

This forced the issue into the open. It also fully explains why imported cars from Japan could be so price competitive and why they could sell, pound for pound, a more luxurious vehicle even with the shipping costs from Japan taken into account.

Gilbert Summers knows all about the fragility of fixed prices. He runs a store in Texarkana, Texas, and has done so for twenty years. He never had any trouble with his prices until 1979.

Up to then housewives and their families loaded up the carts in his store with their weekly shopping, waited quietly while the clerks at the checkouts totaled the price tags, and then paid with cash, checks, or credit cards.

If there were any upsets, they were over delays while a price was checked because the tag had come off, or if the clerk suspected it had been "accidentally" changed, or if a drunk had wandered in and wouldn't go home, or if a couple was fighting over an incident that happened at last night's party.

Most of the time the only noise was that of the cash registers, the piped music wafting overhead, and kids screaming as they played about.

Nobody, but nobody, ever asked to see Gilbert Summers about a price tag.

That was until Hang Ha Dong and family moved into the neighborhood. They are Vietnamese refugees, the survivors of a particularly harrowing boat voyage from Saigon to Thailand.

Hang Ha Dong brought with him his entire family, all twelve of them, including his wife's sister and her aged mother. He also brought with him the habits of a lifetime, one of which is a total incomprehension of the phenomenon of fixed prices.

The first time the Hang family, en masse, visited Gilbert Summer's store was nearly their last.

Dutifully, they loaded up their carts with their requirements, as they had seen the soldiers do in the PX on the U.S. Army base where Hang and Mrs. Hang had worked as cleaners for several years. They hadn't shopped in the PX themselves—they preferred the local market—but they had been in it a few times, marvelling at its stocks.

When they got to the checkout, Mr. Hang picked up a tin and asked how much the clerk wanted for it. The bored clerk checked the price and drawled, "Two dollars and twenty-five cents."

Mr. Hang delved into the cart and asked, "How much for two tins?" The clerk looked puzzled and said, irritably, "Four dollars and fifty cents."

It was Mr. Hang's turn to look puzzled, and he spoke to his wife in Vietnamese. Whatever she replied, Mr. Hang told the clerk that he would offer him $3.98 for the two tins. This was obviously a bit much for Mrs. Hang, because she let forth a gale of Vietnamese at him— and her mother joined in, too.

The clerk wondered what was happening.

Mr. Hang next lifted out of the cart four string bags of oranges. The clerk said, "A dollar-thirty each."

"A dollar-five," said Mr. Hang.

"A dollar-thirty," repeated the clerk, adding: "Can't you read? It says a dollar-thirty on the tag. Where did you get a dollar-five from?"

"A dollar-ten and that's my best price," said Mr. Hang.

"A dollar-thirty," replied the clerk.

"A dollar-twelve, if you throw in the bag of rice at four dollars," said Mr. Hang.

"It's a dollar-thirty for the oranges and five-forty for the rice, as it says on the tag."

"But how much for two bags of rice?" asked Mr. Hang.

"Jesus!" exclaimed the clerk, by this time losing his cool. "Are you nuts or something?"

He decided to explain in simple English (he knew no Vietnamese, having spent his army service in Colorado Springs) how the Texarkana store run by Mr. Summers operated, which he assured Mr. Hang was no different from every other store in the United States of America.

"*You* have to pay the price on the tag. *I* have to check it here. When you've paid, you take the goods home. Until then they stay in the store. Got it?"

Mr. Hang and his family began speaking at once, some to each other in Vietnamese, picking up and turning over items to look at the tags, some to the clerk in English, trying to get the haggle under way again.

The din rose considerably, and other shoppers crowded round to watch what was going on (watching people shouting at each other is a common trait in the West).

At this point Gilbert Summers arrived at the checkout. The clerk explained to him that he was dealing with some weird people who didn't appear to understand how the world was organized.

"What do you mean?" asked his boss.

"They want to haggle over every goddammed can of peas and packet of soup," he told him. "Christ, Gil, they're offering me deals left, right, and center, for two of this and one of that, or three of this or one of the other. I don't know what's going on. Can't they read the frigging price tags?"

"H-o-l-d i-t!" bawled Gilbert above the row.

His whole store stopped.

The checkouts, crowded with carts and people, stopped ringing up the dollars, which in Gilbert Summers's world made it *an emergency*.

He ordered Mr. Hang to take his family out of the store and not to come back. He told the clerk to run their carts back into the shelf lanes and then get back to his desk pronto.

Mr. Hang didn't move.

He was clearly completely bewildered by the strange behavior of the boss man. He knew about hard bargaining from the market square at Lang Foo, but never had a merchant snatched away his goods and ordered him off!

This was clearly a time to try another tack. He put his hand in his coat to take out his wallet.

Gilbert Summers, the clerk, and a half dozen others hit the floor as if they wanted to get through it. When they saw Mr. Hang was holding his wallet and not a magnum revolver they got up sheepishly.

Mr. Hang shoved a piece of paper toward Gilbert. It was his honorable discharge as a cleaner from the U.S. Army back in Vietnam. (Hang was using the "returned soldier" ploy, or rather a "Vietnamese ex-cleaner" version of it).

He explained to Gilbert Summers that he had always liked the Americans and had wanted to be in Texas ever since he had seen a John Wayne film where everybody in it spoke Vietnamese. He had heard that Texas was a land of opportunity where anybody could make their fortune if they worked hard and knew that "a dollar saved was a dollar earned."

"Damn right," said Summers. "As my daddy told me, you-all work hard and live like decent folks and you-all'll get by."

"OK," said a beaming Mr. Hang, happy to have resolved the misunderstanding with such a fine Texan as Gilbert Summers (though he didn't understand why he spoke no Vietnamese). "Now about these oranges at a dollar-thirty. I'll give you a dollar-fifteen if you throw in two tins of tomato soup at thirty-five cents each . . ."

It took many months for Gilbert Summers to get used to Mr. Hang and his family. Likewise for Mr. Hang, who found that if he waited until 5 P.M. each day he could get his fruit and vegetables from the Summers's store much cheaper than they were in the morning (giving him a unique insight into the American concept of the "happy hour").

CHEAP BUT LUXURIOUS

Travel is often a large proportion of the expense for a vacation, especially if you want to reach exotic places.

A travel agency in London specializes in rock bottom luxury holidays.

Clients can get a two-week cruise in first class accommodation for as little as $450 all inclusive. Or they can safari in Kenya for ten days on the "millionaire's circuit" for $525, first class airfare included. Or how about three weeks in the Caribbean in a sun-soaked paradise for $300?

How do they do it?

The agency contracts to buy up all the cancelled holidays at the top end of the market for a nominal sum and they sell on to their clients the vacation at a knocked-down price.

The client states the months when he and his family are free to travel; they must be prepared to go on holiday at seventy-two hours' notice.

But the deal certainly proves that even high-priced services can be consumed at rock bottom rates—if you look for the deal!

NEVER MIND THE WINE, WHAT ABOUT THE MONEY?

A discount wine chain in the U.K. made a name for itself through years of selling good quality French and Italian wines at discount prices. In fact, the prices were so low that people wondered how the chain managed to make a profit.

True, the wine company bought up vast stocks of wine and sold them virtually at cost to the customer.

How did they make their money? On a large volume for a small profit? Not at all.

They weren't interested in making a profit on the wine—that's how they beat the competition.

They made their profits by having a constant flow of cash into their bank accounts, which they loaned to the banks for thirty days until they paid their invoices. The interest of 10 percent on the money exceeded the profit they would have gotten if they had sold the wine at regular prices.

CHARGE IT OR CHARGE AT IT?

Any retailer who accepts credit cards is disclosing that he is prepared to accept a discount on his prices of at least 2 to 3 percent because that is what the credit card companies charge him for the transaction.

Therefore, any cash customer ought to be able to get up to 3 percent off a purchase without a quibble.

If the guy claims that he relies on cash customers to make up his profit targets, tell him you don't believe in subsidizing others and you will therefore pay by credit card instead of cash!

He also found if he bought soup by the case he got a few cents off the per tin price.

Sometimes he sat outside the shop with his family for hours and made trial runs inside to see if the price of cans of soup had fallen in the past hour. Occasionally the clerks would give in to the Hangs just to get rid of them.

Other times, Mr. Hang chose to go in when the shop was busiest and delay the checkout while he haggled over the price of three loaves of bread, or fruitcake (for which Texarkana is famous), or the weekend's groceries.

Gilbert Summers and Hang Ha Dong have gotten along fine since 1979. Their families are soon to be related, for the eldest Summers boy began courting young Miss Hang around Thanksgiving, 1981. She told him that marriage was *the* price tag (and definitely COD only!), but happily for the young lovers his future father-in-law had already taught the good people of Texarkana about taking on a fixed price!

What worked for Hang Ha Dong can work for you. His advantage is that he never believed in fixed prices—they were unknown in Vietnam until, ironically, the Communists took over.

Communist-fixed prices are the final proof of the idiocy of fixed prices. No Communist state knows the real price of anything because their accounting systems do not recognize supply and demand or the value of what is contained in any product. The Communist state arbitrarily fixes hundreds of thousands of prices at the center, and these are used for transactions, irrespective of whether or not they correspond to the costs of producing the goods themselves or the needs of those buying them. The stores sell goods at fixed prices, and if they run out of a good, that's too bad. Hence, there are long lines for some goods, none for others, and masses of the population wish to emigrate at any one moment.

The black market flourishes. Russia is the only country in the world where they shoot you for supplying to people the things they want which the state is too inefficient to provide. What Prohibition did for organized crime, fixed prices in Russia (and Poland) have done for the resistance to all things Communist.

How, then, should you tackle a fixed price?

The simple way to do so is to challenge it!

If you don't ask for a discount for cash, you certainly won't be offered one. (If you are offered 5 percent discount, ask for 7.5 percent.)

If you can think of a way to change the deal, you might be able to change the price. For example, what does the deal include?

> *Delivery and installation:* How much off for transporting and/or installing it yourself?
>
> *Parts and labor warranty:* How much off for forgoing your rights to these? (You can be sure they cover themselves for repairs and defects in their price.)
>
> *Pay now or later:* If there is a delivery delay, how much off for paying cash now—you get the use of my money?
>
> *New or "as new":* If it's $1000 for a brand-new freezer, how much off for a demonstration model, a window model, a slightly bashed-in or scratched model?
>
> *Price for one:* How much for two—or three? This will tell you something about the margin on the price for one.
>
> *Compatible purchase:* Suppose I buy the desk *and* the chairs together? ("OK, I'll take the suit *if* you throw in a tie.")
>
> *Noncompatible purchase:* How much off if I buy the lawn mower *and* a set of pans from the kitchen department? ("How much off the rent of the office if I use your telex?")
>
> *Related service:* How much off if I clean up after you and dispose of the rubbish?
>
> *Gross account:* How much off the price for the pipes if I agree to place all my business with you this year?

AN ABSOLUTELY TRUE STORY

A video recorder supplier has a chain of shops throughout the country, and into one of these one day walked an earnest young man who was interested in the price of a particular model.

The sales clerk demonstrated the model to the satisfaction of the young buyer and quoted him the list price of $600. The man agreed to buy at that price(!), and as the clerk completed the order form the young man told him "his company wanted to use the video for staff training."

As the young man read the order form, a frown appeared across his brow, and the clerk asked what was the problem.

"How many of these forms will I have to fill in? Can't we get the order on a single form?"

The clerk asked him to explain.

"It just seems to be an excessive amount of work to fill in a form for every machine."

"How do you mean?" said the clerk. "Every sale has an order form; of course, if you want two machines we can use the same form."

126

"OK, as long as we can speed it up a bit?"

At this point the sales clerk suddenly realized there was a misunderstanding between them.

"Er, exactly how many video machines are you buying?"

"Why, one for each branch, which is about 2,500," answered the young man, adding: "I should have said to earlier, but I'm in a hurry as this order has to beat our budget year on Friday."

The sales clerk was stunned. He had no idea the buyer wanted 2,500 video machines because he had not even attempted to quibble over the price list or negotiate a quantity discount of any kind, or ask for delivery, or anything like that. The only thing the buyer was anxious about was saving time filling in order forms and beating a budget date!

The clerk quickly wrote out another order with 2,500 on it and the young man signed it. The sales clerk's commission at $50 a machine was worth $125,000 (his company "negotiated" that down to $50,000), but the quantity discount the buyer could have got was worth much more than that. He didn't ask for one, and what you don't ask for you seldom get.

You are unlikely to get very far with the counter clerks in a store. Higher management deliberately gives them absolutely no discretion over price, though it is worth testing this assumption just in case they do have a small margin to work with.

In clothes stores, the counter clerks sometimes have discretion over small things like the price of alterations. Almost certainly, even in big stores you can get the alterations done free if you make that a condition of purchase, particularly if you have already taken up their time looking at lots of suits.

Naturally, they will tell you that it is company policy to charge for alterations—and so it should be if you are daft enough to accept this.

Hence, you must be prepared to ask to see the manager when you are approaching a buy decision. If you can't do that you're sunk. If the clerk tells you that he cannot give you a discount, ask him who can. Invariably, he will tell you to see the manager.

TWENTY FIVE WAYS TO TAKE ON A FIXED PRICE

1. Throw in the accessories and I'll take it.
2. At that price I must get the display stand for free.
3. What discount is there for a regular order?
4. As a new/old customer I want an introductory/loyalty discount.
5. What is the discount for cash?
6. If you give me 90 days credit, I'll buy now.
7. What will you take off for the demonstration model?
8. If you give me a special price, I'll order right now.
9. I want a year's free maintenance, which will cost you nothing if your product is as good as you claim.
10. I want to test it for 30 days free of charge.

11. How much off if we use non-returnable/returnable crates?
12. How much off if I take the end runs?
13. I'll take last year's stock if you take off 15 percent.
14. I'll try it, if you guarantee my money back if I am unsatisfied (How much off for a no-come-back deal?).
15. How much off if I recommend it to my friends/colleagues?
16. What's the discount for two/three, etc.?
17. What's the discount for an exclusive supply agreement?
18. How much off if your people work at my place?
19. How much off if we collect?
20. How much off if we order and you deliver as we need it?
21. How long will you hold your discount prices if we order today? (Hold them for an extra six months and we'll buy.)
22. As we are the first/fiftieth/last purchasers we should get a 20 percent discount.
23. For a discount you can quote me as a reference.
24. As this is a risky/new product, I'll need ten percent off.
25. Only if you have the power to give me a special price, will I order now.

Now, either this is a way of telling you that if you don't believe him about the company's policy on discounts you had better hear it from the boss, or he is telling you that only the boss can/will give you a discount. Either way, you must be prepared to test it.

Why should the boss give you a discount?

First, it's likely that he has the authority to do so, and people who have authority occasionally like to exercise it, especially if from time to time they like to impress on their subordinates the distance between them.

Second, you have probably brought him away from much more important work, and the amount you are haggling for is not worth his time to fight over. If he gives you 5 percent off a suit or a table, he still has a 40 percent markup left for his profit. And if he believes you will not buy without a discount he knows he loses the entire sale.

What is the rational thing for him to do? Agree to a discount! He didn't get where he is by being silly over trifles.

Third, guys who have graduated up from the counter like to keep their hand in when it comes to individual selling. They get promoted because they are good at selling and they are good because they enjoy it.

In management they seldom get a chance to show themselves (and their subordinates) how good they are, so your request to see him could be music to his ears. You are doing him a favor!

I always go to the top guy when making a purchase, though I met my match a few years back.

I went into Austin Reed's clothes store in Princes Street, Edinburgh, to look at their suits. When it came to the buy decision I asked for a discount off the price tag.

The assistant couldn't give it to me, so I asked to see the manager. He came along with a smile and a "what-appears-to-be-the-trouble" look about him.

I told him I liked the suit but not the price, and asked him for a 10 percent discount.

He started chatting and soon had me trying on suits again, and he indicated that I could have 5 percent off the gray suit I liked, but said he thought I looked better in the brown one. He also offered me 5 percent off the brown one *and* hinted at a bigger discount if I bought them both.

That is what eventually I agreed to.

It wasn't until I got home that I realized I had ended up spending more than twice what I intended, had two suits instead of one (I narrowly escaped from buying a winter coat, too), and had been given a 7.5 percent "discount" off an amount I hadn't intended to pay.

And I wore the brown suit only once! That is what comes from chasing a discount and forgetting the budget.

However, I still fight those fixed prices. You should too. It could save you hundreds of dollars a month.

The fact that most people don't bother to challenge fixed prices is no comfort. Sure, there is a time penalty for haggling, and usually we simply do not have any time to spare.

But one consequence of *never* challenging fixed prices is that we do not know how to when we want or need to. It's no good waiting until we are about to make a large-value purchase before we get experience in taking on a fixed price.

In Texas they say that business is about people with money meeting people with experience: The people with experience get the money and the people with the money get the experience.

But as Hang Ha Dong puts it, he didn't go all the way to Texas just for the experience!

ANSWERS
SELF-ASSESSMENT TEST 12

Q.1: a] A good move, because it enables you to push for an extra discount for a third troll. (+ 3)

b] Not so good, because you have used up your leverage for a quantity discount in one go. (− 5)

c] Correct. There might be other special offers—packing and postage to your home abroad free, a 10 percent sales discount off the price tag just for one, and so on—which you should know about before you press for a quantity discount. (+ 8)

Q.2: a] Only if you think you can get a discount for a mint copy, otherwise you'll pay the tag price. (0)

b] This gives you a case for a discount to take the book off the store's hands (as long as it's readable). (+ 5)

c] Yes. A strong move as evidence is a powerful supporter of an assault on a fixed price. If they still say no, leave both copies at the desk and go to a more sensible book store. (+ 10)

Q.3: a] Yes. If you can't face this step then you surely have not got the credibility to get a discount. (+ 10)

b] You are obviously easily persuaded and lack grit. (− 10)

c] If you have ducked out of a], I doubt if you will get very far with this approach. (− 5)

Q.4: a] (− 5)

b] Right! You can see how much we are brainwashed. (+ 10)

c] (− 10)

d] (− 3)

e] Are you serious? (− 15)

SELF-ASSESSMENT TEST 13

Q.1: You are on a sales tour of South Africa, arranging dealerships for your range of industrial pumps. In Johannesburg you are told that your pumps are "too expensive," in Durban, your prices are "unrealistic," and in Cape Town "the dealer's margins are too low." Do you:

a] Telex head office to say the marketing people have got the price structure wrong?

b] Carry on your tour as normal?

c] Request discretion on the margins?

d] Give discounts off the list price in exchange for the order?

Score:

Q.2: You are negotiating the supply of heavy pumps to a power station project, and the contractor tells you that your prices are about 15 percent above the quotes he has from a competing German firm and 35 percent above the prices he is being offered for a totally reconditioned set of pumps. Do you:

130

a] Assure him that your pumps are the best in the world and known to be such by everybody in the business?

b] Tell him that the price is negotiable *if* you get the order?

c] Remind him that your pumps are regularly serviced and have a twenty-four-hour emergency repair service behind them?

Score:

Q.3: You are telexed by a construction consortium that they will accept your bid for earth-moving equipment to be shipped to Jordan if you can reduce your prices by 5 percent. Do you:

a] Offer 3 percent only?

b] Agree?

c] Suggest that it is possible only *if* the bid terms are changed?

d] Decline?

Score:

THE WALLS OF JERICHO
or How to Stop Conceding

Fainthearted negotiators, faced with a challenge to their price, change their price rather than risk deadlock. They have the resolve of a wet paper bag.

Price is a predictable target in any negotiation, and you don't need to be a genius to appreciate why.

Price is divisible—it's counted in nickles and dimes—and many buyers (rightly) believe it pays them to try to shave price a little.

Supermarkets that cut a penny off each delivered bottle can share the savings with their customers or add directly to their profits.

A wine negotiator who concedes a "mere" penny a bottle cuts his own company's cash flow on 50,000 cases a year by 600,000 pennies, or $6,000. That is equivalent to a large chunk of his salary. (Even a penny off per case is worth $500.)

If he concedes a penny a bottle with two of his accounts, he doubles what it costs the company to employ him!

Conversely, if he could get an extra penny a bottle from two key accounts. he costs his company nothing and can spend the rest of the year earning pure profits.

A Middle East go-between on a modest 3 percent commission (some get 9 percent) makes $900,000 on a $30 million turnkey project—if you can get him down "only" half a percent, you can save yourself $150,000.

Is it worth trying a price challenge to save your company $150,000? Of course it is!

Is it worth his while trying to raise you half a percent on your offer of 3 percent. Sure it is. If he gets you to agree to 3.5 percent, his commission for acting as a go-between goes up to $1 million.

Pennies and half percents do matter.

That is why you must expect the opposition to try some form of price challenge—they wouldn't be doing their job properly if they didn't —and if you are not ready for them, you aren't doing your job properly either.

If price challenges succeed, they provide big benefits to the asker. The fainthearted always crumble at a price challenge, and they are a cause of their company's losses—which proves that employing them as negotiators is an expensive luxury.

Of course, if you are buying you should always make a price challenge. Never accept his first offer: Test his resolve! If he crumbles, you gain; if he doesn't, you haven't lost anything.

But what of your own propensity to crumble? What can be done about it?

Quite a lot. You can eradicate the propensity to crumble at a price challenge by learning how to fight back without provoking deadlock. One immediate way to stiffen your resolve is to stop thinking about price in the same terms (and sometimes even in the same currency) as the other guy.

He will ask you to drop your price by so much a unit, or to raise his fees by so much a day. He certainly won't talk to you about the total cost of his price change or the annual cost of his services.

Why?

Because by looking at his price challenge in the small, you forget to think about what it's going to cost you in the large.

He encourages you to think of a single bottle rather than the warehouse full of cases stacked from floor to ceiling. Are you going to think a penny doesn't matter when you multiply it by the half million bottles of wine in your warehouse? That is the *real* cost of giving in to his price challenge.

Use a calculator if you want to see the real costs of conceding to price challenges—and let him see you using it, too.

But seeing the real costs and avoiding them are not the same thing. The per-unit-price ploy is aimed at making the cut more acceptable to you and is not an end in itself.

The other guy's real objective is to achieve a larger slice of the cake for himself, and therefore you need to have some weapons on hand to prevent him from reaching that objective entirely at your expense.

Take the case of Helmut Weber, on his first overseas negotiating tour. Representing a German firm of high technical reputation, he went to South Africa to negotiate new supply and service agreements with his company's existing local distributors and to negotiate new agreements with some new outlets.

THE SQUARE ROOT OF NOTHING!

The 1980–82 air freight price war on the North Atlantic routes saw extensive price slashing by air cargo carriers. If one carrier cut rates to get business, another would go below the cut immediately. This led a third to follow suit and a fourth to jump in with yet lower rates.

Something akin to panic set in when one cargo handler was filling space for an airline at 25 percent off the already slashed kilo prices of the main cargo carriers.

Not surprisingly, this handler's client went bust. But the heavy pressure on rates continued. Except for one company, British Caledonian. To the surprise of almost everybody, they refused to join the suicidal scramble to cut prices.

"It is the easiest thing in the world to go out and fill an aeroplane with the square root of nothing," was how a company spokesman put it. "We have refused to dodge the issue," he added. "If shippers do not wish to pay our rates, they do not get our services. We are not in a rate war on the North Atlantic in any shape or form."

The result?

BCal's air freight revenues rose 36 percent in 1981 as it made an aggressive marketing bid for traffic at economic prices. It was also able to expand its facilities and capacity when all around it other carriers were in severe financial difficulties.

British Airways was forced to withdraw from the cargo business altogether, and other giants had to revise their rates upward.

Obviously, BCal is not managed by price crumblers!

Helmut Weber knew something about pumps; he had just graduated with a degree in engineering. However, he knew next to nothing about negotiating, and nothing at all about price challenges.

South Africans as a whole are not reputed to be handicapped in business matters. The distributors didn't know much about the technical side of pumps, but they knew how to buy and sell them (and most other things) in their territories.

A classic negotiating asymmetry!

You might wonder why Helmut's company sent him on such an important mission when clearly he was less than qualified for it. That was precisely the question I put to the company president, and he said that his wife had insisted that their *son* show what he could do!

Helmut's progress across South Africa was monitored by the long trails of telex messages that accumulated on his father's desk.

If they were read in sequence, the trend was obvious to even the untrained eye, but his father did not need the normal German passion for order to see the pattern of his son's negotiating behavior.

Helmut was a price crumbler.

BROTHER, CAN YOU SPARE A MILLION DIMES?

A Korean construction company submitted a bid for the first phase of a Jordanian building project that was so low even their most hardened competitors just did not believe it.

It was not just rock-bottom—it was positively subterranean! Their competitors could only look on in wonder at the Korean price.

One old hand surmised that the Koreans were going in well below cost in the first phase of the project in order to eliminate the competition, in the hope that they would recoup some profits on subsequent phases.

The Koreans took the risk that the Jordanians would put out the subsequent phases to some other contractor, or that they might insist that the Koreans matched the prices of their earlier bid in all subsequent work.

If this happened the Koreans would have expended something like $40 million for a $24 million income.

Stop Press: The Korean firm went bankrupt in 1982. The Jordanians approached those contractors whose bids had been rejected in favor of the Korean firm to rescue the project. All of them refused on the grounds that "cut-throat competitors" do not deserve a reprieve, and neither do short-sighted governments, who encourage "kamikazes," deserve assistance until "common sense and economic pricing" is accepted in contracts.

Not that Helmut saw it that way. He was working extremely hard in what he considered the most difficult of circumstances. If asked, Helmut would have summed up the problem in one word: *competition.*

Within two days of arriving at Jan Smuts airport in Johannesburg, he was convinced that South Africa was the most price-competitive economy in the world.

Nobody denied the technical excellence of Weber pumps—though nobody praised them outright, either—but everybody told him that Weber's ex-works pump prices were too expensive and that the dealer margins were too low. He telexed Hamburg that he had been forced to cut the ex-works price by 5 percent just to hold the current order level with their largest Johannesburg distributor.

Durban was much worse: "Weber prices are too high and your

135

pumps will never sell at the list prices even if I take no cut myself," was how the boss of the largest engineering parts stocking firm put it. Helmut telexed Hamburg: "Our prices unrealistic. Have increased the distributor's margin by 10 percent and opened up a new dealership."

A new distributor asked him why Weber pumps were costing more this year compared to last, which puzzled Helmut a little, as he didn't know they had sold pumps to that outlet before—he would check when he got home—and as far as he knew, Weber pumps had not risen in price for fifteen months. He agreed, however, to a 15 percent discount and telexed home that he had opened up another new dealership, and an order for one of each pump type was enclosed (the dealer wanted "to try the market" first).

Another distributor told him that he wanted to stock and sell Weber pumps, but "the competition quotes me keener prices than yours and trade is so bad at the moment that I am not reordering anything." This got the distributor a 20 percent discount.

Helmut got different versions of the same story wherever he went, and he telexed Hamburg that he was "compelled" to make discounts of between 15 percent (if he was really lucky) and 30 percent (when he wasn't).

By the time he returned to Johannesburg he was utterly convinced that Weber pumps would never keep a foothold in South Africa if he stuck to the company's "ridiculous" overseas pricing policy.

He was mortified when a distributor in East London rebuked him for "attempting monopolistic exploitation of South Africa's need for good pumps," and he reported by telex that he had conceded a 30 percent discount because the distributor said that his budget for pumps "does not enable me to take on your series."

A Cape Town distributor's accusation of price skimming (as Helmut wasn't even sure what this meant, he asked Hamburg for an explanation) left him depressed and left the distributor with a 15 percent discount.

When an admittedly somewhat sloshed buyer in Bloemfontein charged him with "barefaced profiteering," he realized what it was like to feel guilty *and* framed at the same time, so in response to the claim that "my customers would not pay that price for a pump," he made the usual price concession.

He got to the point where he dreaded anybody referring to the high prices of Weber pumps. So much so that he got in first to discuss his prices almost as soon as he opened the negotiations and kept referring to his prices whenever he thought the distributor was about to raise the subject himself.

He had no doubts that he had identified price as the barrier to securing a foothold in South Africa.

He reported by telex to his father that the marketing men had got this one completely wrong, that the competition was fierce, even cutthroat, and that he had been able to maintain interest in stocking Weber pumps with dealers, but only at the cost of discounts off the list prices and other concessions.

He telexed home shock-horror stories galore about "pump dumping" by the Japanese, the French, and the British. They were all at it! They were going into the dealers and selling them pumps at "below cost" just to keep out Weber's pumps. The representatives of one Japanese firm—he was told this "in confidence" by a Johannesburg distributor—had been instructed to "always go below whatever price Weber quoted for their pumps."

"How can honest men compete with such rogues?" Helmut wanted to know when he telexed the distributor's story to his father, and he asked for a similar freedom so that he could get Weber pumps into that distributor's warehouse. "If the Japanese stoop to low price tricks of that sort, we must show them what a low price looks like!"

When his father read this particular telex he held his head in his hands in despair and refused to see anybody for an hour while he recovered his composure. Then he rang his wife to tell her what an idiot of a son she had given birth to and he telexed Helmut with immediate instructions to return to Hamburg.

When Helmut got back to the office—after a few days' rest, during which his father thought carefully about what he was going to do with him—he was told to report to Fritz, the marketing manager, who gave him a thick pad of paper and a pencil and told him to write out his experiences in detail.

His reports, client by client, were read carefully and sent back to him with comments and questions in the margain. He was told to identify what each distributor had told him regarding the prices of Weber pumps ("their *exact* words, please").

Long after he wearied of this seemingly pointless task he completed it and was ushered into Fritz's office. He realized that he was to be the object of a special grilling and naturally was apprehensive about making a fool of himself.

Fritz put such fears to rest by opening up with the statement that after what Helmut had done to the company in South Africa there was no possibility of him ever making such a fool of himself as long as he lived. Everybody had made similar mistakes (though never on such a scale, he added to himself) and they had all learned how to avoid them.

Getting back from a suicidal freight rate policy to an economic one is not easy in shipping.

Customers do not like taking price increases, especially when other lines are holding their rates down below yours.

One container shipping line decided to break away from the crazy prices that operated in the business in 1982 and imposed a surcharge of $275 a container.

"Rates must rise today to avoid dramatic increases tomorrow, they announced, for rates had to reflect a reasonable return on investment.

"We reinvest our profits to increase efficiency, they claimed, and it is from efficiency that "you, the customer, benefits."

They asked customers to think what would happen to their freight rates in a year's time if the rates war drove the line out of business.

That is what price wars are about: driving the least successful companies out of the market.

But you have a choice before the price war begins: Keep out of it, and run your business without price crumblers!

"In your opinion, what is the big problem with Weber pumps in the South African market?" he asked.

"Undoubtedly, the fact that our prices are too high," replied Helmut.

"OK, let's accept that view for the moment and ask how you know they are too high."

"Because the distributors told me they wouldn't buy pumps at our prices."

"Did they all tell you the same story about our prices, or did they vary their stories," asked Fritz.

"The same story."

"Interesting," said Fritz thoughtfully. "How, then, do you explain that in your reports of each client you mention being given not just one, but several reasons why they think our prices are too high?"

"I don't follow what you are getting at," said a puzzled Helmut.

"OK, I'll show you."

Fritz turned over the top sheet of a flip chart that stood in a corner and read down the page:

"Weber pumps are too expensive ex-works and therefore the distributor's margin are too low."
"That is more than I paid for similar pumps last year."
"The competition quotes me keener prices."
"My budget for pumps won't stretch to your range."

When he had finished he asked Helmut if he agreed that these were sentences from his reports. Helmut muttered, "If you say so," and nodded, though he couldn't remember specifically.

"Are these sentences the same?" asked Fritz.

"They are all about our prices being too high," offered Helmut.

"That, Helmut, is where your mistake is being made. They are not the same. They are all different notes in the same song: "Get Your Prices to Tumble Down." And like Joshua at the battle of Jericho, the dealers only had to blow a note and your prices did precisely that— they came tumbling down."

Helmut thought that a little unfair but said nothing and allowed Fritz to continue his lecture.

"Price was their vehicle for putting pressure on you to make concessions. The fact that you responded by reducing your price does not make price the barrier to the deal, nor does your collapse on price automatically secure you a deal, as we can see from the number of times you offered a price concession and did not secure any business."

"How do you mean?" asked Helmut. "All the deals I got required me to make a price reduction. Perhaps with others I did not go far enough down in price!"

This provoked a visible sigh from Fritz, but he continued patiently. "Ask yourself what interest a distributor has in getting you to reduce your prices to him—leaving aside the question of whether he is telling the truth about the state of the market?"

"Well, I suppose it is possible that he would gain an extra margin if I reduced my price to him and he was able to maintain prices in the market, but that is not how it is in South Africa, as the competition is fearsome."

"How do you know it is fearsome?"

"I could see it, of course," replied a by now irritated Helmut, "and the distributors know best about the market."

"OK, let's take the distributor's budget for pumps, for example. How do you know what his budget was limited to?"

"I remember that one. He told me he had only five percent of his sales in pumps and showed me the racks where he kept his stocks of that Yahatsu range. They took up only three shelves out of the entire warehouse," Helmut replied triumphantly.

Helmut thought he heard Fritz mumble something about "Frau Hubbard."

"And the one about the keen prices from the competition?"

"I heard that from practically everybody," replied Helmut.

"I am sure you did, but did it not occur to you that they say the same thing to everybody? If they told you that your competitors prices were higher than yours would you want to raise or lower your own?"

Looking back on the 1980–82 North Atlantic air cargo carriers' price war, it might be thought that they did not realize what they were doing. That is by no means the case.

The boss of the U.S. Flying Tigers Corporation had no doubts where it would lead. In 1981 he warned customers and carriers alike:

"The shipper in the short term may think he has the benefits of getting low rates, but in the long run he will suffer, because if the free enterprise carriers are driven from the market he will be stuck with the government subsidized carriers, who are well able to sustain losses.

"These are the inefficient airlines, and in those circumstances the price of the service will rise steeply if we are not around to discipline them."

This situaiton, he added, was caused by the "unreasonable situation where airlines are trying to protect market shares at all costs at prices which are totally uneconomic."

"Raise them," began Helmut, and then realized the implication. "I see what you mean," he mumbled.

"Yes, I hope you do. Now consider the one about the customers not paying our price for a pump. How many pumps do we sell each year from this factory—ten thousand, plus all the spares? Who buys them? Is price a barrier for those customers?"

"No, but that doesn't prove we can sell them at our prices in South Africa," suggested Helmut.

"Maybe, maybe not, but I think the chances of South Africa being a different market from the rest of the world are pretty slim, don't you? After all, allowing for exchange rates, I should think that our pumps are more expensive in the USA at the moment, and that is our second largest market. We even sell our pumps in Japan, not far from Yahatsu's main plant."

"So I overdid the discounts a little. Next time I'll be wiser," said Helmut.

"The discounts were only a part of the problem, Helmut," replied Fritz. "You conceded discounts, credit terms, sale or return, free inventories, CIF shipping—the only thing you didn't give away was a promotional budget. All these concessions on top of the price concession. Have you any idea what they add up to in cost? No, don't bother guessing. I'll tell you. As of now, Weber Pumps is giving its products almost free to the richest country in the whole of Africa, while we sell at a profit to everybody else in the African continent, including the reconditioned jobs we sent to Chad. It would be cheaper to dump our pumps in the Rhine—that way we'd save on freight to South Africa."

There was silence for a full minute. Eventually Helmut spoke quietly: "What should I do now?" he asked, resigned to the worst.

"How about getting a job with the competition?" whispered Fritz.

Poor Helmut. It was a heady baptism indeed. It took his company several years to get out of the mess he had got them into.

It wasn't just the price concession he had made, but the way he had crumbled on price and everything else *once he believed that price was the obstacle to a successful outcome for his negotiation.*

Handling a price challenge is one of the two key skills of the successful negotiator—making a price challenge is the other!

ANSWERS
SELF-ASSESSMENT TEST 13

Q.1: a] Every sales negotiator believes this is true at some time or other, and invariably he is wrong. Anyway, marketing will not change its policies from a single telex, so you are wasting your time sending one. (− 5)

b] Yes. What you are hearing is what buyers say everywhere, and you must get used to it. (+ 10)

c] You are weakening under pressure and could end up a price crumbler. (− 10)

d] You are a price crumbler! (− 15)

Q.2: a] Every seller will say something to this effect. If it is true, the contractor will know it; if it isn't, you'll only annoy him. (0)

b] Definitely not! The first step of a price crumbler. (− 10)

c] Could be a good move, because it pays to highlight benefits that separate your package from the others. (+ 5)

Q.3: a] You are a modest crumbler! (− 5)

b] You are a rampant crumbler! (− 15)

c] Much better. (+ 10)

d] Not by telex. See them first, use after c]. (+ 5)

SELF-ASSESSMENT TEST 14

Q.1: You are a specialist in deep-sea oil exploration and have been approached by a consultant engineer in Singapore to join his staff on a two-year assignment. In their letter offering you the post, they quote a salary that is within a few dollars of what you are earning from a local company. Do you:

a] Tell them you want a higher salary?

b] Quote a figure that you would settle for?

c] Quote a high figure and suggest a compromise between that and their offer?

Score:

Q.2: A client expresses strong objections to a price proposal you have submitted. He makes no suggestions as to what could be done about it. Do you:

a] Say no to price cuts?

b] Suggest he make a proposition?

c] Ask him why he is objecting to the price?

d] Make a proposition yourself?

Score:

Q.3: You are negotiating an off-site sales training seminar for a insurance company. They are worried about the aggregate cost and are pressing for a reduction. They hint that unless the price comes down they cannot run the course, nor the three follow-up courses they had planned to use you for. Do you:

a] Go over the proposal with them and see what items they can provide from their own resources to save you charging them for hiring in?

b] Take a firm stand on price, given your outstanding quality and the improvements in sales they will get from the high numbers they intend to put through the program?

c] Find out what their "best price" is and go for that if it is close to your own?

Score:

DON'T CHANGE
THE PRICE,
CHANGE THE PACKAGE
or How to Shape Up
to Better Deals

In 1801, when Lord Nelson's small fleet hove to in sight of the Danish island forts, armed hulks, and ships defending the entrance to the harbor at Copenhagen, there was more than one palpitating heart as his men gazed in awe at the menacing ferocity of what was waiting for them.

Characteristically, Nelson wrote of the Danish preparations that they "only look formidable to those who are children at War."

Similarly, the opposition in a negotiation is seldom as formidable as it looks and almost always looks invincible only "to those who are children at Negotiating."

Those who feel that the competition they face is formidable ought to mind Nelson's judgment and, perhaps, emulate his grit!

Of course, it does not follow that Nelsonian grit is, by itself, enough for success—Nelson almost lost the Battle of Copenhagen, making it one of Britain's bloodiest naval contests. You also have to be good at what you are doing. But if you surrender merely because of what you are up against, then they will ride all over you.

This chapter is about a key negotiating skill: handling a price challenge from a skilled and formidable opponent.

From the last chapter we know why people invariably challenge your price—it's the obvious thing to do!

Helmut Weber's response was to crumble like the walls of Jericho. The guys he negotiated with saw how he crumbled under pressure and inevitably, they didn't confine their pressure only to his prices—they pushed on everything else too: credit terms, shipping and insurance, spares, returns, training, and so on.

If you concede, you open the door to an across-the-board challenge to everything in your package (and possibly some additional issues you had not even thought were negotiable).

Once the price walls tumble down, so does most everything else! Hence, it is important to stick to your price if you possibly can.

How do you do that?

THE KAMIKAZE AIRPLANE BUSINESS: I

One of the world's most highly competitive businesses must be that of airplane engines. Three or four large corporations dominate this market, and the competition is murderous—almost kamikaze!

It began in 1978 when General Electric fought Pratt & Whitney for the engine contracts of the Boeing 767 and the Airbus A310. The giveaways they offered to the planes' users reached 40 percent of the initial prices of the engines!

In 1980 the Saudis were "persuaded" with offers even they could not refuse. They chose the Pratt JT9 over the Rolls-Royce RB 211. Rolls accused their competitors of "buying business."

They claimed that Pratt offered cheap spares, training, free maintenance tooling, free rebuilds on existing engines, free access to worldwide maintenance bases for their aircraft, and even special finance.

And all this to the richest country in the world. Naturally, the Saudis took the deal—if people want to give them millions of dollars for nothing, it sure beats trading them oil for it!

By repeating "no"? By doing without a deal? By having a policy of fixed prices only?

Not at all!

The idea of fixed prices implies fixed packages, and the reason why there is no such thing as a fixed price is because:

There is no such thing as a fixed package.

Everything that is negotiable has different attributes for different people.

Take a chair, for instance:

I see a means to comfortable seating,
somebody else sees an item for decoration,
a third person an antique,

144

a fourth person a stage prop,
a fifth person an investment,
a sixth person some firewood,
a seventh person a pile of old junk,
an eighth person a wedding present,
a ninth person a hole in his bank balance,
a tenth person part of her image,

and so on.

The attributes people see in the same object are as countless as there are people. And as each person's perception of the object is subject to change, the possible attributes of the object for any one person increase with time; today's fashionable furniture is tomorrow's junk.

Also, a black chair may not qualify as a wedding present but might do as a stage prop. Offer to sell her a white chair and the uses may reverse—and may change again when the price is quoted!

People do not purchase objects, they purchase the *services* that the objects provide for them, and these may be tangible or intangible, specific to the person or general to everybody.

Sometimes we put up with an object that meets our needs imperfectly; other times we insist on a most exacting match of our needs with the services derived from the objects being offered.

This is the foundation of all good selling and buying practice: Find out the needs of the customer, fit what you have for sale to those needs, and you'll get their money; find which object provides the services you need and you'll not regret your purchases.

In principle, the price of any particular object, when all else is said and done, is what somebody is prepared to pay for it: You match the service provided by the object with the price they want it for.

If they press you on your price, that may be because they don't think the services they derive from the object are worth what you are asking for them. Alternatively, if they believe the services they obtain from the object are very valuable to themselves, they may be willing to pay a great deal more for it than they tell you.

On the other hand, there are other reasons why they may not agree to your price:

1. Most commonly, the other guy may just be testing how firm you are on price.
2. He may just be mean—some people (and not only the mythical inhabitants of Aberdeen!) abhor spending money.
3. He may genuinely believe you are ripping him off.
4. He may not be able to afford it (the cupboard really is bare).
5. He may like to bargain for bargaining's own sake (good man!).

6. He may want to use your price concessions against your rivals (a "Dutch auction").

7. He may be using price as a camouflage to back out of the deal.

Now you are not likely to know beforehand which of these is behind the particular price challenge you face in your negotiation—yet another dilemma for you as a negotiator!

The first thing to do when you hear a price challenge—as in other critical moments in negotiation—is ask "why?"

You don't need to accept his answers naively, but they give you a better start to handling the challenge than to assume that because he tells you your price is too high (or too low, for that matter) that this is necessarily *the* barrier to the deal and therefore you must cut your price to get the deal.

Cutting your price because of a price challenge could be the worst thing you can do. Looking at the reasons for his challenge, we can see that a simple price change is not your best move in any of them—this was Helmut's real mistake in South Africa.

If they are testing your resolve with a price challenge, it does not make a lot of sense to show them that you have no resolve. They will only press for more, until they are convinced that you have nothing left to give—and as they still may not agree to a deal, you ought to stick at where you started.

Meanness is a very difficult attitude to cope with and it flourishes in small pockets all over the world. It is not confined to any class, race, political system, religion, or nation, nor is any grouping you care to name entirely free from it.

It is most often prevalent among people who know the price of things but not their value, and because reducing the price of something does not increase its value, there is little point in you doing so.

As for the guy who believes that you are ripping him off, there is no surer way to confirm his suspicions than to reduce your prices!

The guy who cannot afford the deal you are offering may be open to another deal; it is up to you to find it (of which more in a moment). The guy who likes to bargain for its own sake is not really a big problem —indeed, in a sense he is the easiest of the lot to deal with.

KAMIKAZE AIRPLANE BUSINESS: II

Airplane manufacturers have also got in on the kamikaze competition act. Boeing snatched the Trans World Airlines contract from Airbus Industrie by making a fuel economy commitment which they are unlikely to meet; even if they do, TWA still gains.

They promised TWA that for every percentage point by which their 767's fuel consumption exceeds their design claims, they will pay to TWA $20,000 a year for each of the ten 767s they will be flying.

If they fail to meet their fuel targets even by 3 percent it will cost Boeing $15 million over twenty years. Thus, effectively, TWA would be getting the ten planes at a discount of $1.5 million each.

Also, Boeing effectively waived the progress payments that TWA would normally have been expected to contribute up to the delivery of the first aircraft in 1985. In other words, Boeing is "lending" TWA money which they hand back as progress payments.

Who says you can't put a deal together?

When you suspect that the other guy is using you as fodder for a Dutch auction with the competition, you will not frustrate this tactic by cutting your prices—as that is exactly what he wants you to do, it must be self-defeating—so don't.

The same is true of the guy who is using a price challenge in order to get out of the deal. Nothing you do on price—except in a totally humiliating fashion—will keep someone in a deal who doesn't want to be there. It's more likely to give him yet another excuse for not agreeing— "If your boat is now reduced by twenty percent in price, you were obviously ripping me off in the first place."

How, then, do we handle a price challenge?

Few deals are decided solely on price. There is almost always more than one variable in any deal, and where there is a variable there is a possibility of a negotiation. Therefore, a price challenge is a challenge to only one of the possibly numerous variables available for negotiation.

We know already that to give way to a price challenge is to invite a challenge to the other variables. So consider the consequence of using the other variables to protect your price.

If the other party wants to change the price variable in the package, it is legitimate for you to adjust the other variables. Indeed, make it a condition for the change in one variable that some others must be changed in compensation.

You can sum this strategy up by the following:

For this package there is one price; for another price there is another package.

I can illustrate this strategy with the subsequent career of Helmut Weber. After his debacle in South Africa, he decided to resign and start again, not with the competition as the marketing manager had sarcastically suggested, but in an entirely different line altogether.

Also, the company doctor advised Frau Weber that it would be better if Helmut left home for a while, which he did with his father's apoplectic scream ringing in his ears: "You're not even suited to be a candy salesman!" Given his father's low opinion of him—though he made allowances for the effect on his father of the four million deutschmark fiasco in South Africa—he decided to win his way back into the family affections by proving that he could make a success out of being a salesman.

And so he did. But it took a lot of hard knocks, bitter defeats, and humble pie. The spur to Helmut's redemption was the German passion for chocolate. It's one of the many products the Germans excel in. (They also excel in the production of sausages, but the ingredients and processes by which they make their sausages are—like that of the Scottish haggis—best left out of delicate conversation. Thus, I have chosen the more aesthetically pleasing subject of chocolate.)

The Germans eat so much sausage and chocolate that it is no wonder they drive around in Volkswagens on their way up and Mercedes when they have arrived—they need strong cars to carry them!

The Germans are very competitive with the Austrians and the Swiss in the production of chocolate delicacies, for chocolate is to the Germans what cheese is to the French—there are hundreds of different types, many eaten only in the locality where they are made.

Chocolate is made from cocoa and cocoa comes from West Africa. The cocoa beans grow in Ghana, Nigeria, Togo, the Ivory Coast, and Cameroon, and are shipped in 130-pound sacks to Europe. There they are processed and sold to chocolate manufacturers, who add their own ingredients (mainly milk and sugar, but also nuts, raisins, cream, jam, and God only knows what else) from their own recipes.

Some of the chocolate is made into popular products for the supermarkets and some into local varieties. The packaging and marketing of these brands is a highly diversified business, with some large companies and lots of smaller ones.

It was into this business, as a cocoa broker, that Helmut threw himself, originally in a quest for his father's approval, but later because he enjoyed it.

This was how he discovered pacakaging. Not the stuff they wrap the chocolate in, but the way that negotiators go about getting a deal.

Chocolate, like pumps and most other products, is no stranger to prices. In a market economy, price is a great storer of information; it is an efficient indicator of a product's standing in relation to supply and demand.

But man does not buy chocolate only on price, any more than he lives by bread alone. The cocoa processors, who buy tons of beans a month, are not just concerned with price. If they were they might very well end up producing an inferior product, and if they won a reputation for inferior—or even variable—quality, their sales would plummet.

Thus, the quality of the beans, and the consistency of that quality, is an important variable in the deals they negotiate with the shippers of beans from West Africa.

Quality is a variable in a technical sense, for not all variations in quality are critical to the production of highly consistent output in each type of chocolate. It depends on the type of chocolate a particular batch of processed cocoa is to be used for.

Helmut had to learn, in buying processed cocoa, to get the right trade-off between price and the minimum quality required in each process.

For instance, cooking chocolate can take a lower quality cocoa than confectionary chocolate. Top-class table chocolate—the kind you would give to a loved one—requires top-class cocoa.

With some processors, the quality control is so reliable that you need fewer sample inspections and risk fewer rejects than with those others whose quality is a bit of a lottery and whose output generates substantial wastage during the making of chocolate.

The quality variable throws up several other related variables: inspection criteria, rejection policy, credit or replacement for rejected batches, payment on delivery or after processing to take account of acceptance levels, and so on.

These variables had to be considered when prices were negotiated. If the processor pushed up his prices, Helmut learned to adjust the package he proposed to take account of the risks his company ran and the appropriate compensatory measures it required either before or after delivery and payment.

It could be that for a particular reason he would agree to a higher price per ton of cocoa if the supplier agreed to accept later payment and a higher inspection standard, and sometimes he did the reverse.

He certainly did not just change his price upward or downward because the processor told him how "fearsome" the competition was or how lousy his prices were.

This does not mean to say that Helmut was not interested in the competition. On the contrary, he made it his first objective to learn about the business he was in and how the industry was organized. He knew about the real competition and how it was faring because he studied it, and consequently he was never hustled by processors or manufacturers and their fairy stories.

In this respect, he lost count of the times buyers told him ("in confidence," of course) about a Dutch, Danish, or Swiss company—the nationality varied each time (he even heard it once about a Japanese supplier)—that "was given instructions to beat whatever price Weber's company offered."

Helmut took an interest in processors out of a healthy concern for ensuring continuity of supply for his customers, the chocolate manufacturers.

If a processor was totally dependent on cocoa supplies from a single West African country, then this was of significance to Helmut, particularly if political conditions in that country were unstable. The prospect (highly probable) or actual occurrence (frequent) of a military coup influenced the way he approached a supply contract both as a buyer and as a seller.

With those processors who were not dependent on a single source for their cocoa, but had several sources, he had to face the question of the compatibility of their cocoas from the different countries that they got it from.

Blending compatibilities could be reflected in the price he was prepared to pay per ton or the credit terms he sought and the prices he could get from the manufacturers—who insisted, like art dealers, on knowing the provenance of the processed cocoa he supplied to them.

Sometimes, in periods of tension or calamity among the West African growers, the payment terms switched one way or another between Helmut and his suppliers.

If supplies were unsettled, the trade-off could be to shorten the payment period; if they were fine, the payment period might lengthen, or it might stay the same and the price per ton change.

There was always the possibility of longer-term contracts for at least some amount of the output of certain suppliers. Helmut had to make a judgment about whether to get locked in at too high a price or risk being locked out if he didn't offer enough.

For each negotiation there was a different set of variables to consider, and the skill Helmut developed was that of packaging the best deal he could out of the deals that were available.

The supplies that were earmarked for Helmut's company—and they could be counted in anything from thousands to tens of tons— could be stored at the processor's place (at whose expense?) or at Helmut's (at whose risk?). It could be delivered into large silos (who paid for them?) or in containers (who owned the containers?).

The negotiators had to decide who was responsible for the processed cocoa when it was not in their stores and what access to what minimum amounts was possible if supplies were needed urgently?

These are only some of the many variables that Helmut learned about in his new job as a negotiator with the cocoa processors, and this represents only half of his job.

He only bought processed cocoa in order to sell it to chocolate manufacturers, and while dealing with one side of a transaction—buying in—he could very well be dealing simultaneously with the other side— selling out.

150

On occasion, Helmut also dealt directly with the retail outlets, though on a small scale (he has ambitions to produce his own chocolate brand—Weber's African Delight).

In selling, the same variables emerge. Manufacturers require consistency and continuity of supply. They may want to vary the supply over a production cycle—they need more chocolate for Christmas than they do for the height of the summer, for instance.

The issues that have to be negotiated as part of a package include who holds the stocks surplus to current requirements and who pays what for the cocoa, and when, between contract and delivery? To what extent can a price variation be traded off in the returns of inferior or damaged supplies? How much of a promotional budget would a manufacturer contribute for its branded products and what effect does this have on the order levels of the supermarket chains?

VARIABLES AND CONSTANTS

What are the *negotiable variables* in your business?

It is well worth you spending some time making a list of the variables you negotiate over in your particular line of work.

Then add to the list all the things you could negotiate over that at present, for one reason or another, you don't.

The list should be a long one. If it isn't, it may be that you are missing opportunities for negotiating better deals.

If you get stuck with a small list, start from the other end and write down all the *non-negotiable constants* in your business—the things you do not negotiate over.

Ask yourself why you don't negotiate over each constant? Who said you shouldn't? What good reason is stopping you? Is it a matter of habit, tradition, custom? Is it an ethical matter? As you ask these questions you will gradually find reason to move those constants into the variables column.

The boss of one of Britain's largest life assurance societies said in 1981: "You need a big crunch every now and again. Out of that you get a lot of ideas. In a big organization it is amazing how many sacred cows are created—and it is hard to slaughter them" [*Fiancial Times,* October 6, 1981.]

How many sacred constants have you got around your organization and its activities in the competitive markets you deal in?

And so it could go on. The variables that emerge from a simple product like chocolate are clearly very numerous.

In the real world, whatever it is that you sell or buy, there may be many variables that you have not considered recently, or at all. It's time you did, because it is in the variables that you will find the defense of your prices.

At the Negotiators' Clinic we require participants to discuss all the negotiable variables in their businesses. The results sometimes surprise even the old hands.

Routine approaches to their businesses can exclude glaringly obvious variables from consideration which must diminish their negotiating ability to package and repackage deals. Constant reviewing of the negotiable variables is a necessity for successful negotiating.

HOW TO WIN PRICE WARS

Faced with stiff competition many negotiators believe that price cuts are the road to salvation—they are in fact the road to ruin.

Every negotiator must eradicate the view that price cuts win business; instead of the first resort they should be the last.

If the competition is tough it is the time to wage a relentless war on *costs*. All costs can be pruned to the bone. Inefficient plants can be closed or reorganized; deadwood can be eliminated: sentimental symbols scrapped; workforces slimmed down and all expenditure that is not connected with the productivity of the assets can be postponed (in some cases for good).

As costs come down, profitability goes up ("a dollar saved is a dollar earned"). With higher profits a beleaguered firm has an alternative to a kamikaze price war.

The beer business, for example, is extremely competitive and it is getting tougher as younger people turn to other beverages.

In some cases, beer companies slashed their prices to grab market share, and seize a temporary advantage which provokes the price crumblers to panic.

The firms that survive usually do so because they resist joining in a price war. They go first for profits and use them to increase their marketing impact.

Distributors and retail outlets can be trained in grass-roots financial management so that they can see for themselves the margins on each of their lines, the turnover per asset they use, the sale per customer, and even the profit per use of shelf-space in their operations.

Everybody must become *cost* not *price* conscious. In this approach, you will find that marketing support is demanded by the guys selling the beer because they want to sell more of the most profitable beer brands. Their attitude changes from demoralized guys looking for price cuts to guys "struggling to be humble" because they are proud of their profitable products.

In one seminar, for a multinational company, the various national divisions produced from their syndicate sessions lists of variables that directly contradicted each other's! It was an illuminating experience to watch the syndicates explain why they had grouped some variables as non-negotiable while their overseas colleagues considered them negotiable.

This was all the more interesting when the Canadians disclosed that they were negotiating on some issues that the English traditionally held out on. The English were not slow to wake up to the real explanation as to why they had lost business over the years in the United States and Mexico—their clients had switched to the Canadian branch of the company instead!

Once we stop seeing price as *the* issue in a negotiation we can really put some good deals together, deals that are good for us and good for them. All the variables in and around the deal can be used to improve the deal and protect our interests.

How?

By concentrating our attention not on the huffing and puffing about price, but on the total shape of what is proposed.

Consider some illustrative variables that are present in most deals. They were present for Helmut Weber in South Africa but he didn't see them, and they are present for you in your negotiations if you look for them.

Take the shape of the *money:*

Can we adjust the way we pay?
What currency we pay in?
The credit terms—30, 90, 120 days?
The discount for early payment?
In advance or in arrears?
The intervals between progress payments?
With revocable or irrevocable lines of credit?
To a third (neutral) party?
Cash on delivery or after acceptance? (Whose inspection?)
Consequences of default?

Or consider the shape of the *delivery:*

In what quantities can it be delivered?
Any advantages for smaller packs/larger loads?
Who pays for delivery and insurance?
If in a container, who pays for damage?
What packaging is used? Possibility of own branding?
How wind-, water-, or rodent-proof are the storage materials?
Who stores surplus requirements?
Who pays for storage?
What minimum loads can be gotten quickly?
What and whose inspection of deliveries is acceptable?

What about the shape of the *specifications?:*

What are the critical specifications?
Can they be varied without risking quality?
Do we need 95 percent reliability?
Is a doubled working life worth a trebled price?
How much do we save by marginally reducing a spec?
Should the extras be standard or some standards extras?
Which features are attractive and which actually used?

153

What about the shape of the *relationship?*:

> Is it worth anything to be a sole supplier?
> Is it better to spread the business among several suppliers?
> How long should a sole supplier contract run for?
> How long should any contract run for and what is duration worth off the basic price?
> If we deal with them solely, how much advertising and promotion will we get them to pay for?
> What about joint promotion?

Is there anything variable in the shape of the *risks?*:

> Who pays for insurance?
> How much insurance should we go for?
> Who pays for replacements and how are they credited?
> Who defines *force majeure*?
> What is a warranty worth?
> Who guarantees quality and inspection?
> What about performance measures and third-party liability?
> Share of insurance pay-outs? What expenses are covered?
> Whose liability for patent breaches, copyrights, etc.?
> Whose liability for local taxes, sundry debts?

Is the shape of *time* a variable?:

> When is delivery to commence?
> Over what period is the contract to run?
> How late is late delivery?
> When do we get access to the product?
> When will proportions of the project be released?
> In what order will things happen?
> The timing of progress reports?
> The closing dates for inspection?
> How flexible is the completion date?

Handling price challenges this way, the guys across the table will learn from your behavior that if they want to change the price, they will have to face the inescapable consequence that you will vary the package.

For you, everything must be negotiable!

There are no circumstances in which you agree to back off a price unilaterally. This is negotiation, not a Dutch auction in which you keep shouting out lower and lower prices until somebody agrees to take the deal.

If the guy does not like your price for the package you propose, then you are happy to quote him another price for another package.

It may be that the new package you propose meets his needs more closely than the original one. In moving to alter the shape of one or more of the components of the deal, you could be moving closer to what he really wants.

His price challenge is a signal that there is something wrong with the proposed package. That is how you must interpret it.

If the other guy insists that he is flying a different signal, then, like Nelson at the battle of Copenhagen, put the telescope to your blind eye and tell him you really don't see the signal!

The rule that Helmut Weber had to learn ought now to be abundantly clear:

Don't change the price, change the package!

ANSWERS
SELF-ASSESSMENT TEST 14

Q.1: a] A strong move if you are confident they need you badly enough to make an offer and you are not too fussy whether you get the job or not, but as you don't tell them what would be acceptable they don't know how far to pitch it. You would need to explain why you accept their rate from your present employers but reject it from them. (+ 5)

b] A definite move but vulnerable to a "split the difference" response. (+ 3)

c] No! This indicates weakness in your position and will likely get a negative response. Better that they reply to b] with a compromise than you to offer one yourself. (— 5)

Q.2: a] A negative move. Does not give them anywhere to go but to back off their price expectations or deadlock. (— 5)

b] Implies that a price cut is possible in principle. He should go in tough on you and get a compromise. (— 10)

c] Good. You need more information about his reasons for objecting to the price. (+ 10)

d] Weak. Don't offer price cuts just because they ask for them! (— 15)

Q.3: a] One way to break a deadlock at no real cost to you (unless your charges for these items are padded). (+ 5)

b] A strong defense of your prices is essential if you are to have credibility in the negotiations. A good lead into a]. (+ 8)

c] That only teaches them to make price objections. (— 5)

SELF-ASSESSMENT TEST 15

Q.1: You are in the market to buy an executive jet for a small courier air service you intend to set up out of your hard-earned savings and small borrowings from a local bank. The company selling new and used aircraft of the type you want is located on the seventy-second floor of the World Trade Center in Manhattan. The president's office is as big as an aircraft hangar, and the carpet pile is up to your ankles. The elegantly dressed man behind the twenty-foot mahogany desk sits in front of a Picasso original. There is a Henry Moore sculpture in one corner of the room and a fountain spraying quietly in the other. Do you:

a] Think you will get a bargain price?

b] Wait and see?

c] Believe you are likely to be pushed to the top price?

Score:

Q.2: The man who has come to see you wears a beautifully cut Saville Row suit and wears Gucci shoes. If asked to rate his status, would you rate him:

a] Low?

b] High?

c] Indeterminate?

Score:

Q.3: When he leaves, how would you rate him (high or low) if he:

a] Waited at the curbside for a cab?

b] Had your secretary call him one?

c] Got into a compact car he had parked round the corner?

d] Got into a chauffeur-driven Rolls-Royce?

Score:

ALL THAT GLITTERS ISN'T GOLD
or How to Resist Intimidation

Have you ever wondered why some corporations go in for highly expensive waste space? They locate themselves in glass palaces downtown, in the most exclusive real estate they can find, or out in the wide open spaces of the far-flung suburbs, surrounded by acres of pretty flowers and healthy trees.

The entrance to the glass palace is like a scene out of Cleopatra: Vast columns rise toward the heavens, marbled staircases wind majestically upward, fountains and waterfalls abound everywhere, and there is solid dark wooden furniture dotted about like little fortresses on a plain. The only thing missing is a trumpet voluntary announcing arrivals.

Batches of people cluster at the mouths of high-speed elevators and the doors swish open and shut, disgorging and swallowing their fare effortlessly.

Behind the front desks sit immaculately groomed receptionists chosen presumably for their perfect smiles and expensive teeth, as well as their ability to suffer boredom gladly.

Nearby, the security guards hover, looking busy but doing nothing much. Each is turned out like a Marine drill sergeant who has had nothing else to do since his last war.

When the phone rings, it does so quietly; it is answered with manic precision before the second bell.

When you arrive for an appointment you are treated as if you are in danger of becoming a lost parcel. And just in case you have an identity crisis while on the premises, they give you a pass to tell you, and anybody else who asks, who you are.

If they are really pulling out the stops, they take a quick photograph, seal it with plastic and pin it on your chest so that you look (and feel) like an immigrant at Ellis Island in the 1920s.

When you go anywhere you are escorted politely by a junior clerk (or a spare gorilla out of security).

BIG AND LITTLE CONS

Practically every known con starts with the use of props. That is why the use of props in business runs a thin line between probity and fraud.

Just because a guy is living in a penthouse suite does not mean that he is productively using the funds he collects each week from gullible investors.

He may just be using each week's "contributions" to pay the bills for his exotic life-style so that he can con new contributors to pay his bills next week.

More than one real-life bankrupt flies the Atlantic by Concorde—it makes creditors less anxious about their money if they associate the person with the trappings of wealth and power. If the bankrupt switched to economy stand-by tickets to save cash, the creditors would begin to worry about their money.

There is a constant stream of programs on TV about dubious business dealers who drive Rolls-Royces and Mercedes and live in small palaces. Hence, caveat emptor.

Also, there are several religious cons that involve substantial transfers of wealth to high-living "saints"—the more material wealth they display the more their followers are convinced that they are divine.

The source of the problem is a logical distortion: The successful have high living standards and conspicuous evidence of wealth (yachts, helicopters, country houses, and so on) hence, so the "logic" runs, people with high living standards are successful.

Almost all cons rely on that sort of "logic" in the minds of the marks. If you are intimidated by the other (honest) guy's props you are a victim of a mild con. If this results in you settling for less, then the con game has worked.

Elevators, corridors, and waiting rooms are furnished to give you the impression that you are passing by Big Events that are taking place behind the closed doors that hum with purposeful activity. The way the staff moves about is proof that something is happening.

When you get to the guy you have come to see, you enter an office as large as an aircraft hangar with carpet pile up to your ankles. It also has the odd Picasso or Van Gogh on the wall and some tasteful sculpture in the corner.

158

This is the moment when you make your most important mistake.

You foolishly believe that all the trappings of corporate wealth you have seen are for the benefit of the guys working for the outfit and are their reward for loyal service to the corporation and an exhibition of their successful endeavors.

Nothing could be further from the truth! It has nothing to do with the comfort of or praise for the employees, loyal or otherwise. If they benefit from working in such munificent surroundings, that is an unavoidable and minor consequence of the main objective of all the splendor.

Everything you have seen has been put there especially for *you*. It is your perceptions that they are working on. Everything you see from the moment you step through the front door is pure theater. You are being had by props, all carefully designed to create the right impression in the minds of visitors.

The purpose of that design? Simply to *intimidate* you! And unless you are very strong minded, or prepared, you don't stand a chance.

Why?

Because intimidation of this kind works.

The building oozes with success. Power creeps out of its every pore. You are seduced into asking yourself: "If they can spend that kind of money on this kind of foyer, what must they be making out there in the harsh competitive world that I am struggling in?" (Leading to: "Boy, do I want to do business with this company!")

One thing you feel for sure. They are making a lot more money than you are: How do I know that? Because you are on your way to see them; they are not on their way to see you.

And if they did visit you, how would your entrance and foyer compare? A tiny orange crate of an office, an old desk and chair, and last month's rent overdue?

You either have a bigger glass palace than they have, in which case you wouldn't even notice the splendors of theirs, or you haven't, in which case you do. If you notice it, you're half way to being conned. It'll get to you and when it does, it will influence your attitude toward the way you go about doing business with them.

You'd better believe that this is true. It's your impression of their strength that they're working on.

Why?

Because through intimidation they subtly get you to undersell yourself. In its extreme form, this kind of intimidation can turn you into a cowering cheapie.

Once you've been through the intimidating treatment and are in the presence of the Very Important Person who has granted you some of his precious time, there is no doubt that you are likely to be grateful for whatever he feels you are worthy of. And that is before he has even begun his pitch (it doesn't matter whether he is buying or selling).

Covert intimidation is the least talked about aspect of the negotiating relationship. Volumes have been written on overt and actual intimidation through the use of threats and so on. Yet covert intimidation is probably more prevalent and is certainly more effective in that the person who is intimidated in this way is less likely to realize it and, not realizing it, is less likely to resent it.

If someone bullies you to take a lower price, you resent their exploitative behavior—especially if you might have to take the deal as well. But if they psych your perceptions through covert intimidation, you cannot resent them for what you do to yourself, can you?

Some sales training programs prepare the participants for some

---

ON BEING HUSTLED

A young manager decided to invest his savings in land zoned for house building, which he saw advertised in a New York paper. He visited the site, where the broker assured him of the stiff competition for the lots, recently zoned by the state for housing development. He was not persuaded by this but was marginally interested in the proposition.

However, as he was talking over the deal another man entered the room and interrupted their conversation, asking to buy some of the lots (including the ones that he was interested in) for a house-building program. The broker told the man, who apparently was a local builder, that he would have to wait a moment.

The builder replied that he was ready to place an order for the unsold lots there and then, and he ought not to be kept waiting as he had the bank behind the finance.

The young manager, hearing this, was aware that if building commenced on the site, any lots he owned would realize an early profit to him on his investment (and therefore he could afford to buy more than he had originally intended).

He told the builder that he had first option on the lots in question and that he was about to write a check for a signed title agreement. This he did.

The builder was not too happy about this and demanded to have the right to purchase the surrounding lots. The young investor left the two men in the office in argument about the remaining lots and their price.

He felt very pleased with himself, and this feeling persisted for about a year, until it became obvious that no houses were being built in the area he had purchased. Had the builder changed his mind? Or was he the victim of a setup by the broker and a so-called builder to hustle him into believing there was competition for the unsold lots? (What do you think? No prizes for my guess!)

It took him five years to get out from under with a capital loss of three fifths of his savings.

---

forms of intimidation by buyers but not for others. They cover those aspects of buyer behavior that are designed to intimidate the luckless seller who is unprepared for them.

The tactics used by such unscrupulous buyers are by now well known in the folklore of the downtrodden salesman.

Ask anybody who has been out selling in the real world about his atrocity stories of how buyers can behave, and he or she is bound to include one or most of the following:

> You will be kept waiting outside his office, or the appointment will be postponed, rescheduled, or will clash with another he has with a far more important person than you.
>
> When you do get in to see him he directs you to a seat that is smaller than his.
>
> It's also lower down—and probably wobbly as well.
>
> Also, you are facing a brightly lit lamp or the sunny window.
>
> The door will be left open and you can hear people moving about outside. The secretaries might walk in and out looking for papers.
>
> The room is too cold, too hot, too stuffy, too open, or too drafty (and guess who is sitting in one?).
>
> The phone rings incessantly as you make your pitch.
>
> There are other interruptions, such as staff knocking loudly on the door and entering to discuss business or social affairs with the buyer.
>
> The guy tells the secretary to hold his calls for a couple of *minutes*—indicating that your time is nearly up—and he'll keep looking at his watch.
>
> Other times, he meets you in the foyer or the waiting room with other people milling about and proceeds to conduct a conversation.
>
> He gets your name and that of your company wrong repeatedly.
>
> He looks bored—painfully bored—and stares as if he is not listening.
>
> If you hand him some literature he throws it casually to one side or doesn't study it at all (though he will certainly spot a blemish on it if it is torn, stained, or written on).
>
> He will avoid touching any samples of your product and will only give them a cursory glance. He certainly will not show any interest in seeing them operate.
>
> He will make disparaging remarks about you, your appearance, your weight, your hair loss, your teeth ("Do you smoke a lot?"), your accent, your ethnic origins, your background.
>
> He'll do the same about your product, your company, your deliveries, your quality control, your invoicing, your previous promises, your superiors, your employees, your track record, and your chances this time.
>
> He'll do the opposite about the competition, using their first names and personal details of their background ("Did you know that Henry, their marketing boss, won a gold in the Olympics? Of

course, he's a fit, good-looking man for his age, and he never lets me down").

He'll also praise their products, their efficiency, their accounts, their integrity, and their prices.

He'll ask you questions aimed at identifying your social inferiority—which clubs you belong to, what cars you drive, whether you have been to the Seychelles, whether you know the president of the steel company in your home town, what do you think of the Hotel Al Khozama in Riyadh, how are your stocks going and which way will the Dow Jones go, what do you think of the Archbishop of Canterbury's library, whether you have seen the price of gold this morning, who is your broker, your banker, and your tailor, and so on.

He'll stall over decisions, announce he doesn't make them and the guy who does is not available.

Next time you go there you have to begin again with somebody else; if he has higher status than the first guy, you are in for a tough fight over the deadlocked issues, and if he is of lower status it's going to be even tougher.

He'll require everything in writing and all your prices have to be your "best prices."

The purpose of these tactics is to intimidate you into a submissive attitude. Every seller has to learn how to cope with buyers who use these methods.

Fortunately, some sales training programs show you how (and buyer's programs teach them the counters), and you'll pick up some ideas from Thank-God-It's-Friday seminars with your colleagues.

But these well-known stress tactics of buyers are small change compared to the self-induced intimidation that comes from downgrading yourself because of the way the other guy's corporation spends its money on props.

These latter tactics are far more intimidating because they operate in your mind as "own goals." You see, down deep you really want to acquire the trappings displayed in the corporate headquarters yourself, and when you see them around somebody else, you assume that the other guy has them already because he is better than you or has more power than you or knows what he is about.

I was given a very clear example of the power of subtle intimidation through the use of apparently expensive props when I was involved in negotiating the sale of a hotel in the Highlands of Scotland, just across the water from the Isle of Skye, in 1976.

The owner had offered me a commission if I could close a sale with the third set of buyers he had tried to negotiate with, the other two falling out after meeting him.

I had driven up overnight from Edinburgh to be ready for the arrival of the prospective buyers the next morning. Five minutes before the meeting was due to begin, the owner began to get anxious, as the other side had not yet arrived.

We could see about four miles down the road toward Fort William, and no cars were coming our way. Was it a no-show? I too was a trifle anxious, as I was to get my commission for arranging a sale, and without the other party there would be no negotiation.

At one minute to twelve we heard a loud noise approaching. In swooped a helicopter, right into the hotel's car park, and set itself down a few yards from my Mercedes—which the owner had been impressed with on my (quieter) arrival the night before.

There is no doubt that it was a magnificent entrance for the buyers to make. They totally upstaged me in the eyes of my client, and in doing so weakened his resolve (but not mine!) on price.

I am certain that this knocked about $20,000 off his aspirations for what he thought he could get for his hotel. He literally fell over the buyers for the two hours or so they were there, and clearly no longer regarded them as the "mugs" he thought they were going to be in our conversation over dinner the previous night.

The helicopter had intimidated him.

He believed he was dealing with *real* money when he talked to those guys and was more than grateful when they treated him and his business with some respect. This made him feel almost like the kind of guy who one day would ride around in a helicopter!

If he had thought about it (as I did on my way home by car) the cost of hiring a helicopter for a round trip from Glasgow via Fort William was about $850. If that knocked $20,000 off the top price the owner was looking for the hotel, it had to be a good investment.

And it was. The buyers got extended credit on part of the sale price, a generous assessment of stock at valuation, and were required to pay a very low deposit on contract.

Also, I had difficulty in getting my full fee out of him!

I had pressed hard in the negotiations for a price about $6,000 more than the owner finally settled at and also for stiffer terms. He instructed me to accept the lower price and the softer terms and even suggested publicly that I was threatening his deal!

When the agreement was signed and it came to my turn to get paid, he had the impudence to suggest I should take a smaller fee as I had not got as much for the hotel as he had anticipated.

Fortunately, I had a signed letter from him confirming my fee, and I waved it at him. Also, in view of his attitude, I insisted on cash, and told him I was quite prepared to load the Mercedes with Scotch if he didn't have the money on hand. We settled on a bit of each, with the whiskey valued at the same terms he had given to the new owners.

Intimidation through props is not easy to combat.

Why do you think women dress up the way they do and paint on expensive makeup—with the skills of a Michelangelo, in some cases—if not to intimidate the male sex as well as their own?

How many doors are opened for unattractive crones? How many for the rest? Have you ever seen waiters *not* dancing to the tune of a beautiful woman's glances? It's pure intimidation, and it works!

In business you make status judgments all the time. Practically everybody—with the possible exception of bankers who know what real money is, who has it, and what it should or should not be doing—equates the trapping of status with the possession of power.

That is why there are so many burned fingers in the negotiating business and why so many people are conned every day by acting upon what they think they are seeing.

Every hustler knows about intimidation. They know that you judge the quality of someone by the possessions they have around them. If you notice and are impressed by ostentatiously visible possessions, you are almost hooked, and the rest is easier than it would be if you weren't.

What will intimidate the average negotiator? Any or all of the following:

- A prestige headquarters, exquisitely furnished
- A list of international offices
- An executive jet—or better still, two—or a helicopter
- A yacht cruising in the Mediterranean or Caribbean

IT DOESN'T ALWAYS PAY TO BE AN MBA

A multinational shipping consortium faced a severe drop in earnings caused by the world trade recession of 1980. It decided to rationalize its operations and called on the various national components to submit survival plans.

The U.S. end of the operation took the problem on board much in the manner of a Harvard Business School case study, that is, as a problem to be solved rather than a fight for national interests.

They set up a ten-man survival team, seven of them with MBAs, and produced a detailed survival report for the meeting. In presentation terms it was a well-produced document—spellbinding, even!—and was supported by a slide projection program.

The other members of the consortium were less than impressed with the hundreds of man-hours that had been used in producing the report, with its obvious professionalism.

They recommended that the U.S. office be de-manned by 15 percent, as they obviously had too little to do if they could produce such magnificent reports with their available staff.

- Rolls-Royces and other gas guzzlers
- Minions running round at the beck and call of the boss
- Expensive clothes, accessories, and gadgets
- An obvious ability to get other people to fawn
- A facility to talk in large numbers and work out percentages of awkward sums fast
- Association with "important names" in society
- Evidence of cash resources, credit cards, and lines of credit
- The appearance of being unrushed and unworried
- Evidence of constant international travel
- A much larger business than the negotiator's
- Some evidence of kindness and respect from the "big guy" with a reputation for ruthlessness toward others.

All of these are pure intimidation. They are the business version of see-through blouses and tight jeans (indeed, it is not unknown for ostensibly non-business intimidation to be used to facilitate a negotiated outcome).

The antidotes?

Recognize the signs of intimidation for what they are. Don't psyche yourself into becoming a victim of your own fantasies. All that glitters is not gold, and the apparent access to props is no proof of the actual power relationship between you and the big guy in the corporate suite.

If you are not intimidated you have nothing to worry about, no matter who you are dealing with. In a practical sense you can steel yourself against their intimidation by avoiding any overt references to their props. You give the game away if you make it obvious how impressed you are with the props, for this automatically acts to strengthen the other guy if he basks in your approval and you gratify his self-esteem. Hence, do not exclaim how wonderful their building is or even make a remark about the view from his office (no matter how magnificent it is —that's why they pay for it).

If you are there to see a head guy and you are kept waiting, always ask the receptionist to use the telephone to ring home, the office, or your next appointment. That will change her attitude toward you (remember, she is part of his team, not yours) and when the boss hears what is delaying your admission it undercuts his tactic of keeping you waiting.

If the wait is likely to be a long one (he is delayed at an "important" meeting, i.e., his lunch, a round of golf, or coffee and doughnuts with the blonde in accounting), make some more phone calls (think of the money it's saving you). If you really want to fight back, make a long distance call by direct dial. Or better still, ask to be connected to the telex room!

165

Whatever else you do, do not read the magazines they leave out for visitors in your predicament, because that is your first step in the dance to their tune. I always bring a book to read in these circumstances, so when he looks out of his door he sees me immersed in something from the top ten list (hardcover, not paperback), but certainly not *House and Garden, Vogue,* or his company's annual report.

One guy I know fights back by going to sleep; he says it gets him into the right unintimidated mood! Another guy only talks business, never anything personal, with clients. That way he can't be intimidated by the often entirely phony international jet-set image his clients like to create for the impressionable.

He finds no need to explain himself as a person or to account for his worldly adventures. He just sticks to the deal, the whole deal, and nothing but the deal. So should you.

Beware, however, of trying to out-intimidate the other guy with your own props and phony lines.

Stick to the use of your skills in negotiating and leave the manipulative moves to others, because it is sufficient for you *not* to be intimidated by what they do. It is not necessary for you to work out how to intimidate them by what you do.

If you're good at your job, that is all the intimidation you require, for there is nothing so awe-inspiring as a richly deserved reputation for being good at your business.

ANSWERS
SELF-ASSESSMENT TEST 15

Q.1: a] You have not been intimidated by the props of power. You live in hope. (+ 5)

  b] The right approach to a deal. His props may hide an imminent financial disaster unless he can off-load some planes quickly. (+ 10)

  c] You have been intimidated and deserve to pay more. (− 10)

Q.2: a] Surely a trifle perverse! (0)

  b] You've been intimidated. (− 10)

  c] Good. You do not judge status by props. (+ 10)

Q.3: a] High: (0) (he should have ordered one); Low: (− 5).

  b] High: (0) (a power prop is not status); Low: (− 5).

  c] High: (0); Low: (− 5) (absence of a prop means nothing).

  d] High: (− 5) (intimidation!); Low: (0).

SELF-ASSESSMENT TEST 16

Q.1: You manage a small engineering plant, and one of your large customers owes you for three deliveries. You feel you are getting the runaround from his accounts department. Another delivery of parts is due next week. Do you:

a] Tell his accounts department that you will hold back the next delivery unless they pay up?

b] Continue to demand payment for the overdue accounts?

c] Tell the user department that you will hold back delivery until the overdue amounts are paid?

Score:

Q.2: A smaller supplier of valves has delivered a batch which failed your quality control test; you put them into your own workshop for corrective machining. Do you:

a] Demand a reduction in the invoice for your machining costs and warn them about future quality?

b] Deduct your costs from the invoice and pay the balance?

c] Pay the invoice but demand a guarantee on future quality?

d] Wait until you hear from them about their upaid invoice?

Score:

Q.3: The supplier demands payment in full. He argues that your machining costs are excessive and that allegedly rejected work should be returned for their inspection and replacement. Do you:

a] Reject his invoice again and insist on your reasonable costs being met?

b] Tell him that if he insists on full payment you will cease to do business with him in future?

c] Pay the invoice but demand a guarantee of future quality?

Score:

ON BEING
RUSSIAN FRONTED
or How to Cope
with Threats

Consider young Lieutenant Wolfgang Mueller's predicament in Paris in 1943. He was dining with his girl friend in a bistro just off the Boulevard St. Germain, in the Rue De Bac, when his colonel walked in and took a fancy to his companion.

He called Wolfgang over and ordered him to go for a walk, to which order Wolfgang protested. The colonel told him: "Either you do as I say or I will have you sent to the Russian front *tonight*."

"*Mein Gott*," said Wolfgang. "The Russian front! Anything but the Russian front!"

And he went for a long walk.

Why?

Because Wolfgang believed that the colonel fully intended to get his way or send him to the Russian front, which, Wolfgang also believed, would be absolutely disastrous to his interests.

If you believe that the threatener fully intends to carry out his threat and has the capability to do so in such a way that you are damaged by the consequences, it is bound to influence your judgment about the appropriate course of action for you to follow. If this causes you to alter your previous intentions in any way, you have been "Russian fronted!"

168

When was the last time you were Russian fronted?

You may remember your feelings of resentment at being forced by circumstances to accede to the threat. True, you have a choice, but the choice is between something so unpleasant that the alternative, unpleasant as it may be, is less unpleasant than the Russian front.

What is the role of a threat in negotiation?

The evidence is overwhelming that threats, sanctions, and their counters are familiar features of negotiating practice.

They are used frequently in many negotiations—industrial relations, international conferences, commercial disputes, domestic altercations, and so on. Sometimes they are used as pressure tactics in the aftermath of a deadlock; other times they are a part of the negotiation itself.

Threats and sanctions can be used as substitutes for negotiation, such as in hijacking and kidnapping; though the more you can get the hijacker or kidnapper into a negotiating relationship, the more likely you are to resolve the issue without giving in.

To see the tactical use of threats, consider the case of a small components firm that had not received payment for the last three deliveries it had made to a large Brazilian engineering corporation. All three deliveries were on time and all of them were accepted by the customer's quality control people.

Naturally, the firm had chased the various departments concerned for its money and had been fobbed off by various managers, including the accounts department, each time.

The managers of the small firm were of the opinion that they were getting the proverbial runaround from the corporation's employees, who gave no explanation as to why payment was delayed—they only made vague references: "It's in the system." The failure to pay was causing a serious cash-flow problem, and they did not have the resources to sustain themselves beyond a few weeks.

The next delivery of components was due in two weeks' time, and a letter was sent to the head of the particular division that used the components, informing him that until the previous accounts were paid delivery would not take place. The day before the delivery was due, a check for the outstanding amount arrived without explanation or apology. The small firm had successfully *threatened* the larger firm.

However, threats can sour a good relationship and make a bad relationship worse by leading to outright warfare and mutually damaging behavior. Nobody likes to be threatened. In fact, the chances are very strong that a person who is threatened will resent it so much that he or she will make a counterthreat, *even if the implementation of that threat will lead to large mutual losses for both parties.*

169

For once a threat/counterthreat cycle gets underway it is very difficult to reverse it into a reward/counterreward cycle. Threats beget threats, probably more often than they produce compliance.

A North American aircraft corporation, for instance, received a batch of valves from a supplier which failed to pass its quality control sampling test. Following procedure, every item in the batch was individually inspected; the failure rate reached 24 percent.

The rejected valves were remachined on site and the supplier was notified that its charges had to be adjusted downward to take account of the itemized additional costs of labor and machine time to the aircraft company. They were also issued with a warning on quality standards.

The supplier refused to accept a reduction in their invoice and insisted on full payment. Allegedly defective materials should be returned to them for remachining or replacement, they argued, and they did not accept the customer's machining costs, which they considered overpriced compared to the costs they would incur in their own plant for the same work (this also told the supplier something about the cost margins between their work and their clients, and suggested that they were quoting for work too cheaply).

The aircraft corporation threatened the supplier that unless they agreed to cut their invoice by the stated amount and guaranteed quality for the future, their contract would be terminated forthwith and the supplier would never earn another dollar from them again.

After a delay of some weeks, the aircraft corporation received an invoice for the same amount by certified post and a demand for full payment within thirty days, otherwise the supplier intended to go to court over the issue.

A week later the supplier received a check, along with formal notice of their removal from the list of approved subcontractors.

Neither side has done business with the other since.

The corporation *threatened* the supplier and the supplier *counterthreatened* the corporation. The corporation *implemented* its threat (not to do business with the supplier); the supplier didn't have to implements its threat (to take the corporation to court).

But who, if anybody, won?

The capacity for people to act irrationally—that is, against what a disinterested onlooker would judge to be in their best interest—is not related to the level of intelligence of the parties.

WHEN ARBITRATION IS WORSE THAN ROBBERY

Yarrows, the British warship builders, were nationalized in 1977; for several years they fought hard for what they considered to be a just compensation.

Yarrows valued their shipbuilding assets at $28 million and the British government valued them at $11 million (at least that was the total compensation they offered).

Two other formerly independent companies also contested the amounts of compensation they were awarded. However, one of the former yards settled with the government—under protest—and a week later, Yarrows followed suit.

They had been disappointed that the new Conservative government did not endorse their fight against the previous Labour government's nationalization formula.

They were also advised that the only recourse open to them was to go to arbitration. If they did so, they were told, there was no assurance that any award made would be any better than what they had at that point, and there was also the risk that it might be worse.

Faced with that as an alternative, Yarrows decided to settle for what they could get.

They had been Russian fronted.

Geniuses can engage in mutually destructive behaviors when they are in contest over something—who discovered something first, for instance—so it is not surprising that "mad" behavior is commonplace among the rest of us. When threats appear in a negotiation there is a higher chance of deadlock than when they don't.

There is a lesson here: Avoid making threats in a negotiation. They are often unproductive for being made explicit.

As a professional negotiator, I almost always raise at least one eyebrow (two, if the timing of the threat is utterly ridiculous) when a threat is clumsily articulated by the other guy.

Why?

Because I regard it as a sign of impatience, of amateurism even, that the other guy thinks I need to be reminded of the power balance between us.

Threats are put-downs, like drawing attention to my accent or my clothes. If he thinks I need reminding of the power balance, he is either trying to intimidate me or he has no respect for me as a negotiator.

On the other hand, when a negotiation is in deadlock—or stalled due to a party's tactics of prevarication—it may be that only threats will get things moving satisfactorily. In this circumstance the threatener regards the risk of upsetting the overall relationship as less damaging than letting things slide indefinitely. It all depends on context.

Some types of negotiation involve the frequent use of threats and counterthreats by both parties. International disputes between countries and labor disputes with managements are two familiar contexts in which threats and sanctions (or implemented threats) are regular features of their dialogue.

In business negotiations threats are also common—much more so than is admitted—though they are often disguised or buried in subtle hints, and the parties can miss them when they are made.

Anyway, properly prepared negotiators are aware of their vulnerability in a deal without the heavy-handed having to remind them.

The purpose of every threat is intimidation, and there are two ways to intimidate people by using threats:

> You want the kids to cut the grass, so you threaten them with no television for a week.

This threat is a *compliance* threat that compels the kids to do it or else.

> Your spouse wants you to stay home and sober, so you are warned if you go out to expect the house to be deserted when you return.

This threat is a *deterrence* threat that prevents you from doing it or else—you may do most anything else instead.

To illustrate the difference between these types of threats more clearly, consider the unhappy (for the hostages) experience of hijacking or political kidnapping.

An aircraft hijacker's demand for the release of terrorist prisoners (or a similar demand) is a compliance threat; the passing of a law that requires a mandatory life sentence for hijacking is a deterrence threat.

How should we respond to threats? This is a very difficult question to generalize about.

The question that must be uppermost in a negotiator's mind when contemplating making a threat is:

> What is the likelihood of the threat succeeding as an intimidator?

That depends, as with much else in negotiating, on the context of the threat. Specifically, it depends on two interrelated but nevertheless distinct factors:

1. The credibility of our intention to carry out the threat, and
2. The capability of the implemented threat to damage the other party.

These have both objective and subjective aspects.

If the threat has high credibility and its capability to damage us is extensive, we are likely to accede to the Russian front tactic.

There is no point mincing words about this: If they have you over a barrel, the prospect of resistance to their demands is purely academic.

But if they have you that way cold, why are they negotiating with you?

On the surface there is no reason, but if you examine it more carefully you will see that your position is not as weak as it looks.

In the unhappy circumstances of a hijacking or kidnapping, your only chance of getting out from under without giving in is to find something to negotiate about.

The hijacker holding a planeload of people hostage needs material things from those he is threatening. He needs fuel to get away, he needs food, water, and perhaps medicines while arrangements to meet his demands are made (you can spin that out to increase his dependence on your goodwill, which has the effect of lowering the pressure on you, too), and he needs good communications, otherwise his threats slacken by an inability to reinforce them.

Experience suggests that long negotiations between the authorities and the hijackers weaken the pressure from the latter and produce a stalemate, and the longer the stalemate the more the hijackers will reduce their demands (down to a final one—escape).

The hijackers can increase the pressure by carrying out their threats to kill hostages (though each execution lowers their leverage), or they can avoid the pressure of a stalemate by changing location. The first may provoke a violent ending to the hijack; the second weakens the pressure on the original target.

The delay in gaining their ends also increases the chances that they can be disarmed successfully by special antiterrorist units. The hijackers get tired, jaded, and mentally stressed as each hour passes. The assault troops are well trained, rested, and fresh, and need only be brought into contact minutes before the assault.

In the case of a kidnapping we are in an entirely different environment. You know where the hijacker and his hostages are—sitting out there on the tarmac with the world's TV filming every move—but you don't know where the kidnapper's lair is.

The kidnapper issues demands from a secret hideout, shuns physical or visual two-way contact with his target, relies on his own resources of food and water, and is able to cut out if things go wrong.

But the kidnapper's Achilles' heel is the line of communication between him and the target for whatever it is that he is demanding.

If it's money he wants he has to get it delivered somewhere without being arrested in the process of collecting it. Negotiations on the means of delivery, the denominations of the currency, the dropping zone, and the involvement of the authorities all take time.

The longer the time these negotiations take, the greater the chance of the authorities releasing his hostages.

The more difficult problem occurs when it is something political that the kidnapper is after—release of colleagues in prison, dismissal of a government official, distribution of relief to the poor, publication of a message by the media, ending of some program that helps a racial or religious minority, and so on.

For reasons of state, many governments refuse point-blank to negotiate under the duress of a kidnapping for political demands on the grounds that this will lead to repetition by other ruthless and determined groups.

For tactical reasons, the authorities might pretend to be negotiating with the kidnappers when in reality they are using whatever information they can glean during the negotiations to catch them. Or they could be negotiating in earnest, but a slip by the kidnappers could give the authorities another option.

So, in general, if threats are used against you in a negotiation, it does not necessarily follow that you are trapped cold.

If you have some room for maneuver you have a choice, *however limited*. Identifying that room, and expanding on it, is a task you have to face if you prefer not to comply with their demands. Otherwise, you are stuck with the lesser evil they offer you as an alternative to their Russian front.

In negotiating, each party has a veto—you don't have to agree to whatever is being offered—though this may have consequences for you. The plant could go on strike, they may try to get their way by force, you might have to do without supplies, you might be taken to court, and so on.

CHEERS!

Around Christmas time in Britain, one or other of the breweries are regularly faced with wage demands from the unions; regularly, this ends in a prolonged strike.

The union chooses the run up to Christmas time because this represents the peak of the buying cycle for booze. The management tends to resist because if they give in under one Christmas threat they can be sure that the unions would be back every Christmas with other demands.

Does the consumer go thirsty? Not at all. Why?

Because the other brewers that are working normally get stuck with extra shifts to get their beer out to the pubs to take up the sales lost by their competitor.

Why do they take advantage of their competitor's predicament, when rational consideration would suggest that they stick together against the "common enemy"?

The answer is that they find it profitable to do so, and also because that is what has happened regularly at Christmas for years past.

FLEET STREET, BLOODY FLEET STREET

A similar situation exists in Fleet Street, London, where the major national newspapers are printed. Each employer faces the same unions but negotiates with them individually.

If a newspaper suffers an industrial stoppage when it tries to de-man its notoriously overmanned work force, the others stand by and try to sell more newspapers.

The result: They are all held over the barrel by the unions. Why do the unions take advantage of the inability of the employers to stand together? Because that way they ensure that their members are the highest-paid employees in Britain.

It is legitimate in a negotiation to draw the attention of the other guy to the consequences of his persistence with a deadlocked position, though there are ways in which this can be stated without provoking the charge that you are threatening them.

Timing is the essence of making clear the consequences of deadlock without necessarily creating resentment. In commerce, you have the option to take your business elsewhere. The implicit threat to do so is present in every negotiation and is widely accepted as being legitimate. By legitimate I mean that it is regarded as being within the norms of everyday negotiating.

The acceptability of the implicit sanction of not doing business if you fail to agree is a matter of degree. The buyer (or seller) uttering the "killer" sentence—"You'll have to do better than that"—implies that if you don't or can't, you won't get his business.

That *might* be acceptable as a negotiating tactic if it is confined only to a relatively small transaction out of your annual turnover with him. If you say that not only will he not get your business in the case in dispute, but he will not get *any* business from you at all, the sanction threat begins to move toward being unacceptable and you run the risk that your threat may dig him deeper into his position precisely because he resents your blackmail and cannot be seen giving in to those tactics.

If you use the threat of possible large-scale damage to his business in pursuit of a relatively minor matter, he is likely to perceive your intentions as being hostile to him and his interests, and his reaction could produce an equally negative response.

His quandary is (and ought to be) that if he appears to give in to a large-scale threat over a relatively small matter, how does he protect himself in future?

If you threaten that you will stop him from doing business with everybody else in town, the territory, the country, the continent, even the world, your threat is pure blackmail, assuming that it is credible. And if it isn't credible you cannot possibly retain his respect.

As large-scale threats are less credible in pursuit of small objectives than they are when in pursuit of large-scale objectives, there is a natural limitation on using them in this way without provoking legal intervention, public hostility, or outright disbelief that you intend to do what you threaten.

If a guy in a bar says "Pass me the ashtray or I'll kill you," it is unlikely that you would take him seriously (you would certainly doubt his sanity or sobriety, or both). Most people would pass the ashtray without such a heavy threat, but a lot of people wouldn't if they were treated that way. (In some bars that could be fatal.)

The United States—or for that matter, the Soviet Union—doesn't use the threat of nuclear *attack* when in dispute with a smaller, non-nuclear power. They reserve the nuclear option for retaliation if they are attacked by the other.

If you compared in 1973 the absolute capacities of the United States and North Vietnamese militaries to inflict damage on each other, there is no doubt that the U.S. arsenal of nuclear weapons made it by far the more formidable of the two.

However, *using* nuclear weapons is not the same as *having* them. The North Vietnamese could, therefore, safely disregard the U.S. nuclear arsenal in their calculations of the balance of forces between them.

The magnitude of the threat ought then to be relative to the issue at stake. This is more true the earlier in the negotiation the threat is made: When a threat is a last resort it has more legitimacy (i.e., it is more acceptable as a negotiating norm) than when it is the first resort.

To open up early in the negotiation with a threat is likely to raise the other party's eyebrows, if not their hackles! It provokes more resistance than it overcomes.

Actually implementing a threat may also impose costs on the party doing the threatening—for a start, you would have to do without their services, and they yours, at least in the short run.

This is also your opportunity, because it is rare to find the dependence only running one way. Most of the time, just as we are vulnerable to a threatened action from the other guy, he is vulnerable to some form of threatened counteraction from us.

No wonder, then, that most threats do not provoke immediate compliance—they provoke retaliatory counterthreats instead.

One of the most devastating counters to a threat is to imply that it does not concern you all that much if the threat is implemented. The other guy has to contemplate whether you are bluffing and what the cost is going to be to himself of implementing the threat.

If, however, you are the only supplier of a particular product which the other party must have (say, a drug company negotiating with a hospital), there is a strong moral pressure present (often backed up by legal deterrence) for you not to exploit that position and make "unreasonable" demands.

Market economies normally have legislation to limit monopoly powers, though the limitations vary across different types of monopolies, and may be applied with more or less vigor by the administration. For instance, labor monopolies tend to be less regulated than corporate monopolies.

A DISCOUNT, OR ELSE!

A hotel chain selling a branded vodka in its bars decided to widen its profit margin on sales by increasing the discount it got from the supplier.

The negotiations deadlocked when the vodka people insisted that the chain was already on a top discount and anything more "would make it unprofitable to supply them at all."

The hotel chain was adamant in its demands because it had been offered by another company an "own brand" vodka at a higher discount.

The "unprofitable to supply" statement of the vodka people was taken as a threat to withhold supplies. In fact, the so-called threat became the main issue at the next meeting, but the suppliers heatedly denied they had threatened anything at all—they were "just drawing the attention of the hotel chain to the financial realities."

The hotel negotiators insisted on a larger discount and added that if they did not get one they would stop buying the branded vodka altogether.

The vodka people took this as a threat—"blackmail" they called it—and the negotiations broke down.

The hotel chain changed its vodka suppliers, and customers were offered the in-house brand when they asked for the other company's (well advertised) vodka. This did not always go down well with those customers who asked for vodka by brand name.

It might have been possible for the hotel people to get a better financial deal if they had simply switched from a demand for a discount to a demand for extended credit. This (minority) view was expressed at the time but was over-ruled once some of the hotel chiefs got their backs up at the alleged threats not to supply them with vodka.

Casual remarks can be taken as threats, and can be thrown back as a challenge. If the negotiations break down the threat may have to be implemented.

A threat raises the costs of disagreement, assuming that the threat will be implemented if we disagree and is not just a bluff. If you are dependent upon the other guy, you are vulnerable to a threat from him.

Wolfgang's problem was his dependence on his colonel, who had the power to decide where Wolfgang fought in Hitler's war.

Being dependent upon the other party increases the possibility of being Russian fronted. It follows that lessening your dependence improves your chances of being able to defy threats, ill-timed or otherwise.

Chain stores that place their orders with small suppliers can get a lot of negotiating leverage into their hands if they can come to represent the bulk of a small supplier's sales. They can do this by placing large orders—which the small firm may at first be grateful for—or by offering credit to buy machinery and such like.

They can (and often do) squeeze down the price of the goods they buy from totally dependent sources by threatening to cut them off as a supply source. They also take longer credit and insist on higher quality.

At the very least, they can determine the supplier's policies in areas where normally you would not expect to find them operating (e.g., in hiring standards, trade union membership, even ethnic balance).

They also tighten the squeeze on dependent suppliers by locking them into exclusive purchase agreements, thus preventing them from expanding out from under their dependence by acquiring other customers.

The threat to cut them off need not be made incessantly, because every time the smaller company looks at its markets (or lack of them) it gets the message. So the latent threat to cut them off—through, perhaps, the occasional demonstration of the disciplining of a troublemaker—is enough to get the desired result.

Many a large business has grown by swallowing up smaller suppliers that either needed cash for expansion or got into debt to their customer.

Breweries often pick up hotels and bars because their owners fall into debt to them; retail stores acquire clothing manufacturers because they become so dependent on their customer that they cannot survive at the prices imposed on them for their clothes; petroleum companies take over garage outlets, and franchise operations acquire faltering businesses or the real estate left after debts are paid off.

You can save yourself a lot of grief at the negotiating table if you refrain from getting too dependent on one source and thus increasing the costs to you of disagreement with the other guy on what he regards as being a substantial matter.

All threats boil down to some version of the Russian front: They force you to choose between unpleasant alternatives.

If you believe they have the power to damage you and that they will do so if you don't comply or are not deterred, you will be Russian fronted.

However, unlike Wolfgang, you might have a choice.

ANSWERS
SELF-ASSESSMENT TEST 16

Q.1: a] If you can wait it might be better to do so, *up to a point*, because fighting for the money has risks. (0)

b] The wrong guys to pressure. Accountants are unlikely to worry about missed deliveries—it gives them an excuse for delaying payment further! (− 10) c] Put the pressure on the guys who feel it sharpest; they will put pressure on accounts for you. (+ 5)

Q.2: a] The course most likely to lead to a negotiation. (+ 5)

b] Might work if they decide not to fight. Otherwise, it reduces the pressure on them if they do fight. (0)

c] The weakest move, unless the sum is trivial. (− 10)

d] Changes a grievance into a mere late payment. (− 5)

Q.3: a] The course most likely to lead to negotiation. (+ 5)

b] The move with the highest risks of total breakdown. Unlikely to succeed. (− 10)

c] The weakest move, unless the sum is trivial. (− 5)

SELF-ASSESMENT TEST 17

Q.1: You are in dispute with a shipper who has managed to lose a twenty-foot container between your factory and Benghazi. This is the second shipment that has been lost—the first turned up weeks behind schedule—and the Libyan client is threatening to cancel the contract unless you deliver on time. In a meeting with the transport agents that is long on verbosity and short on details, do you:

a] Insist that they admit liability?

b] Ask them why they let you down on this occasion?

c] Ask them how they can claim to be efficient when it is the second container to go missing?

d] Tell them their schedulers are hopeless?

Score:

Q.2: You are a contractor in East Africa and the project is running behind schedule. The minister in charge constantly interferes with the project, changes his mind on details, holds up papers needed to clear supplies through customs, and makes untrue and slanderous public statements about your company's efforts. As a last straw, he issues a public warning that he will cancel the contract and arrest your staff for malingering, corruption, and, most ludicrous of all, spying! The local TV asks you for a comment. Do you:

a] Tell them what you think of the minister's mental age?

b] Deny the charges and give your side of the story?

c] Say "No comment"?

Score:

Q.3: You have been negotiating for some months with the land
over the rental of your office. He has made tough demands and
cannot budge him. The negotiations are taking up a lot of y
time and you are fed up with the arguments. Do you:

a] Accept the rent because it is close to your top price?

b] Decide to fight him in any way you can?

c] Look for another office?

d] Have another go at finding a negotiated solution?

Score:

THE LAZARUS SHUFFLE

or How to Cope with Deadlock

Deadlocks are a familiar experience for negotiators.

They occur frequently in negotiating; in extreme cases, they can occur over every single point at issue.

Sometimes both parties are unprepared to compromise or they have not discovered anything suitable to trade off. This provokes the kind of deadlock that endures, and no amount of time spent trying to unlock it seems to work. The parties get entrenched where they are and the negotiation grinds to a halt.

In some circumstances, the relationship of the parties degenerates into outright hostilities that kill the prospects of a deal. And there is nothing deader than a dead deal. Except perhaps the parties, if they end up killing each other.

In business, it is not uncommon to find that some former clients will have nothing to do with each other, even though they were once trading frequently, because of some unbridgeable gulf that opened up between them during the course of their dealings.

It dosen't always take much to do this—you missed a due payment by careless oversight; you pressed just too hard for a rebate; you let the other side down in special or commercially embarrassing circumstances; or your interests clashed diametrically on an issue.

On other occasions the differences are long in germinating—constant letdowns, frequent bickerings, startling revelations and accusations and such like gradually erode the trust between you, and when that is gone the entire relationship collapses.

Also, it is not unusual for negotiating relationships to exist in an atmosphere of suspicion and hostility. The parties bring with them to the negotiations their reputations, or the history of their "atrocities" on friends or predecessors of the other party.

Cease-fire negotiations, for example, are never easy, and they are made even less easy by the images of the two parties in each other's perceptions. The Arab–Israeli conflict is an obvious case in point; the splintering of Lebanon is another, as are the differing traditions of Ireland and the histories of India and Pakistan.

Intractability is not monopolized by political conflicts. The scope for intractability in everyday business is limitless. The issues may be less serious—in life-or-death terms—but the fact remains that soured relationships stay sour.

The question asked in this chapter is: Can we get a "yes" or "maybe" instead of a "no" or "never"? This amounts to asking whether there is anything we can do in our negotiating to get back from the dead.

There is. We can try the Lazarus shuffle!

How does this work?

Basically, it is an attitude rather than a prescription. It aims at separating the negotiators from the emotional tensions and commitments of the issues in dispute and shuffling them slowly toward a settlement.

Why?

Because people are the biggest problem in negotiating! They bring to the negotiations their hopes, fears, prejudices, and offensive behaviors. If they came without these there might be fewer deadlocks, but then the people would hardly be normal.

How do we achieve this remarkable result?

Let us work our way through the Lazarus shuffle and see what pointers it has for our negotiating behavior.

Having chosen to negotiate a settlement, we have by implication abandoned the alternatives, which include legal remedies, violent confrontation, outright warfare, guerrilla action, sabotage, blockade, boycott, bribery, demonstration, hunger strike, legislation, or just some good old publicity.

If for good reason we reject the alternatives as being inappropriate, excessive, or too risky—or if we have already tried them and failed—and we commit ourselves to a negotiation, this must be our *only* means. In other words, we must approach the negotiations in good faith and with an open mind.

If the real estate company wants to increase your rent or shorten your lease, you have the alternative of fighting them. You can refuse to pay up or to leave—even barricade yourselves in—or you can threaten to go to court and seek a legal injunction to prevent them from repossessing the property.

PRIVATE COMMUNICATION
MIGHT PREVENT PUBLIC BLASTING

In 1980 the British Airport Authority raised the landing charges on aircraft using Heathrow Airport, London.

The eighteen international carriers who use Heathrow protested in the strongest terms, both privately and publicly.

The issue became very heated between the carriers and the British government, and much abuse flowed across the media about the motives of the agency that raised the charges.

The carriers decided to sue the Airport Authority for imposing "illegal and excessive" charges.

The Airport Authority boss issued a statement, saying, "Differences between partners should be settled by negotiation, not by public and expensive squabbles."

The spokesman for the carriers replied: "We would not have recourse to litigation if there had been any prospect that your authority or the Secretary of State would have been willing to settle the differences between us by negotiation, but in view of the Airport Authority's statement we are prepared even now to enter into negotiations upon any sensible and realistic basis to reduce charges."

If the option of negotiation was present, there was no need for media blasting or litigation.

But whose responsibility was it that the issue blew up? The Airport Authority, which unilaterally hiked the landing charges, or the carriers that got cross about it?

They too can engage in similar behavior. They can send in their "heavy" squad to intimidate you, cut off your utility supplies, or get a repossession order from a court.

The publicity value of your predicament ("Rogue Landlords Terrorize Defenseless Families") is contrasted with theirs ("Scofflaw Tenants Snub the Law"). The grievance cycle is going to escalate rapidly if this behavior is the sum of the relationship. Each side takes a public position and seeks to strengthen it relative to the other. The consequence of this is to weaken the possibility of negotiating a compromise, because any compromise by either party is a defeat, a loss of face, a comedown, and so on.

Fighting them may not be your first best alternative. It might not be your second or third best alternative, either.

It certainly helps your prospects of negotiating a settlement if you have not done anything (or at least haven't done enough) to set the relationship on such a collision course that you are both straining at the leash to get at the other's jugular.

Your behavior, therefore, does influence the prospects of a settlement. Provocative behavior does just that: It provokes! And what is regarded as provocative is not within your control—it is the other party's perception of your actions that counts.

Who can provide you with the best description of how they perceive your actions? The other guy, of course! So ask him questions—incessantly—about how he sees the situation, and don't argue over anything he says. He may get repetitive, but you'll soon know what you are up against.

When I say "find out how he sees it," I do not mean that as a prelude to surrender. You need to know his views if you are going to find the bridges between your side and his.

You, quite rightly, see a rent increase as a reduction in your standard of living (and an increase in the landlord's—who by your definition is richer than you are, as he owns what you are renting).

He—quite rightly, too—sees the rent increase as a means to preserving the integrity of the property by funding the necessary repairs. His ownership of the property gives him responsibilities which he can meet only if there is an adequate income from the rents, and to expect repairs in any other circumstance is to reduce *his* living standards (and increase yours).

A bridge to think about is present: Both of you want to maintain your living standards, and an adequately maintained and repaired building is common to the living standards of both of you.

Attacking the other guy is no way to make him conducive toward helping your interests when his own are at stake.

It never ceases to amaze me to listen to negotiators attack the other guy—ofttimes ferociously—when their strategy requires the same guy to compromise his interests in some way. Why they think that abusing him makes him warmer toward them, I do not know.

If you attack people, they will defend themselves. That ought to be self-evident.

"It's your fault," "No, it bloody well isn't," "Oh, yes it is," and so on—these are fairly familiar attack–defend cycles. So is the (bad) habit of point scoring:

> "Before I respond to what passes for a proposal from you, I cannot let you get away with the snide and ridiculous remarks you made a moment ago."

The result? Certainly not peace!

The taking of firm stances is a form of attack. If you declare a firm, unalterable position, it is more than likely that they will too, and there you will sit glaring at each other across the battlements.

It is a negotiating tactic (discussed along with the other tactics in the next chapter) to make a public commitment to a position and use that as leverage on the other party, who is supposed to appreciate the fact that as you are unlikely to move off your declared position without considerable loss of face, he had better accept your position.

Playing chicken with a dedicated (irrational) opponent in fast cars on a highway is also a fast way to die. In negotiating, a mutual chicken game is known as deadlock.

"I will *never* pay an increased rent!" is one way to provoke the response: "I'll see you in hell if you don't!"

Firm declarations of commitment are to be avoided in moves to unlock deadlock. A moratorium on public statements would greatly assist the negotiators (Sadat and Begin meeting in total privacy at Camp David, for instance). No interviews with the media during delicate labor or commercial negotiations is always a good policy.

How can we state our perceptions if we do not let the opponent know of our feelings?

Feelings tend to be resented if they are presented in the form of an attack, but there is a world of difference between saying that you feel let down and accusing the other party of screwing up your business.

You can always translate statements from accusatory attacks into more acceptable feelings.

"You've ruined my delivery schedules!"
"You let me down on this occasion."

The very translation of attack language into neutral statements of our feelings highlights the perceptions we have of the problem and suggests ways in which it can be tackled.

It is the problems that require solution, not the attacks that need responses. Highlighting what the problems are suggests ways in which the bridges can be made.

For the problems to produce solutions it is necessary for you to understand clearly what it is that the other guy is interested in. This may require some very careful questioning on your part:

"Let me be clear about what it is that you need."

or

"Are you suggesting that we arrange dual inspection on site on weekends?" followed, if the answer is affirmative, by "What do you mean exactly by *dual* inspection?"

Once you are both discussing *how* something should be done, as opposed to *why* it wasn't in the past, or *why* they don't trust you to do it, you can move on to discuss what sort of packages would be possible that could incorporate the safeguards both of you legitimately are seeking. (You can see that this is really a chapter for those who have graduated from merely stating grievances to proposing remedies!)

However, the road to dissolving the deadlock cannot be traversed without first defusing the causes of deadlock, and the most productive way to do this is to ask questions.

Now, questions can be either helpful or irritating; they can soften up a deadlock or ice it over. It's a matter of content, tone, and timing.

Much has been written by psychologists on the role of questions, and my summary here is more in the form of a whistle-stop tour than a comprehensive treatise.

Lets look at some no-no's.

If you want to start or continue a fight, ask provocative questions, show them you don't believe their answers, ask sarcastic supplementaries, challenge their veracity, contradict their answers, interrupt them before they have finished, and discuss their answers with one-liners (examples include: "Rubbish," "Crap," "Lies," "Oh, my God," "You must be joking," "You don't really believe that," "Remember, you are under oath," "Tell the truth, now," "Be honest," and "If you think I'll fall for that one, you must be out of your tiny mind!").

Any attempt to use questions as battering rams against the other guy's position is bound to be self-defeating in the retaliation that it provokes. Before long, you will be up to your necks again in accusations.

The same applies to questions that are directed in an antagonistic way, such as:

- *Loaded* questions ("Do you believe you are always right?")
- *Impertinent* questions ("How long are you going to continue carrying on about nothing?")
- *Perry Mason* questions ("How can you claim to be innocent when you have just admitted to five cases of missed deliveries?")
- *Boomerang* questions ("Don't you agree with me that your lot made a monumental screw-up of the scheduling?")
- *Gotcha* questions ("Wouldn't you do *aything* to save your country's reputation?"—whether you say "yes" or "no" they've gotcha!).

To see why the content, tone, and timing of questions is so important, we must consider the purpose of questions in the Lazarus shuffle. A question can imply that:

- You want to receive information.
- You want the other guy to think about the implication of something by his answers.

- You want to give information.
- You want to defuse tension.
- You want to facilitate communication.
- You want to make a decision.

The same is true, hopefully, for the other guy.

Moving the discussion into a question format has a number of advantages, not the least being that it releases the tensions associated with deadlock.

Hence, as your questions are aimed at ending a deadlock, it follows that you will make the most progress if your questioning style facilitates your aims rather than undermines them.

It is best to start with questions that open up the discourse rather than track it into a monosyllabic exchange. Closed questions can be answered with a single word: "yes," "no," "maybe," or "never." They must be avoided, especially in the early high-tension part of the negotiation.

Open questions are preferable because they require more than one-word answers and invite the other guy to expound his views at length—the length of the answers increasing as the hostility level drops.

Once you both get talking, the tension will begin to drain, if only slightly at first, until it is at a manageable level.

You might remember how to ask open questions by prefacing your questions with the key words in Kipling's little ditty:

> I keep six honest serving men,
> They taught me all I knew.
> Their names are *What?*, and *Why?* and *When?*,
> And *How?* and *Where?* and *Who?*

The purpose of the dialogue is to lead yourselves to a break in the deadlock. This suggests that the next step is to get agreement on the next step!

You can do this by summarizing the benefits of an agenda, a time-table, an exchange of views in a "safe" environment, a procedure for adjudicating issues, a forum for discussing informally at high level, the main headings of an agreement, and so forth.

The questions that is posed after such a summary is of this type: "Is it possible to agree to proceed in such a way?" The answer *leads* the negotiation to the next stage because the question is a *leading* question. Such questions have to be carefully placed, leaving the way open for the other guy to step back if he is not ready to commit himself. If badly timed (often by being put too early, before the tension has dropped), it can backfire.

In this sense, leading questions are *permission seeking* ("Could/Would/Should we do it this way?").

You can use questions to get at the other guy's perception of the facts. Psychologists call these *directed* questions. They require something more than yes-or-no answers, but may not elicit a great deal more information than the specific answer to the specific question. For example:

"What sum of damages are you seeking?"
"When did our services drop below the standards you expected?"
"How many man-hours were tied up in the search for the compressor?"

Their counterparts are *nondirected* questions, which leave the other guy discretion on how much he wants to inform you by his answers:

"How do you calculate the consultant-day rates you charge?"
"What benefits do you see in applying an equal opportunities code to my part of your operations?"
"Why do you insist on our bids remaining at a fixed price for twelve months?"
"Would you outline for us how you assess the losses on the Jordan contract?"

Another version of a nondirected question is *barometric,* in that it gives you information about the other guy's feelings, state of mind, or degree of flexibility:

"How do you feel about training black labor for the South African project?"
"Do you mind if my colleagues sit in on our discussions?"
"How does the idea of a twelve-month lease option strike you?"
"Is there any scope at all for relaxing the documentation procedures within the construction compounds?"
"Have you any views on our making a new site agreement with the union?"

The barometric question is often a good lead-in to a decision because judging by his response, you can make a proposition that could form the basis of a joint decision. That decision may only be a look at the implications of what you have uncovered by testing his feelings and attitudes.

The skillful use of questions is aimed at opening up the discussions from the narrow tracks they have been on or shifting them from the massive issues of principle they have broken down over.

Questions suggest potential packages of proposals on how the dispute can be resolved (partially or wholly) or outlines of what the proposals could look like.

Instead of concentrating on too narrow a package, your best interests are served by opening up the field to as many packages as you can think of. The very fact of searching for packages increases the confidence they have in your intentions, without committing you to any specific solution. (After all, *everything* is negotiable!)

The dispute can gradually come to be recognized as a mutual problem. Once it is in the domain of being a mutual problem it can easily slide into being recognized as suitable for a mutual solution.

The next step is the trickiest: fixing it so that some criteria are chosen against which the proposed solutions will be tested. This is to prevent the negotiations from falling back onto brute strength, pressure, or force for deciding who gets what out of the deal.

The search for acceptable criteria for deciding issues separates each side's threat capacity from the criteria to be used for deciding the issues that separate them.

Criteria for this purpose could include:

1. Comparability with similar solutions (what is a "similar" problem and is it analogous?).
2. General concepts of fairness (what is fair?).
3. Maintenance of traditional differential treatments—the weakest get the most support (what is "weak" and how much is "most"?).
4. Accept the given standards laid down by third parties—for example, government legislation, club rules, referee's reports, independent surveys, technical specifications, and so on (how is applicability decided?).
5. Previous decisions (but which "precedents" should be followed and which created?).
6. Equality of sacrifice or gain (how is "equal" defined?).
7. Separate the issues and deal with them individually or link the issues and take the lot together on a "win some, lose some" basis (what happens if each has advantages and disadvantages?).
8. Majority votes to decide (referendum—who sets the question? Absolute majority or qualified majority? What constitutes a fair vote? Who can vote in the election?).

COMMUNIST COMPETITION HURTS

The German and Soviet governments began consultations in 1978 on the impact of cut-rate Soviet merchant shipping on the German shipping industry. The matter was negotiable because the cut rates were being applied by the Russians on the traditional trade routes of Germany to the Central American west coast and were not based on economic pricing, but solely on the Soviet need for hard foreign currency.

The Association of German Shipowners noted with despondency in 1981 that no progress had been made to solve the real problem.

The announcement by the Soviet government that it was extending the transshipment facilities of the Trans Siberian Railroad—thus cutting further into Germany's Far East liner trade—caused consternation among the German shipowners.

They wondered whether it was worthwhile continuing the negotiations with the Soviets and stated: "If no concrete results can be obtained, other means must be sought to bring a solution."

What the "other means" were to consist of they did not say, but it did not appear to include continuing to find a negotiated solution!

NEGOTIATING WITH SOVIET OFFICIALS

U.S. Ambassador Gerard C. Smith summarized his negotiating experience with the Russians on arms control and related issues as:

1. Avoid a preference for spectacular summits as against more mundane sessions at a lower level—the time pressure is on Western leaders who need a summit success most.
2. Have only one channel of negotiation; "back door ones" leave the official negotiators in the dark.
3. Don't expect quick results.
4. Don't put up inequitable propositions—they create distrust where there is already a surplus of it.
5. Only put up propositions that are to be supported by the negotiators—negotiations are not seminars.
6. Understand the different negotiating styles—Russians make political speeches, Americans look at detail.
7. Americans ought not to worry too much about leaks—the Russians don't have any because they have a closed society.
8. Refrain from generating over-optimistic expectations about the results for domestic purposes—they reduce your bargaining power.
9. Don't interfere with the negotiating process once it has begun—leave it to the negotiators.
10. Don't worry about elusive results—the negotiations themselves are worthwhile.

[U.S. Congress: *Soviet Diplomacy and Negotiating Behavior,* U.S. Government, 1979]

Of course, the selection of criteria is itself a negotiating problem (as the questions in brackets suggest), but the act of searching for criteria helps you toward a settlement if you take each obstacle in turn and apply the Lazarus shuffle to it if deadlock threatens.

If they have problems in accepting a particular criterion, then go step by step through the shuffle. Either an amended criterion or a new one will suggest itself.

The one thing you must avoid is attempting to solve a deadlocked position without some criteria against which to test the proposed solutions. Otherwise it will come down to a con or an intimidation.

If the issue remains deadlocked or the proposed solution is still unsatisfactory, you might have to return to the first step of the shuffle and reconsider whether you prefer the negotiated outcome to the alternative means that are available for getting a decision.

There is no dodging this requirement: If the alternatives are *worse* (in the sense of having unattractive consequences or providing little chance of making much difference to the outcome being offered) you are bound logically to take the negotiated outcome or continue with the negotiations (though of course there is no accounting for our "irrationality").

To do otherwise is to fall back onto pure subjectivism: "If the bastards won't give in to me, then screw 'em!"

If the alternatives are better for you (i.e., they have manageable consequences or offer a good chance of securing your goals) you are logically bound (with the usual caveat for irrationality) to choose them—as long as you take into account the damage this might do to your relationship with the other guy.

Clearly, for example, one alternative to agreeing to the landlord's new lease or fighting him is to move out altogether. Giving up is not entirely dishonorable if you have tried and, having failed, you prefer to use your life for something more constructive than beating yourself against a brick wall.

Accepting the fact that we can't win 'em all is no disgrace as long as we try our best to do so!

This sometimes is the best outcome of the Lazarus shuffle.

You become so separated from the emotional ties to your original entrenched positions that you see no point in trying to fight or to rescue them, and you decide to fold up your tent and depart.

For we don't always get what we want or what we deserve.

That, after all, was much the fate of poor Lazarus himself!

ANSWERS
SELF-ASSESSMENT TEST 17

Q.1: a] What good does that do?   (− 15)

b] The first step to finding a negotiable solution.   (+ 5)

c] Argumentative questions only get you a fight.   (− 5)

d] If they know that it won't help and if they disagree, it won't find your container.   (− 10)

Q.2: a] You obviously want to go to jail! (— 15)

b] You rarely win public arguments with politicians. (— 5)

c] Correct. You clearly need some behind-the-scenes clout, and the best way to get it is not to make it difficult for political friends to support you. Public rows entrench people in positions they find difficult to move from without losing face. (+ 10)

Q.3: a] Should be resorted to only after d], c], and b]. (— 5)

b] Only if it is likely to produce the result that negotiating hasn't managed so far, otherwise you are using up energy better spent in your business. (0)

c] Could be the only alternative to a]. (+ 3)

d] Everything is negotiable! But recognize that you can't win 'em all. (+ 5)

SELF-ASSESSMENT TEST 18

Q.1: You are in the midst of a very tough labor negotiation and you believe that the union does not fully appreciate the seriousness of your commercial plight. A local TV reporter asks if you have a comment on the union press conference, where the official spokesman declared that you were trying to bluff them with your poverty, but in reality you would pay the twelve-dollar raise or take a strike. Do you:

a] Decline to comment publicly?

b] Go on camera and say they are talking through their hats?

c] Tell the reporter to see one of your team who has had training in TV interviews?

d] Offer to give a full interview in a hour or so after you have checked with your team?

Score:

Q.2: You have been negotiating the sale of light vehicles to a courier business. Just before you wrap up the final package for joint signature, they ask for the vans to be delivered sprayed light blue. That happens to be the production color of the vans and would require no change in your programming or costs. Do you:

a] Tell them it will cost them extra for light blue?

b] Tell them light blue is "no problem"?

c] Ask them how important is it that the vans be blue?

Score:

Q.3: The union has demanded that long service vacations be awarded to employees with thirty years service or more. Your personnel department tells you this will affect 5 employees out of 3,000 over the next three years. Do you:

a] Agree if they drop their claim for a safe working bonus?

b] Decline to consider it this year?

c] Agree if they confine the award to veterans and the handi-capped and the company chooses when the men take leave?

Score:

GAMBITS, PLOYS, AND TACTICS
or How to Use
and Resist Them

The one sure thing about negotiating is the fact that there is always room for surprises. No matter how long you have been at the game, somebody, somewhere, will teach you something new about your business sooner or later.

Take the game of chess, for instance. There, the rules are well established, the moves of the pieces strictly determined, and the limits of the board unanimously agreed. Yet there is no end to the combinations of moves that are possible.

Grand masters and beginners learn something new about chess every time they play. Each game is different, for no two people will make the same moves in the same game no matter how long they play.

And there is a vast literature on chess. I have several volumes on the game, relics of my student days when I learned the game because Patricia (she of the dedication!) liked the game, and there was no way I was going to be left a wallflower while she played with somebody else!

Negotiating, however, is not a form of chess. There are no agreed rules. The moves of the players are by no means restricted. And there are no *limits* to the game—everything, but everything, is negotiable!

Yet there are similarities in that, as with chess, there are some well-established combinations of moves that players can learn.

The most famous in chess are in the opening phase: the Ruy Lopez (been around since the sixteenth century), the King's and the Queen's gambits, the Nimzo-Indian, the Sicilian, the disappointing (to me at least) Scotch Gambit, the exotically named Giuoco Piano, and many, many others.

In this chapter I discuss some of the more well known of the negotiating moves that have not yet been covered as separate topics. The cognoscenti among you will already be familiar with most of them—though by the nature of negotiation you have most probably come across variant forms to the ones I describe here.

For beginners, this chapter should be studied carefully, for you can bet your last two cents that you will see some, most, or all of these moves played before you are in the business much longer.

In negotiating there are two major objectives of all tactics, ploys, and gambits:

1. To alter your opponent's perception of the strength of *your* position; or
2. To alter your opponent's perception of the strength of *his* position.

The moves you undertake can work at both objectives singularly or together. To the extent that you succeed in either objective, the more likely the deal will be to your advantage (which, note well, does not *necessarily* mean that it will be to your opponent's *dis*advantage—you both may gain from finding a deal different to the one either of you first thought of).

What follows is a summary of the main negotiating moves to secure either of the two objectives.

People begin negotiating with their prepared positions more or less worked out, if only to the extent that they have decided they are "agin" whatever it is they think you are going to propose.

Taking a determined opponent head-on without some softening up is bound to lead to a deadlock. Hence, the questioning techniques of Chapter 17 are very relevant here.

In this case, the targets of your questions are the *assumptions* upon which the other guy has based his position and the *conclusions* he draws from his assumptions:

> "Could you just run over the reasoning behind your claim for compensation?"
>
> "Assuming, for the sake of argument, that I accepted your charge that some of my boys were drunk on Saturday, how did that affect the work of my riggers on Monday?"

If you question him in a constructive way it is likely that you will find (and he will articulate) weaknesses in either his assumptions or his conclusions (and if he is badly prepared, both his assumptions and his conclusions).

And, if there are no weaknesses in his case, you had better be clear in your mind exactly what you are up against. More than one stupid management blunder went to court when it could have been settled quietly if the facts had been gleaned by the negotiator when he had the opportunity to ask the appropriate questions.

Having gotten clear in your mind what it is you are up against and having decided to contest their demands by negotiation, there are several tactics you can bring into play to secure your position.

A common one is "death by a thousand exceptions." This is a very popular ploy in the British Civil Service and is used as a means of blocking, slowing down, and eventually killing legislation they consider to be too radical (they copied it from the Celestial Chinese Empire and its sentence of death by a thousand cuts).

In this ploy you must look for the *anomalies* in their proposed solution to the problem. The more anomalies you can find, the less credible their proposition. The world is full of good ideas to solve all sorts of universally recognized problems, but almost all of them fall victim to the complications (and the costs) of administering them.

A big problem for any negotiator is to find that the guy he is dealing with lacks, or more recently, *claims* he lacks, authority to vary the terms upon which he proposes you do business.

This is a very powerful tactical position for him to be in. He forces you to change your expectations of the deal or to find a way to get to the authority level he claims he lacks.

Some unscrupulous guys use this tactics to good effect. They make a provisional deal with you "subject to board approval," and then tell you the board did not approve everything. The items not approved by the board must be amended before agreement can be reached.

Usually the rejected items are some of the concessions that they made originally, but which they now propose to claw back. Often you will agree to the amended package; that's why they try it on so often.

YOUR SCHEME WON'T WORK—TRY MINE

"You are suggesting that you inspect each and every delivery on arrival at the compound. Have you any idea just how many hours of work that would involve? Are you prepared to have your inspectors on hand at two, three, four in the morning in case the trucks come in without notice from customs at Mosul? And what about the Iraqi security men when you start busting open containers looking at loads at night only three miles from a military camp—they'll think you're trying to start a coup or something. Is it safe to have containers opened on the site outside working hours? What about supervision? We'll also need a license for night working, and that'll take weeks to get from the Iraqis.

Later:

"So we agree that you confine your inspectors to a random day check only, and that you telex the driver concerned before he leaves Italy to give him time to make his domestic arrangements for the additional delay he will face once he gets here?"

SPEAKING HYPOTHETICALLY

"Suppose for the sake of argument and without committing either of us to anything definite, we were to consider reopening what is for us the settled question of compensation for war damage. Would you be prepared to release our diplomats and their families forthwith?"

Later:

"Our agreed proposal can be summarized by saying that *if* you release our diplomats and their families by tomorrow noon, we will publicly announce the setting up of a joint commission to review the claims for World War II war damage that you have submitted and to report our findings to the United Nations in due course."

Can you beat it by asking if they have full authority to settle? Not always. If he says no, what do you do? Ask to see the organ grinder! But perhaps he is not available, and even if he is, he too might also require "board approval."

But you ought to find out as early in the negotiation as possible exactly what authority the guy has and has not got. If he has to fall back to the board for final approval, you had better make sure you do not give everything away in your bargaining with him, otherwise when they come back for that little extra it's going to cost you something extra for the deal.

However, "no authority" is a useful tactic. If you do not have discretion you cannot exercise it!

Many companies bind their representatives to routines and procedures that strictly limit their authority. Partly this is a bureaucratic convenience and partly it is a negotiating defense against nibbles at their prices or conditions:

"Sorry, but we can't discount on orders less than ten thousand dollars."

"It is not company policy to vary the terms of hire."

"You would need the finance director's approval for that and he's in Indonesia for three weeks."

197

> "The details you are asking for are confidential to our company and cannot be disclosed."
>
> "To pass this consignment I would need a departmental authorization and a quality certificate."
>
> "We do not accept returns after thirty days."
>
> "Our terms are strictly net."
>
> "We are bound by the Smelter Association's rules on scrap prices."
>
> "You have raised a legal issue and I need to check with our solicitors first."
>
> "We would need government approval for a variation in the license conditions and that could take months."

You, too, can give yourself limits, real or imaginary, to suit your circumstance. As long as they are credible you have little to fear. How many times have you heard/tried:

> "I had better check with my spouse before deciding."

You are advised, however, to be careful in *challenging the authority* of your opponent. Nothing is more likely to win you an enemy for life than to impugn the authority of the other guy or question it in some way that implies you do not believe he represents the true views of his constituents:

> "Are you sure that you were speaking for your company when you made that last remark?"
>
> "Hadn't you better check with your people first before making such a threat?"

Nobody likes to be challenged in the role they are playing, and it could spell trouble if he decides to take umbrage at what you are implying or if he regards your question as an attack on his credibility.

He might need an excuse to demonstrate his authority negatively. If he shuts off your supplies for a week you might feel he has made his point.

If you go over his head because you are convinced he is not representing your position accurately to his superiors, he could structure his bosses' views with a damaging, not to say slanderous, report on your behavior.

One of the strategic decisions you have to make in a negotiation is whether to take each issue by itself or to link them together and treat them as a package that stands or falls as an entity.

There are some circumstances when one strategy is more appropriate than another.

In the European Economic Community, France long stood for *linking* the outstanding issues between Britain and other members. Britain has a surplus of oil over its domestic requirements and most of the European fishing grounds are off its coasts.

The EEC tried for several years to get agreement on a common fisheries policy for the member states which from the British point of view threw open its traditional fishing grounds to non-British trawlers. Naturally, in these circumstances Britain preferred to settle the fish issue on its merits (which successive British governments were convinced would lead to a favorable solution for its national fishing industry).

The French took the view that if Britain wanted concessions from the EEC on fish—the concessions consisting of a fishing policy that the other states would not veto—then Britain would have to make concessions on its oil policies. In other words, from the French point of view the issues were to be *linked* in the negotiations, implying a trade-off between them.

Britain took the view that these issues were separate and not linked, and it did not accept the need to make changes in its oil policy in order to avoid a French veto on its fishing interests.

Similarly, in your negotiations you must decide which approach will pay you the most dividends

Linking has the advantage that it enables the most room for trade-offs, one issue against the other, and also it gives you a fallback position so that if agreement is not reached in total on all the issues, you reserve the right not to proceed with the deal. This puts the maximum pressure on the other guys to reach agreement across all the outstanding issues.

However, separating the issues also has the advantage that it prevents the other guy from using a disagreement on one issue, perhaps only a minor disagreement, as a means to press you for concessions on another issue. If the issues are separate he cannot use the threat of deadlock on individual issues to stop agreement on others.

In separating the issues the parties must reach agreement piecemeal and forgo the scope for wider trade-offs. Parties who feel strongly about individual issues will insist on separating them; those who feel weakest will push for linking.

Sometimes linking is the only way to get progress on the issues, which is why separating them can be useful if deadlock is preferred to compromise and "surrender" (i.e., anything less than the most favored position).

One way to weaken the other guy's perception of his position is to engage in tactics that give credibility to your own position. Among the most common of these is the declaration of a *public stance*.

A public stance carries the risk that if you back off from a declared position you will lose face and be made to look a trifle soft, which will undermine your credibility for the next round.

However, there is a knife edge between the risk of losing face and the possibility of making the other guy believe that you really mean to stick to your position—otherwise, he ponders, why would you make such a public announcement?

If he believes that you have taken a public stance because you fully intend to see this issue through to the bitter end, he may alter his expectations of reaching an agreement on or near his terms.

The trouble with public stances is that both sides can make them and usually do in response to each other's press handouts!

If you have both made public statements of your positions and hinted that no compromises are possible, the tactic will make it less likely that you will get a settlement, or at least an early one.

A word here about the media. The working journalist is a bored but talented creature with a frantic imagination. He sees everything in headlines: sensations, dramas, crises, catastrophes, and general mayhem are his, or his editor's, images of how the world should be reported. Hence, trying to use journalists for *subtle* plays in the negotiating game is kamikaze behavior. If you call an adjournment, they will report it as a walkout; if you say the other side is not moving very far, they will claim you have accused them of being sluggish; if you say you cannot accept their terms in their present form, they will report you as adamantly "refusing to bow to blackmail"!

You might as well learn now: The media is no place to conduct a negotiation. It is read or viewed by people with the subtlety of a main battle tank. The journalist reports on the level at which he believes viewers can best be reached, that is, "Wham, bam, go get 'em, Sam."

Moral: Stay away from the media in the midst of a negotiation. Better still, stay away from the media.

The passion for publicity is endemic in politicians, particularly those who feel that their charisma is essential for all good deals to be concluded.

Britain has more than its share of politicians putting their oars into negotiations they would be better to keep out of. No sooner do they smell the possibility of a headline-grabbing deal than they call a press conference to announce that it is almost signed.

Prime Minister Callaghan did this for domestic political purposes in 1979 with the so-called Polish shipbuilding deal. He announced the $207 million order for twenty-two ships before it was signed; the Poles, noting his public stance, correctly surmised he couldn't afford not to get the deal, and promptly stung the British for another $2 million worth of concessions, just before the final signatures were made.

This is an example of *quivering quill*—the other guy knows that at the end of a negotiation there is a lot of "end of haggle" euphoria building up and that this makes you vulnerable to a squeeze for something extra as their pens hover above the contract.

Prime Minister Thatcher made Callaghan's mistake on her visit to Oman in 1981. She announced that the sheik had agreed to buy British war planes for about $200 million and that her Ministers would negotiate the details. In time, the value of the order diminished in size until it was embarrassing.

Negotiators have different valuing systems—it's as if they worked in different currencies. You work in big money (dollars) and he keeps talking about *peanuts.*

Some guys have become millionaires through peanuts, and I am not just talking about some notable sons of the state of Georgia.

What's a peanut? Something *you* regard as small change.

So what? Why make a fuss over nothing? Because the other guy wants it; and if he wants it he must value it; and if he values it you ought not to throw it away for nothing!

Peanuts are hardy perennials and they are constantly forgotten about by the guys you will meet—perhaps even by the next guy you negotiate with.

The most common play for the peanut ploy is when you are negotiating for one thing and the other guy introduces a minor detail or associated item which does not cost very much compared to the main deal. He asks you to include the minor item in the deal.

What do you do?

Yes. You agree.

IF WE AGREE NOT TO SEEK ELECTION, WILL YOU PROMISE NOT TO LOOK FOR BUSINESS?

A large British construction company in 1981 was chasing for a $185 million share of $525 million hydroelectric and irrigation project in Peru.

The negotiations with the Peruvian government reached a delicate stage, with the contract hanging in the balance and the defeated competition still hanging around in case the deal fell through.

A British government minister went to Peru on an official visit, and his department released the news of the hydroelectric deal being "close to signature."

The industry press was alarmed at this premature announcement and thought it could be enough to put the British company out of the running.

A ground swell against "political salesmen" is visible in the construction and aerospace industries, and the general view is that politicians making trade promotions abroad do more harm than good.

You are selling widgets by the score and he asks for them to be painted black. The widgets are worth $550 wholesale, and painting them costs you nothing, as you have a warehouse full of black widgets.

What do you do? Usually you will say, "No problem."

But the fact that it costs you next to nothing to meet his request is not the point. You ought to realize what he has done. He has gotten a concession from you which he may value very highly indeed—perhaps he must have black widgets to suit his corporation's color scheme—and you have not tried to get something from him.

The peanut can also be used to get something from you that *does* cost you cash: He wants break-bulk deliveries all over the place; he wants a slightly larger swimming pool than standard, or some special-effect tiles at each end; he requires forty-five days' credit instead of thirty—and then he takes forty-eight days, creeping up to fifty; he wants to squeeze another thirteen guys into the training session, asks for extra copies of the manual, and wants you to work through dinner the night before, all for the same fee; and such like.

Now, all of these adjustments can be ways of changing the shape of the deal to get agreement, but they become giveaways if they are treated like peanuts and handed over to the refrain of "No problem."

You have to stay awake as a negotiator to watch out for those peanuts slipping past you. Ask yourself what they are worth to him before you calculate what they are worth to you.

The more he values the peanut the more valuable it is to you irrespective of the actual cost on your balance sheet, because a valued peanut gives you negotiating leverage when you need it most—when you are pressing for a buy decision.

But if you give your peanuts away, you may have nothing but real money concessions to work on when it comes to the crunch.

There are several defenses against peanut ploys. The most common is to have separate budgeting systems:

"Sorry I can't give you bedrooms for your party, because that comes under a separate department from banquet suites."

Or to have a printed price list.

"As you can see from the price list, if you want to buy parts for the motors you have to take them in packaged quantities."

Closely associated with the peanuts ploy is that of salami. Now salami comes in thin slices, and that is how they approach the negotiation: a thin slice at a time. They get a bit here and a bit there.

They open with a request for long service leave for thirty-year employees, then they try to extend that to twenty-five-year employees, then twenty-year, fifteen-year, ten-year, and down to five.

They get you committed to one exception, then press you for others, or press you to extend the same exception to other cases.

Sellers get a trial order from you for a tiny slice of your business and then spend their time trying to extend the size of the slice.

Buyers raise the quality by a few degrees or change a minor specification, they alter the quantity or the delivery terms, and generally work at widening the scope of the deal from where it started. Eventually you find yourself doing much more work for the same money.

How to defend yourself against salami?

Salami back!

Tie every salami concession with qualifications ("thirty-year men with war service," "twenty-year men with war service and unblemished records," and so on). This won't, of course, stop salami altogether, but it will slow down the retreat backward!

Sometimes I am asked whether it is good negotiating practice to walk out of a deal because of the impossibility of moving the other guy or because of what he is trying to do to your position.

I know a politician who walks out of caucus meetings with a frequency that has succeeded only in diminishing her credibility. At first it was a traumatic experience, but after the tenth time everybody expected it—indeed, relished provoking it—and it is now a waste of time.

SALAMI IN REAL ESTATE

The shifting fortunes of real estate development in both North America and Europe have shaken up what had been a fairly stable business.

Tenants used to pay fixed rents for the duration of a lease and that was that.

The shortage of prime office space has shifted the power balance toward the landlords.

In the early 1970s leases ran for twenty or thirty years without provision for rent reviews. The landlords were also left with the management expenses and taxes.

Inflation, expanding government spending, and rapidly changing demand conditions have changed the basic landlord–tenant deal.

Leases are increasingly "net," not "gross"—that is, the tenant has to pay some, if not all, operating expenses of the building.

The duration of leases has also shortened to as little as three or five years (with two-year leases appearing in London in 1981).

This enables the landlord to get compensation for inflation by rent renewals or to find new tenants at up-to-date rents.

Where leases were for longer duration, the landlords of San Francisco in 1980 got three yearly *upward-only* rent review provisions written into their tenants' leases. This innovation is now spreading salamilike across the country.

A typical "hard" lease is one that has a ten-year duration, with a rent review in the fifth year and the tenant having to meet all increases in operating expenses of the building plus a commitment that 25 percent of the gross rent is to be raised automatically in line with the consumer price index.

[Details, *Economist,* February 7, 1981]

In negotiating, walking out is likewise a short-lived asset—do it once or twice in a relationship and you might just put enough pressure on the other guy to influence his thinking and move him toward you.

Do it more than that and you will have the opposite effect. Get a reputation for it and they will laugh silly at your antics, and not always behind your back!

There is also a danger in adjourning too often. Adjournments in some negotiations are absolutely necessary—the negotiation takes several months, for one thing, and there is a genuine need for consultations with your specialists.

However, bear in mind when you adjourn that the competition could get in to see the other guy while you are away and might just sew up a deal, in which case you are out, or they might make propositions to him that he will then use to pressure you, in which case you are poorer.

Also, adjournments create expectations that there will be some movement by the next meetings. After all, you did adjourn, among other things, to consider their requirement that your documentation be prepared in Arabic and English. If you return without showing signs of movement you may cause resentment.

If you adjourn constantly to seek instructions you are vulnerable to a call to send in the organ grinder!

Negotiations have to end sometime, and it is important that you have a capacity for handling the close sequence, otherwise you will waste a lot of time negotiating with Fred when you could be out seeing Bill or home in bed.

There are two major closing tactics common in negotiating: *concession* close and *summary* close. They work either individually or in tandem. Their objective is to convince the other guy that there are no more major movements possible from your side and that the deal being offered, as negotiated by you both, is the only one you can settle on.

In the concession close, you will offer a small, specific, and conditional concession. The condition is that they agree to the package as it stands.

To highlight what the package is you summarize it, perhaps embellishing it a trifle with references to how much movement has been made by both sides and how much progress you have made since you began the negotiations.

If the summary is enough to get agreement, all well and good. If it isn't, you can follow up with the concession close.

What about *last stands* and *final offers?*

Ironically, it is the most inexperienced negotiators who use the more difficult closes most frequently. Among these is the "final offer" close:

"And that's my final offer!"

The problem is that they use this at the wrong time. This means that they are not convincing and consequently they are taken to the cleaners for using it.

204

A final offer close implies that unless the terms are agreed as they stand you prefer not to do a deal at all. If that is not true you simply ought not to try to force them to believe it, for they won't if they suspect you are bluffing.

And even if you are not bluffing, they need not accept that your terms are a final offer. Why should they?

They may respond in much the same way as John Paul Jones at the Battle of Flamborough Head in 1779. When asked by the British captain if he had surrendered ("struck his flag") he replied with the immortal words:

"I have not yet begun to fight."

If you push too soon for a close you may be told by the other guy that he has not yet begun to negotiate!

In the close you have to watch yourself carefully. There are several little ploys that squeeze more out of you. Among these we have the "Oh, dear," "Split the difference," "Yes, but," and "Gimme a kiss."

In the "Oh, dear," the guy comes back to you after the deal has been agreed with a hand-wringing performance about the new stock you ordered coming into the warehouse with a price surcharge on it, and if you still want the deal he will have to add this to your bill. He will be full of apologies, even confide his disgust at the sudden price change and tell you "they" (the suppliers) did this to him last year and he lost a good customer.

If you believe him, you pay; and even if you don't quite believe it has anything to do with you but are pressed for delivery, you'll pay.

"Split the difference" we have seen earlier, but it's worth trying the line that you can't afford to. At the very least, get them to state what split they are suggesting: If they say fifty–fifty, go for eighty–twenty. Don't open up with an offer of a split or they will use that to cut the split in their favor.

"Yes, but" is an irritating ploy if it is used too much. It is a variation on "quivering quill." They tell you that they agree with your proposals, *but* there is a problem with Clause 12. You concede on Clause 12 and then they "yes, but" you again on another clause, and so on. This is most effective when the guy is agreeing "subject to board approval," for which my earlier remarks apply.

"Gimme a kiss" is a tough one to beat in the close. He tells you how much he has done for you—"I even got the special invoicing you wanted through accounts and that motor spec changed to suit your engine rooms." All this may be true, and the more he presents his concessions to you as a *personal* favor the more effective the "gimme a kiss."

Naturally, he didn't do all these favors for nothing, and neither did he have to do them, but he "likes you" and "wants to do business with

205

you." So he asks for a personal favor in return—not a lot, but something that he values: just a little "kiss" on the cheek!

"Could you do me something in return?" he asks. "I need written confirmation of the order for this month's budget, so could you sign this standard order now? Also, how about signing the provisional next-purchase clause—no commitment, of course, but you did mention this as a possibility and it will go down well with my boss."

Sometimes the "kiss" is expensive, because it involves real money, and sometimes (beware) it involves a slightly shady maneuver just on the edge of an unethical act.

Whatever else you do in the negotiation, make sure that you get an agreement on what you have agreed and write the agreement out yourself. Don't rely on them to do so, because you can bet your commission that if they write it they will edit it to suit their understandings, and some of the little peanuts you got will disappear, along with some of the major concessions, too.

I have never yet seen a contract that was written by the other guy that did not need revision to truly reflect the actual agreement we made.

ANSWERS
SELF-ASSESSMENT TEST 18

Q.1: a] Probably your best bet, because negotiating in public is rarely helpful—it entrenches each side in their statements of the moment long after the moment has passed.   (+10)

  b] You are looking for a fight, aren't you!   (− 10)

  c] Risky, as you will be held responsible for what he says by your company. Best to stick to a].   (− 5)

  d] Better than b] or c], but still vulnerable to the remarks in a] as it draws you into public stances. Why not send the union team an outline of the company's position?   (− 3)

Q.2: a] A tough move that is negotiable to some other concession.
        (+ 5)

  b] Weak! You've just had a "peanut" done on you.   (− 5)

  c] Yes. Gives you information. You could then go to a] or demand some other concession, even a trial close on the deal.   (+ 10)

Q.3: a] Depends on how costly the safe working bonus is likely to be and how long you can hold off a "salami" on the long service leave.   (0)

  b] A tough move, which they might accept if they have other things they want from you. Depends on the power balance.
        (+ 5)

c]   The only way to deal with what looks like it is becoming a
salami is to do a reverse salami—add conditions that they will
have to negotiate off to extend the concession.   (+ 5)

SELF-ASSESSMENT TEST 19

Q.1: You are in Selangor (Malaysia) negotiating on behalf of a European consortium to build a satellite station for the government.
You have brought along your colleagues (two Dutch, one French,
and one German) with you; and the Malaysian team consists of six
experts and three officials. How many foreigners are there at the
meeting?

1   4   5   9   13   14

Score:

Q.2: You are the marketing director of a plastics company and your
board wants to get into the lucrative markets in the Middle East.
You are arranging a business trip to Kuwait, Abu Dhabi, Jiddah,
and Baghdad. You have ten preliminary appointments arranged by
the various Arab embassies with import agents and government
departments. Each appointment should take no longer than two
hours. Air travel between each city is excellent. How many days
should you allot to the tour?

10   12   15   17   20   25

Score:

Q.3: The Japanese company that has invited you to Tokyo to explore
the possibility of them buying coal from you meets you at the
airport with a limousine and takes you to your hotel. En route they
check on your arrangements and the head man asks his lieutenant
to make all the necessary arrangements for your return flight. He
asks for your air ticket and tells you that everything will be taken
care of. Do you:

a]   Regard this as an example of typical Japanese courtesy?

b]   Ask them to route you out via Hong Kong?

c]   Tell them you have an open ticket and there is plenty of time
to worry about returning home, having only just got here?

Score:

THE LONELINESS OF THE LONG-DISTANCE NEGOTIATOR

or How to Negotiate Abroad

Business travel is only romantic and exciting to those who seldom or never undertake it. Professional negotiators regard travel as a chore. The suitcase life is less than glamorous for those who suffer from crushed shirts, creased pants, and stale socks.

Four- and five-star hotels pale as attractive watering holes after you have stayed in your first six dozen. Sheraton, Hilton, Holiday Inn, Crest, Trust House Forte, Hyatt, and others are excellent hotel chains that are built and run to a sound formula.

If you were to wake up with a slight bout of amnesia, there is nothing in the hotel room that would tell you immediately in which country you happen to be parked at that moment.

And it is the similarity of each hotel within its own group that they regard as their strong selling point: You, the customer, know exactly what you are getting for your money (generally of a high standard, as every negotiator's spouse will confirm who gets onto one of the trips as a bonus). The cozy familiarity of your regular chain is a comfort no matter how strange (to you) the country you are in.

Airports are something else. They have a similarity that is not altogether welcome: They often seem to be places where people are delayed on the ground for times that are directly proportional to the duration of their flights.

Go into any airport lounge and watch the hordes spend their time incessantly checking their watches against the wall clocks; or try the bars, where you sit uncomfortably on wobbly chairs while you drink more than you should at tables littered with empty bottles and dirty glasses (I exclude Schiphol from this charge in Europe, Atlanta in the U.S., and the new Singapore airport in Asia).

Only the masochistic regard air travel, especially the peripherals that accompany it, as a relaxation.

No matter how good the airline you happen to be flying on this time, if you fly enough with them, eventually you will be let down—badly—and you will hear all kinds of atrocity stories about your favorite airline, airport, hotel, and country.

You can always tell the professional traveler from the rest: He seldom talks about the mechanics of travel or the dodges he has learned to make travel bearable—unless, of course, he is shooting a line at a party.

Why?

Because listeners who are amateurs would think he was showing off, and professionals would think him boring. Anybody who is impressed with the chat is clearly gullible or sexy, and, hopefully for the line pusher, both.

However, international business requires air travel, and if you want to get into (or stay in) it you will have to get used to its burdens.

If the burdens were known and predictable and there was nothing else to concern yourself with, then negotiating would indeed be without its moments of excitement. Fortunately, international business is not a mere extension of the habits of sellers and buyers in the place where you live. It is a confusing mixture of cultures and behaviors that has separate norms for each people and each country.

The international negotiator has to spend some time learning that the backyard he comes from is not the extent of the human achievement of this century. There are other places, vastly different, that have their own perspectives on what constitutes the right and the wrong way to be civilized.

Learning about the ways of the people in those other places is a task of the utmost importance in the career of a negotiator.

Little can be learned out of a book, but the longest journeys must start with a single step, and this chapter will cover some of the points that the negotiator ought to be aware of before trekking out into the wide blue yonder.

For a start, let us be clear about one thing. People in different countries are different for good reason: They are the product of centuries of successful struggle to survive as a cultural entity in the conditions that dominate the territory and climate of their birth.

Those of our predecessors in the human race who are no longer with us as distinct groupings were extinguished by those that are. The habits, behaviors, outlooks, codes, and laws of the peoples of the world are different because different circumstances require different forms of adaptation.

Hence, when you enter what to you is a foreign land, its foreignness is precisely an expression of that different history:

> *You are the foreigner to them; you have the strange habits and outlook; you are the unknown factor in their midst; and you are the odd one out.*

Forget this and you will be a poorer negotiator.

Obviously, it helps to know something about the country you intend to do business in. You could do worse than read about the histories of the countries you visit (preferably written by their own historians—history, like football, attracts devotees of one partisan view or another, and while it makes for colorful opinions it does not do much for objectivity).

You could also try to learn some simple words of the language—even the short words used for politeness are better than none at all.

You will soon become aware of the stress of long distance negotiation. Leaving one's home territory can be an alarming experience, for the journey into the unknown is both exciting and worrying.

The stresses of traveling only add to the worry: Will the connection with the 3:30 P.M. flight to Miami be made; is the guy with a beard a Castroite hijacker; is my confirmed reservation worth the paper it's telexed on; are the police as tough as they say; what will I do if they require a bribe; will I be met at the airport; will my bank drafts clear in time; how much money do I need for the taxi; have I got everything with me?

And that is before you think about what you are there to transact!

Once you are on your own, thousands of miles away from your home base, you are bound to feel isolated and lonely.

You will inevitably feel you are in unfamiliar surroundings and forget that it is you that is unfamiliar, not the surroundings—they've been there all the time.

How, then, should you set about coping with the situation?

By getting your "learn" motors into high gear and leaving them on "alert" for as long as you can.

It is you that has to learn about them and their lands. They have already adapted to their surroundings, which is why they, their families, and the people they are part of live there successfully.

Apart from the language problem, there are other problems of communicating that can be missed in the precise translation of words.

"Yes" means something different in London than what it means in Cairo. In London it means a deal is agreed; in Cairo it can mean that the other guy *wants* the deal to be agreed. The difference is subtle but awesome if the non-Egyptian takes it the same way as he would from the guy next door in Brooklyn.

For the Egyptian, it is a sign of bad faith to say that something is not possible just because events might conspire to prevent it from happening. If you say no because you know it cannot be done, then you are saying, in effect, that you don't want it to be done. So you say yes as an expression of your intentions, not your commitment.

Negotiations with Arabs are likely to be characterized by mundane irritations. The Arabs are a desert people. They take their time to trust a stranger. Hence, there are—to Westerners—inordinate delays in getting things moving. Sometimes this is sheer inefficiency, but generally it is the way the Arabs pace their dealings.

If you go to the Middle East, do not go in a hurry. Nor should you go cold. Arriving in Kuwait or Baghdad or Abu Dhabi with nothing more than a hotel reservation (that alone could be your first mistake—reservations only count when you have the key in your hand) and a few days to make calls on the ministries and local firms is the height of naiveté. The trip could leave you very hot, tired, lonely, and out of pocket by about $2,000 a week.

You need introductions—at the very least you need names and addresses of local businesses. To try to get them on the ground is going to wear out a lot of shoe leather, taxi money, and trouser seats in waiting rooms. Arabs are almost always late for an appointment—if they say 10 A.M., expect to see them at 11 P.M.; if they say Tuesday, be ready to catch them on Friday; and if they say June don't book up a holiday in August!

This is one reason for the phenomenal growth in the number of go-betweens in the oil-rich Middle East. They lubricate the path for you, arrange the meetings, sit in on the deals, discuss the terms, and act as an agent.

LIFE-OR-DEATH CONCESSIONS

When the oil companies were negotiating with the Libyans in 1971 they were up against a force they did not understand. That force was the militant expression of Arab–Islamic revolution. The issues themselves are not relevant here, but the behavior of the Libyan negotiators is.

Major Abdul Salaam Jalloud led the Libyan team that demanded renegotiated prices for its oil. They were within two cents of reaching an agreement. Jalloud offered to make the two-cent increase a temporary one, adding "I may be killed" for doing so.

211

Now in Western culture, a guy saying he will be killed by his colleagues for making a deal outside his limits is unlikely to be taken literally. If you told your pals that your spouse would kill you for being late again, you would not cause them to warn the police—and if they did, the police would need convincing that they weren't all drunk.

In Libya, the issue is not so clear cut. When Major Jalloud said he would be killed (he repeated the statement four times in as many minutes when he was pressed to compromise even one cent), it is highly likely that he believed it himself.

Of course, a guy telling you he will be killed for compromising below a target is not the same as a guy telling you that *you* will be killed for not agreeing with him! But the burden is just the same: If the other guy is going to be punished for accepting a compromise, you had better be clear on your responsibilities if the statement is credible. This marks a shift in the rules for which your background might not have prepared you.

Claims that concessions are suicidal for the other guy are not, of course, confined to Arab regimes. They have been known in Europe. For instance, the German negotiator Matthias Erzberger, at the 1918 armistice talks in the railroad car in the French forest of Compiègne, was murdered later for negotiating in the virtual surrender of the defeated German Army.

Naturally, it costs you. They call it "commission"—so does your head office. It's risky though, for obvious reasons; the more so if you import similar methods into your own country.

Another country for which patience is required is Japan. Never go to Japan in a hurry. They will play you to your deadline and then squeeze as the clock ticks away and your plane revs up on the runway.

Also, the Japanese are well prepared. They study the companies that come to negotiate with them. And they do this on a different wavelength from the average western negotiator.

In the West, a company is successful if it is profitable. If it isn't, for some reason, they feel weaker than when it is. In Japan, a company is successful if it has a large and growing share of a market. If it hasn't, they feel weaker than when it has.

The Japanese are interested in the market share of the company they are dealing with because that is how they assess its strengths. If it dominates the market they accord it higher standing than if it doesn't. If it is small but growing they are more impressed than if it is large but stagnant.

When two cultures come together the Japanese often come out on top because the Western firm chases its profit objectives and does not utilize its market share strengths.

Nor do they, in the main, study closely the Japanese firms they deal with (apart from credit references, etc.) and this lack of knowledge surprises Japanese negotiators.

True, they will show you a plant, but you will learn nothing that way. It's what happens in the market that counts. So get briefed!

The Japanese will take their time once they know you have a deadline. Hence, book a one-way ticket only and show not the slightest interest in the date of your departure.

Do not try to impress them with your busy schedule, and only partake in a minimum of social activity in the evenings, otherwise they will wear you out each night until, through the combination of sensory deprivation, or even satiation, you are ready for plucking.

High-living hell raisers sent to Japan to negotiate deals are probably a better bet than your quiet suburban guy who has never said "boo" to a goose—at least the hell raiser can stand the pace, whereas your quiet guy may discover what he has been missing and enjoy himself to the point of forgetting what he is there for.

NICE ONE, TOKYO

In Australia they have lots of iron and coal. In Japan they have none and must import it all. Who, then, is in the strongest bargaining position?

Right, the Japanese!

How do they achieve this remarkable result? By making the Australian negotiators go to Japan to do the deals. Once there, the Australians are negotiating at a Japanese pace while their minds remain operating at an Australian pace.

The Japanese are in no hurry—they live there! The Aussies are in a hurry because they don't.

Australians like Australia. Hence, after a short while they like their affluent and sunny selves to be firmly planted back in Oz near the pool, the beach, the barbecue, the wife, and the kids.

The Australian coal companies have not always exercised their strengths as seen by the Japanese. They have most of the coal Japan needs, and this ought to be reflected in the price. Instead, they have gone for their own needs, seeing Japan more as a means to their own ends than as a customer desperately anxious to get its hands on long-term coal supplies.

Hospitality is a devastating tool in negotiation. It lowers the social and foreignness barriers and disarms distrust and caution. Once you feel socially obliged you are halfway to being easy with the concessions.

Also, hospitality can have a confusing role in some cultures. A Spaniard giving you a small gift is making a socially approved gesture of politeness. True, this can get out of hand in some other parts of the world, though it is all a matter of scale. A leading Filipino journalist, Teodoro Valencia, explained the well-known social habits of local businessmen in the Philippines by saying:

> Our hospitality is not an attempt to bribe—it is just our way. In my country $1,000 is not a bribe, it is a gift. [*Economist,* March 20, 1982]

How you cope with the social habits of the people you negotiate with is best left to common sense and *advice* from old hands in the territory. You should know all about the country's standards of behavior before you arrive there. You should also have thought through how you intend to handle yourself, bearing in mind the possibilities for gaffes and the consequences for getting things wrong. In most countries, jails are unpleasant places, but their unpleasantness exponentially increases inversely in proportion to the per capita income of the country concerned.

Communist regimes also operate at a very slow pace, but this has different causes than that of the Arabs or the Japanese. Communists, in the main, are bureaucratic in outlook, and this must be understood if you want to do business with them. Unlike the bureaucracies in some corrupt and incompetent countries, Communist bureaucracies are overladen by a ruthless political regime that may not be efficient at pandering to the peoples' wants, but they are very efficient at punishing deviance.

Communist officials operate in teams and within hierarchies. The bureaucrat's goal in life is to avoid responsibility—to pass the buck—and the best way for him to avoid responsibility for his actions is not to act at all, but if he has to act, to make sure—doubly and trebly sure—that his action is unlikely to be laid at his door when the time for accounting arrives.

BAKSHEESH, BACKHANDERS, AND DASH

You will not spend much time in certain parts of the world before you come up against petty bribery. If you hang around long enough and have the right contacts, you will also become aware of *big* corruption, but that's another story (and I don't want my book banned for discussing it).

In West Africa they call petty corruption "dash." If you want *anything* done by an official you ought to know about dash, because if in your innocence you don't, you will wait ages for even the most routine of transactions.

Airplane reservations in Ghana (and Nigeria, etc.) mean nothing unless the guy at the front desk has been paid his dash—a few cedis or whatever—out of which he pays the guy in the back office for the use of the rubber stamp, or his signature, or even a glimpse at the passenger list. Likewise with hotel rooms, appointments to see the boss, the civil servant, the tax accountant, or to use the telex.

This is common practice wherever you have to use the services of people who by virtue of their positions can extract a few dollars here for a few favors there.

In Egypt, the ministries are riddled with locally created monopolies. Maps are not published openly, but are kept in locked drawers to be extracted for

214

"a little something"; statistical tables are treated likewise (i.e., sold page by page like a man who found some ancient scrolls), and official forms and licenses can be little gold mines to the clerk who is in charge of them.

In India, the fastest—indeed, sometimes the only—way to move paper through the bureaucratic labyrinth (courts, tax offices, even railway stations) is be paying a *baksheesh* (tip or bribe):

> Baksheesh! Baksheesh!
> Sixteen Annas, one Rupee
> One Rupee, One Baksheesh!

How you approach this petty corruption is a personal matter, but don't moralize about it unless you *never* give tips to taxi drivers, waiters, and the kids who find your golf ball!

The Communist negotiator's tool kit consists of:

- A well-documented set of rules and procedures that are strictly adhered to because deviance has no defense.
- A strong sense of protocol that shows deference to his own superiors and recognition of yours.
- An obsession with paperwork—everything has to be recorded in writing. All proposals must be made in writing; all changes must be made in writing; all promises, specifications, and amendments must be made in writing.
- A passion for minutes and for reports, with signatures obtained for everything. This includes joint communiqués and statements of intent, and consequently much time is spent in drafting and redrafting the reports (check each one carefully because they write to please their superiors rather than to record what you said for posterity).
- A layer of committees to approve or disapprove of the proposals. You get through one level and there is another one, Kafkalike, waiting to take over, with the "experts" each having a say, sometimes a long one, complete with detailed technical interrogations that show no regard for your commercial secrets.
- A total lack of personal commitment to the deal and to you—bureaucrats constantly change jobs or can be called to account for being "too friendly" with the capitalists, so under no circumstances offer personal "kindnesses" (especially anything smacking of a bribe) or get personally involved even with friendly negotiators ("entrapment" is no joke).

The entire psyche of the Communist state official is motivated by making sure that the job he does for his government has the least chance of being regarded by anybody, now or in the future, as being disloyal.

Risk aversion is rampant in a Communist negotiator, and his ideological suspicion of capitalists compels him to check everything and, having checked, to pass the decision elsewhere, if he can, preferably to

215

as large an official body as possible, because the more people he implicates in the deal the safer it is for him.

There are variations, of course, among the Communist states—after all, even the Communists have been unable to suppress the national instincts of their people. Indeed, there is a case for believing that most Communists are nationalists first and Communist second.

A Polish Communist once told me that the reason why East Germany was so successful as a Communist country was because the Communist system there was run by Germans!

The things Communist states have in common are worth noting. They prefer to deal with the top personnel of a company, as their whole life-style leads them to look upward to the top of the party. They do not like discussing politics with western negotiators any more than they discuss politics with their own people.

If you want to know what the Chinese think of Vietnam, don't ask, just read the *People's Daily*. Your "conversation" with the newspaper will produce more meaningful answers than trying to talk with your opposite number. Above all, *never ever* try to joke about their politics—out of such misunderstandings you can be detained or deported.

In Europe the negotiator has more in common with his opposite number from another European country. However, there are variations.

The Germans are grossly efficient and well prepared, so if you deal with them you had better be well prepared too. They study closely the financial aspects of a deal and do not take risks with their money.

Partly this is explained by the way German industry is financed. In the U.K. industry is financed by share issues to the public. In Germany the banks are the major suppliers of funds and, being bankers, they study any proposition from a conservative banker's viewpoint.

They examine every proposal carefully and prepare thoroughly beforehand to tease out the wrinkles, expose the risks, and generally see that the arrangement will be a tight ship financially.

Therefore, German negotiators like certainty in business affairs and prefer sound propositions from sound companies with sound prospects to the other kind. In this sense they are like the Dutch, and like the little Dutch boy at the dike, they act early to protect themselves if something appears to be going wrong with a deal.

The French are—well, French. They only speak French in business matters even if they can speak fluent English. I listened to a French official conduct an hour-long seminar on the EEC in London in flawless English. Some weeks later I attended a briefing in Paris for English-speaking businessmen at which the same guy spoke only in French, through an interpreter!

Their top guys are good, very good. They are well educated and proud of it. They know how to make money and are surprised if you

216

don't. They are keen on partnerships rather than working for foreign firms, and they hold you to the small print of a deal come hell or high water, which is somewhat less than they do when they find a deal is going against them. Then they are capable of wantonly breaking the deal's conditions, ignoring all appeals to the contrary, and sitting tight until you give in or compromise. If they can get leverage on you they will, because they believe in linking separate issues if it suits them. In sum, the French are past masters of the runaround. They invariably turn up late for the excellent meals they are famous for and attempt to intimidate you with their life-styles.

The Scandinavians are the exact opposite of the Gallic peoples as negotiators. They are far more reserved than other Europeans—though underneath the reserve is a streak of earthiness. They are exceptionally polite and take time to loosen up in a negotiation. They live in sparsely populated affluent economies and deep down intend to survive as independent peoples whatever else happens to the rest of the world.

They can be hard negotiators. Consider the deals they have struck with the oil companies in Norway compared to the deals the same companies got from the "experienced" British, or see how their shipping industries fare compared to the shipping industries of some larger countries. In sum, they are very good at protecting their own interests, without pushiness and arrogance.

THE CIRCLE OF NEGOTIATING RELATIONSHIPS

Negotiators for Third World governments and Western mineral corporations have seen a significant shift in their relationships over the past 30 years. The balance of power has changed since the first concessions were granted during the colonial period.

In the first stages of the relationship, the company was given a concession, that is, an absolute right to remove from the territory primary resources for a fee or a royalty per ton removed.

Several revisions have been negotiated, basically concerned with the demands from the host authority for a greater share of the income from its mineral resources.

The major inhibitions on the rapid spread of these revision agreements was either technological or monetary.

The more the mineral operation concentrated on simple ("steam shovel") operations, or the greater the facility for raising necessary funds from international agencies, the greater the bargaining position of the host government.

The other major barrier to host country development has been the lack of access to Western markets, without which there is not enough demand to justify a host monopoly.

But the picture is patchy across the extraction sectors in Third World countries. Some countries manage to tie their contracts to the establishment of local "downstream" capacity, others to local participation in the equity of the

217

mineral companies. In addition, the government has renegotiated both royalty and taxation liabilities with the mineral companies.

The final stage has been the movement over to management agreements, where the corporation manages the exploration, commissioning, and extractive contract for a fee from the indigenous (usually nationalized) company and arranges the marketing of the output (again, for a fee).

This reverses the original relationship, but the parties have found a way of living with these changes.

There is a lot I could write about the British styles of negotiating (remember, the British Isles have the English, Welsh, Scots, and Irish traditions in them, and they are all different where it counts), but the Brits are having such a bad time in business at present that I see no need to expose their negotiating foibles to further assault from the successful negotiators of other lands!

However, a few pointers to two of the British nations are in order. The English have a reputation for being gentlemen. They are also distinctly amateurish compared to the Germans, and they are not as fast on their feet as the Americans. They tend to get better deals with poorer countries than they do with richer ones (compare the ex-Empire with the EEC!). They do, however, believe strongly in fair play. The English have a word for refraining from doing in the other guy when they have him over a barrel—they call it statesmanship.

The Scots come in two kinds: those who work from Scotland and those who live elsewhere. The latter are better at negotiating than their more homely brethren, mainly because the home-based Scots model themselves on their English neighbors in business matters—though they bring their unique canniness in matters financial to that relationship—while the expatriate blends in with the best practice wherever he is located. Also, he likes winning, which is why he left Scotland in the first place.

With the United States we enter a melting pot of negotiating traditions. North Americans are deal seekers. "Go get a deal" has replaced "Go West, young man" in Fortune's litany.

The frontier now is in the marketplace, and it is run in traditional Western fashion. There are good guys and bad guys, with sheriffs to keep the peace but who otherwise mind their own business.

Their entire commercial ethic consists of sellers offering deals, megadeals, and supermegadeals. Everything is hyped. Even the hype is hyped! "Buyer meets seller" is the reality of the world's largest market economy. They worship success because nothing succeeds like success, and a failure is a no-no. Worse, failure is anti-American. When you're down you're out.

Make a comeback and you're admitted in again. If you don't try

218

to make a comeback you prove the point about being anti-American, which is something close to having leprosy or yellow fever.

Hence, negotiations in the United States are a bit like the annual Rose Bowl game. In the huddle you are expected to plan your play and then make it. Tactics are permissible, indeed expected. If you go one up, well and good; if you don't, he will.

It's a game. It's a spectators' sport. It's a high-energy hassle from the moment the other guy walks into the room grinning like a Cheshire cat and saying: "Have I got a deal for you, or have I got a deal for you!"

Despite his busy schedule—sign of a successful man—he has time for a deal. True, he might increase the pace of his speaking, get excited about the moves, even shout a little (North Americans love shouting—it's the Mediterranean influence), but he will be looking for that deal right up to the moment when the elevator doors close.

The American understands the principle of trading. That is what negotiating is for them. It's only when they get diverted by their analysts (emotional, not financial) that they fall into deeply irrelevant psychological plays.

Hence, if you negotiate in the United States, keep your head down in the huddle as you learned to do in the streets you grew up in and above all, keep it away from the analyst—at least until you make your first million dollars!

Finally, in negotiating with anybody from anywhere about anything, you will find you do better if you treat them with respect. If you do otherwise they will tell you to buzz off.

If, on the other hand, you avoid provoking that reaction, then you will find in the main, on average, and through the long run that

Everything is negotiable!

ANSWERS
SELF-ASSESSMENT TEST 19

Q.1: There are 5: you, two Dutchman, one Frenchman, and a German. The Malaysians are in their own country. If you answered 5, take 10 points.

Any other answer, deduct 10 points, unless you answered 4 because you are Malaysian yourself (in which case, have a bonus of 5 points).

Q.2: Certainly not 10.   (− 10)

Twelve is too tight, given the Arab attitude to time.   (− 8)

Fifteen is still risking it.	(− 5)
Seventeen is just about workable.	(+ 3)
Twenty is safe.	(+ 5)
Twenty-five suggests you are a risk minimizer.	(+ 8)

Q.3: a] It certainly is Japanese courtesy (not to be underestimated in importance), but it has another purpose—to find your deadline for departure. Japanese love running non-Japanese negotiators to their deadlines. (− 5)

b] You really have fallen for the ploy. (− 10)

c] Good. If you value your coal you would protect yourself this way with the Japanese. (+ 10)

THE NEGOTIATOR'S CHECKLIST

In this summary chapter I have collected the salient pointers to effective negotiating behavior and tactics that are discussed in this book. You may remind yourself of the main points and drawn upon them as circumstance and opportunity dictates. You can also check back to the relevant chapter if you want to revise a point. How you play the shots in any particular situation is something only you can decide, but by bearing in mind the following pointers you will be able to make more winning decisions than losing ones. And that, after all, is what you're about as a negotiator!

Chapter 1
The Worst Thing You Can Do to a Negotiator

1. The worst thing you can do is to accept his first offer.
2. Make a negotiator happy—haggle.
3. A deal he works for is a deal he is happier with.

Chapter 2
Why You Can't Negotiate a Grievance

4. Don't just state a grievance, negotiate a remedy.
5. Tempers are never calmed by being tested.

28. Soft negotiators open modestly, move a long way, and frequently make large concessions. They are terrified of deadlock.

29. Toughness pays. If he's selling, squeeze him; if he's buying, say no.

30. Don't give discounts to people who need your business.

31. A tough stance is much more likely to provoke a soft one than a tough one.

32. If you're soft you have to work harder to get the same amount of business as you would if you were tough.

Chapter 9
The Negotiator's Most Useful Two-Letter Word

33. The negotiator's most useful two-letter word is *if.*

34. Negotiating is about trading, not conceding.

35. In negotiating, both sides have a veto.

36. Negotiating involves both sides in a voluntary consent to a joint decision.

37. Never concede anything without getting something back in exchange.

38. Nothing, absolutely nothing, is given away free.

39. You can't afford to "split the difference."

40. Because it's "fair" doesn't make it "equal."

41. Preface all your propositions with *if*: "*If* you agree to this, *then* I will agree to that."

42. If they want something from you, it ought to cost them.

43. How do you educate your opponents? Put a price on their demands.

Chapter 10
Who Has the Power?

44. Power matters: It is the very essence of the negotiating process.

45. Power is in the head, and in negotiating there are two heads: yours and the other guy's.

46. If you believe they have the power, they have it (and they have you, too).

47. Untested assumptions may credit them with more power than they have.

48. All negotiating moves are about structuring the opponent's perception of his and your power.

49. The competition is never as fierce as the buyer claims.

50. Buyers always challenge prices, invariably have "better offers" from the competition, and never admit to needing anything—it's the nature of the beast.

51. Sellers are always in a hurry, warn you that stocks won't last, prices are due to go up, and that demand for their products is bouyant.

52. Sellers ought to avoid disclosing instant availability of supplies—it's worth a discount to help clear the shelves.

53. Buyers ought to avoid disclosing urgent needs—it's worth a premium for early supply.